DISJOINED

PARTNERS

DISJOINED PARTNERS

Austria and Germany since 1815

PETER J. KATZENSTEIN

UNIVERSITY OF CALIFORNIA PRESS
Berkeley   /   Los Angeles   /   London

University of California Press
Berkeley and Los Angeles, California

University of California Press, Ltd.
London, England

Copyright © 1976, by
The Regents of the University of California

ISBN 978-0-520-30423-9
Library of Congress Catalog Card Number: 74-30526

Designed by James Mennick

For Gerda, Johnny, and Gerhard
and
to the memory of Merle

CONTENTS

	Tables and Figures	viii
	Preface	xiii
I.	Introduction	1
II.	The Probability of Political Autonomy	9
III.	Aristocratic Pattern (1815–1848)	35
IV.	Conflict Pattern (1848–1870)	66
V.	Hierarchical Pattern (1870–1918)	97
VI.	Voluntaristic Pattern (1918–1938)	132
VII.	Structural Pattern (1938–1945)	163
VIII.	Pluralistic Pattern (1945–1970)	177
IX.	Counterpressures and Political Autonomy	199
X.	Conclusion	219
	APPENDIX. Political Unification, Political Fragmentation, and Cultural Cohesion in Europe Since 1815	227
	INDEX	259

TABLES AND FIGURES

Table 1.	Two Dimensions Defining Different Degrees of Political Autonomy: The Austro-German Case (1815–1970)	15
Table 2.	Elite Migration to Austria: Top-Level Decision Makers by Place of Family Origin (since 1740)	49
Table 3.	Relative Distribution of Austrian Attention: Average Foreign News Coverage in Two Austrian Papers, 1816–1849	54
Table 4.	Relative Distribution of Austrian Attention: Average Foreign News Coverage in Two Austrian Papers, 1831–1870	78
Table 5.	Five Indicators of Capability: Ratio of Austria-Hungary/Prussia, 1840 and 1860	87
Table 6.	Relative Distribution of Austrian Attention: Average Foreign News Coverage in Two Austrian Papers, 1873–1912	101

List of Tables and Figures

Table 7.	Evaluation of Germany in Government Speeches and Newspaper Editorials in Austria, 1853–1918	104
Table 8.	Categories for Symbols of Common Identity	107
Table 9.	Strength of Austrian Symbols of Common Identity as Measured by the Ratio of Direct Plus Indirect Austrian Symbols over Direct Plus Indirect German Symbols	109
Table 10.	Rank Order of Emigration and Casualty Figures for Different National Groups in Austria	117
Table 11.	Relative Distribution of Austrian Attention: Average Foreign News Coverage in Two Austrian Papers, 1900–1938	135
Table 12.	Evaluation of Germany in Government Speeches and Newspaper Editorials in Austria, 1918–1938	139
Table 13.	Political Coordination between Austria and Germany, 1922–1933	150
Table 14.	Membership Figures of the Austrian Nazi Party, 1928–1938	171
Table 15.	Casualties Sustained by Five Countries in World War II	174
Table 16.	Austrian and German Casualties in World War II	175

Table 17.	Relative Distribution of Austrian Attention: Average Foreign News Coverage in Two Austrian Papers, 1933–1969	181
Table 18.	Evaluation of Germany in Government Speeches and Newspaper Editorials in Austria, 1946–1970	183
Table 19.	The Growth of Austrian Self-Identification 1956–1970	185
Table 20.	The Growth of Austrian Economic Attachment to the Second Republic	188
Table 21.	Austrian Attention to Domestic and Foreign News, 1815–1970	200
Table 22.	Austria's Foreign Communications and Transactions as Percent of Domestic Total	201
Table 23.	Transactions and Communications between Austria and Germany, 1815–1970	204
Table 24.	Changes in the Heterogeneity of Austro-German Transactions and Communications since 1815	208
Table 25.	Long-Term Trends in Evaluations and Self-Identifications in Austrian Newspapers	210
Table 26.	Political Unification and Fragmentation as Outcomes of the Balance between Communications and Transactions	252

List of Tables and Figures

Table 27.	Average Percentage Rates of Growth of Communications and Transactions per Decade in Ireland and Norway (1870/1910, 1920/1960)	253
Table 28.	Changes in the Relative Acceptance Indicator as a Measure of the Intensity of Transactions and Communications Flows between England-Ireland and Sweden-Norway, 1913–1968	255
Table 29.	Changes in the Relative Acceptance Indicator as a Measure of the Intensity of Culturally Cohesive Areas, 1913–1968	256
Figure 1.	Symbols of Common Identity in Austrian Government Speeches, 1860–1917	108
Figure 2.	Symbols of Common Identity in Austrian Government Speeches, 1919–1938	140
Figure 3.	Symbols of Common Identity in Austrian Newspaper Editorials, 1919–1938	142
Figure 4.	Long-Term Trends in the Attention of Austrian Newspapers to Foreign Events, 1815–1969	205
Figure 5.	Two Indicators of Political Communications between Austria and Germany, 1822–1970	214

PREFACE

Truth is where the individual mind comes to rest. What about the prior journey? The central idea that originally started this research seemed simple and plausible. The absence of full-fledged integration of Austria and Germany since 1815, I thought, provided an interesting case, untypical of the pervasive political integration in contemporary European politics. The central idea that finally emerged from my research is equally simple and plausible. The absence of full-fledged integration of Austria and Germany since 1815 provides an interesting case typical of the pervasive political autonomy in contemporary European politics. This drastic change of mind took a long time to complete, longer than I now care to remember, largely, I suspect, because both ideas seem so simple and plausible.

This book applies some insights and methods of contemporary social science to the analysis of a historical problem. The choice of the level of theoretical abstraction, type of empirical documentation, and methods of analysis will be a source of unease—to the social scientist for its excessive preoccupation with historical detail, to the historian for its inexcusable predisposition for ahistorical generalization. I am cheerfully sympathetic to both reactions since I regard intellectual unease as an ingredient indispensable in the formulation and testing of new ideas.

Parts of Chapter II and the appendix of this book were published in modified form as an occasional paper of the Western Societies Program of Cornell University.

This study owes much for its support to several institutions. Harvard University's Faculty of Arts and Sciences gave me the funding for a year of research in Vienna. There the Stadtbibliothek permitted me special access to its collection of newspapers. A supplementary grant from Harvard University's Center for European Studies partially financed a content analysis of these Austrian newspapers. The Center for European Studies and the Center for International Affairs at Harvard provided office space, secretarial assistance, and most important a large measure of intellectual stimulation essential to distraction from and improvement of my own work.

Support from many individuals was no less important. Günther Anger, Elisabeth Arzberger, Helmut Blechner, Rainer Brandstätten, Gerald Gaschler, Klaus Luif, Margret Macco, and Edwin Wurm assisted me in coding the content of Austrian newspapers. William T. Bluhm, Hartmut Kaelble, Gerhard Katzenstein, David Laitin, Peter H. Lyon, Richard L. Merritt, Gebhard L. Schweigler, and Mack Walker read successive versions of the manuscript in their entirety. Bernhard Badura, Cal Clark, Stephen D. Krasner, George H. Quester, Richard N. Rosecrance, John Ruggie, Lawrence Scheinman, and Sidney G. Tarrow commented on drafts of Chapter II and the appendix. I have benefited greatly from their many suggestions and criticisms. By sheer force of intellectual osmosis I have learned from my friends at the Center for European Studies how to construct an argument.

Karl W. Deutsch and Joseph S. Nye supervised this project as a doctoral dissertation. They read interminable drafts and spent long hours with me discussing problems of integration theory and central European politics. From their contrasting approaches to the study of politics I have learned more than is reflected in the following pages.

Dorothy Whitney contributed valuable editorial assistance. But the greatest thanks go to Johnny Fainsod for her tenacious battling with my Teutonic prose. Kathy Schwarz, Scott B. Heyman, and Mayerlene Frow did wonders in deciphering illegible drafts and typing them with skill and speed.

The greatest of all thanks, finally, go to Mary. Her steadfast refusal to become either slave or expert may not have accelerated the process of writing; but it has made writing an eminently enjoyable experience.

I

INTRODUCTION

FOR MORE than a hundred years the German Question has been Europe's problem. Situated in the heart of Europe, Germany has, in the course of less than a century, kindled three wars of rarely equaled destructiveness. Too strong when united and too dissatisfied when divided, it has remained a source of fear and suspicion to enemy and friend alike. Germany's catastrophic defeat in 1945 and the onset of the Cold War soon thereafter seemed to have ended its hegemonic aspirations no less than its national achievements. But economic reconstruction in Germany and political realignment in Europe make such a future less certain. With the gradual disengagement from central Europe of the two superpowers, will the potent force of German nationalism pose the German question to the rest of Europe once again? Or is the present fragmentation of central Europe a more permanent outcome?

Although they have differed in the solutions they have proposed since 1945, West German policymakers have uniformly agreed on the basic nature of the German question. That question, they thought, was created by the divergence between domestic and foreign pressures. The different answers they have offered were all based on the conviction that domestic choice would eventually prevail over foreign constraint. The political reintegration of the components of central Europe, similar in language and culture, could be delayed, not prevented. In the early postwar period, the two antagonists in West German politics,

Konrad Adenauer and Kurt Schumacher, agreed on *Wiedervereinigung in Frieden und Freiheit* (reunification in peace and freedom) as a moral and political postulate.[1] Until the mid-1960s the successor generation of political leaders shared this view. On the Right, Franz Josef Strauss asserted that "we are not ready . . . to abandon our national rights and human liberties by accepting the present division in the country and perpetuating the *status quo*."[2] In the Center, Chancellor Erhard concurred: "the claim to represent all-Germany must remain inviolable";[3] similar views were expressed by his successor, Chancellor Kiesinger. On the Left, one of the most important spokesmen of the Social Democrats, the late Fritz Erler, agreed: "Not only is the division of Germany today a reality but also the fact that the German people will not accept this division in the long-term."[4]

This belief in the probability of the reunification of Germany has also characterized Chancellor Brandt's Eastern Policy. In return for a gradual increase in social, economic, and cultural exchanges between the Federal Republic (FRG) and the German Democratic Republic (GDR), his policy amounted to a formal recognition of existing political boundaries in central Europe. Newly elected in 1969, Brandt stated in his first speech before the West German Parliament:

> In the coming years the political task will be to maintain the unity of the nation by relaxing the tensions which mark the present relations between the two parts of Germany. . . . Twenty years after the foundation of the Federal Republic and the GDR, we must prevent a further growing apart of the German nation, that is, we must try to move from living side by side [*Nebeneinander*] to living together [*Miteinander*].[5]

1. Hans-Peter Schwarz, *Vom Reich zur Bundesrepublik: Deutschland im Widerstreit der aussenpolitischen Konzeptionen in den Jahren der Besatzungsherrschaft, 1945-1949* (Neuwied: Luchterhand, 1966). Arnulf Baring, *Aussenpolitik in Adenauers Kanzlerdemokratie* (Munich: Oldenbourg, 1969).
2. Franz Josef Strauss, *The Grand Design* (New York: Praeger, 1966), p. 18.
3. Quoted in Ferenc A. Váli, *The Quest for a United Germany* (Baltimore: Johns Hopkins University Press, 1967), p. 59.
4. Fritz Erler, "Politik und nicht Prestige," in *Sicherheit und Rüstung: Beiträge von Fritz Erler und Richard Jaeger* (Cologne: Verlag Wissenschaft und Politik, 1962), p. 39.
5. Willy Brandt, "Regierungserklärung, 28. Oktober 1969," in Bundes-

Almost self-consciously, it seems, Brandt avoided two alternative images, the prosaic promise of mutual indifference (*Ohneeinander*) and the problematic prospect of mutual confrontation (*Gegeneinander*). The recognition of the existence of two German states sets Brandt apart from his predecessors; the reassertion of the existence of one German nation unites him with them.

Policy analysts abroad have given great weight to the way in which political actors in Germany have defined the German question. In his influential analysis of alliance policy, Henry Kissinger, for one, argued, "The fate of the 17 million people in East Germany is one of those intangible issues that can remain quiescent for many years, only to erupt suddenly and dramatically.... It is against all probability that a large and dynamic country can be kept divided indefinitely in the center of the continent that gave the concept of nationalism to the world."[6] Zbigniew Brzezinski took essentially the same position in assuming that the domestic potential for reunification would remain unchanged until gradual shifts in the international system would permit reunification at some future time.[7]

Political actors and analysts inside and outside of Germany subscribe, then, to what seems to be an intuitively plausible view. There exists a natural—that is, highly probable—trend toward political unification of culturally homogeneous states. The reunification of the current fragments of central Europe, this view suggests, is prevented by only one critical factor, the current international system. The main argument developed in this book takes issue with this view. There exists no natural trend toward political unification of culturally cohesive regions. The historical record of the last 150 years substantiates this conclusion. The political unification of Germany and Italy in the middle of the nineteenth century has been taken erroneously as

---

ministerium für innerdeutsche Beziehungen (ed.), *Texte zur Deutschlandpolitik* (Bonn: Vorwärts, 1970), IV, 11.
6. Henry A. Kissinger, *The Troubled Partnership: A Re-appraisal of the Atlantic Alliance* (New York: McGraw-Hill, 1965), pp. 210, 216.
7. Zbigniew Brzezinski, *Alternative to Partition: For a Broader Conception of America's Role in Europe* (New York: McGraw-Hill, 1965), pp. 137-139.

the only model for the future course of events in central Europe and, more generally, in other culturally cohesive areas. The political fragmentation of Sweden-Norway and England-Ireland at the beginning of the twentieth century points, however, in the opposite direction, not toward unification but fragmentation. And in outright defiance of what is thought of as intuitive plausibility, over the last century and a half a number of states that were culturally cohesive and politically divided—states such as Spain and Portugal, the United States and Canada, and Australia and New Zealand—have shown an undisguised unwillingness to move toward political unification. Political developments of the past thus point to the political autonomy as much as to the political integration of culturally homogeneous states. It is, therefore, possible that the three Germanies in central Europe— West Germany, East Germany, and Austria—are today in the process of finding peace in pieces. What needs to be explained, then, in central Europe and in other culturally cohesive areas is the resilience of the politically autonomous nation-state. With growing interdependence why does integration not succeed autonomy? Why do partners remain disjoined?

This book will offer some answers to that question and test them against data provided by one important case. With regard to central Europe the German case per se is too complex and too heterogeneous to serve well for purposes of analysis. Switzerland, the Netherlands, East Germany, West Germany, and Austria— all have been parts of "Germany" at one point or another. The Swiss and Dutch cases are relatively uninteresting, because they predate modern politics in the era of industrialization, and because they exhibit few deviations from a pattern of amicable indifference. The case of East Germany and West Germany poses analytical problems of the opposite order: the relevant time period is too short and there are few variations from a pattern of hostile involvement.[8] The case of Austria and Germany since 1815, free of these different liabilities, seems the fairest testing ground.

---

8. One crucial aspect of the East German–West German case is analyzed in Gebhard L. Schweigler's *National Consciousness in Divided Germany* (Beverly Hills, Calif.: Sage Publications, 1975).

Comprehensive research of processes of unification and fragmentation in Austro-German relations since 1815 would have to examine, at a minimum, four pieces of the puzzle: Prussia, the Rhineland, Bavaria, and Austria. This book focuses only on Austria. Considerations of research economy account in part for this restrictive focus. But the main reason is the fact that in Austria, in contrast to Germany, the issue of Austro-German relations was a matter of vital political concern for the entire period.

Terms such as "Austria" and "Germany" naturally cover different geographic areas in the period since 1815. This raises questions of terminology that should be confronted at the outset of analysis. "Austria" will designate the non-Hungarian western parts of the monarchy before 1918 as well as the First and Second Republics thereafter. "Austria-Hungary" and "Dual Monarchy" will be reserved for references to the eastern and western parts of the empire before 1918, while terms like "Austrian Empire" and "Austrian Monarchy" are used as synonyms for "Austria." When talking of the Austrian people, "German-Austrians" will be used to describe the Germans in the monarchy, especially those living in the Alpine provinces, in Bohemia, Moravia, and Silesia. After 1918, the citizens of the First and Second Republics will be called "Austrians." By contrast "Germany," whether it is used before or after 1871, refers to the areas united under the Second Reich of 1871-1918, Weimar Germany and Nazi Germany. The people living in these areas will be called "Germans" or, at times, "Reich-Germans."

This retrospective ahistorical distinction between "Austria" and "Germany" would be problematic for an analysis primarily interested in the continuity of historical developments and the gradual unfolding of Austro-German relations since the beginning of the nineteenth century. Although inspired in part by these traditional concerns of historians, the primary focus of this analysis is somewhat different. It treats Austro-German relations not as one case but as a series of comparative cases of states whose sizes have changed. Strictly speaking, on the basis of this analysis it is, therefore, not possible to draw inferences across major historical watersheds such as the reorganization of Austria-Hungary in 1866-1867, the formation of the Hohenzollern

Empire in 1871, and the destruction of both empires in 1918. But the presentation of the empirical material in distinct case studies has the advantage of permitting numerous tests of the explanation of the persistence of political autonomy which is set forth in the next chapter.

This book concentrates on the persistence of Austrian political autonomy since 1815. For an analysis of Austro-German relations, the image of cultural cohesion and political unification as mutually reinforcing, unidirectional processes is intellectually misplaced. Austro-German relations since 1815 reveal instead a balance between unification and fragmentation. This balance is reflected in a set of counterpressures which helps explain the persistence of Austria's political autonomy. But during the last 150 years, a number of discernible swings have occurred between the poles of unification and fragmentation. In the second half of the nineteenth century, for example, Austria and Germany lived side by side in close mutual relations that never resulted in any serious attempt at full-fledged political unification. During the interwar years, the structure of the international system was the major obstacle for the serious drive then afoot toward Austro-German unification. And all the available evidence since 1945 points toward political fragmentation, a trend which the current structure of the international system encourages. Although it falls short of full unification or fragmentation, the Austro-German case since 1815 is instructive for an analysis of the forces that lead to the enhancement, erosion, and persistence of political autonomy.

This analysis plays down two frequently encountered answers to the political and intellectual problems posed by the disjoined partnership of Austria and Germany. The first answer adduces the constraining effects of the international system as the only important factor that has shaped Austro-German relations in the past. Backed by the brooding presence of the Soviet Union, this argument runs, the Austrians were naturally compelled to accept the independence of their own small state. But what was "natural" after World War II was "unnatural" after World War I. During the interwar years the confining effects of the international system on Austro-German relations were also potent.

France, instead of the Soviet Union, was the big power insisting on Austrian independence then. Since, in the nineteenth century, France had been a lesser enemy of Austria than Russia, one might expect the Austrians to have been more accommodating to the wishes of the former, not the latter. History, of course, tells otherwise. Austrian desire for political unification with Germany was much greater before 1945 than after. To be sure there existed important differences in the nature of international constraints. After 1945 Austria found itself at the dividing line of a bipolar international system, while it had been at the center of a multipolar one during the interwar years. French hostility at the end of 1918, furthermore, was constraining in a manner that differed from Soviet occupation after 1945. Although these differences in the international situation contribute to an analysis of Austrian policy, they conceal crucial changes in domestic affairs. An exclusive focus on foreign constraints disregards, then, domestic choices without which a full explanation of the relations among disjoined partners cannot be made.

A second answer, similarly flawed, concentrates on the impact of dramatic forces not from without but from within. During the last hundred years, this argument suggests, German nationalism in Austria, enhanced by the trauma of partition in 1918–1919, rose continuously until 1938. It was only natural that the costly interlude of Nazi rule between 1938 and 1945 convinced the Austrians of the virtues of political impotence and independence. But here again what was "natural" after 1945 was "unnatural" before. The Austrians suffered two costly wars and two traumas of partition. Yet after 1918 and after 1945 they reacted in very different ways. In part that difference can be accounted for by the character of the lost war. Austria's political involvement was far more important in World War I than in World War II. But an adequate explanation of the disjoined partnership of Austria and Germany cannot be fashioned from isolated, spectacular events in history which have led to opposite consequences at different times. The effect of the international system and of spectacular domestic events on the political choices of political elites and mass publics cannot be altogether ignored. But, on the whole, the explanation of disjoined partnership offered here focuses on more continuous and less spectacular processes. These processes point to the prevalence of counterpressures and political autonomy as the central feature of disjoined partnership.

Since no fact harbors any meaning on its own, the task of the empirical study of politics lies in making the unintelligible intelligible, in discovering intellectual order where there seemed to be only disorder. This process inevitably entails simplification, abstraction, generalization, in short, a reduction of complexity. The description of Austro-German relations since 1815 should, therefore, be preceded by an explanation of the relations of disjoined partnership. Only then can answers be provided for the questions of why Austro-German relations were marked by so many counterpressures in the past and what these counterpressures portend for the future.

II

THE PROBABILITY OF POLITICAL AUTONOMY

IN CENTRAL Europe and elsewhere the relations between culturally cohesive states are widely believed to be marked by only one powerful force, political integration. The point of departure of this book is the persistent gap between aspiration and achievement, prediction and verification. The core concern is the permanence of political autonomy of culturally homogeneous states in the twentieth century. Why do partners in international affairs remain disjoined? Why do states not integrate?

For the Austro-German case illustrative evidence suggests that the answer to this question lies in the presence, persistence, and pervasiveness of counterpressures. These counterpressures have occurred within as well as between two distinct sets of political and nonpolitical variables—summarized by the Austrians and the Germans in the terms "political nation" (*Staatsnation*) and "cultural nation" (*Kulturnation*). The "Austrian Odyssey"[1] since 1815, if traced on a map, would chart a collision course of Austria's political autonomy and cultural identity on the one hand, and its quest for political integration and cultural assimilation with Germany on the other. The central argument of this

1. This is the suggestive title of a book by a British journalist, Gordon Shepherd (London: Macmillan, 1957).

book points, then, to two different types of counterpressures neither one of which, taken by itself, can explain autonomy, but both of which, taken together, make its persistence highly probable.

AUSTRIA AND GERMANY: A CASE IN COUNTERPRESSURES

Austro-German relations since 1815 have on the whole stopped short of full-fledged unification or fragmentation. Instead, counterpressures within and between nonpolitical and political variables have resulted in more subtle shifts in Austria's political autonomy. Numerous examples exist of counterpressures between Austrian and German elements within these two sets of cultural and political variables. These counterpressures are very much in evidence, for example, in three features frequently associated with the concept of a cultural nation: shared history, ancestry, and culture.

Like most peoples, the Austrians have always thought of themselves as a special group. In nostalgic remembrance of imperial glory, in painful awareness of political separation from Germany, in healthy respect for a regained sovereignty, or in faint indifference toward all things political—there has always been some identity to which the Austrians have aspired. But a common identity, be it Austrian or German, presupposes a common historical experience. Yet what in the history of Austria and Germany was shared? The colonization of eastern Europe by Germans and Austrians, the German Confederation of 1815, the storming of the *Düppeler Schanzen* in 1864, the Dual Alliance, *Nibelungentreue* during World War I, and the demands for unification during the interwar years? Did these provide a common historical experience? Or did dissimilar experiences prevail? The expansion of the Habsburg dynasty into central and eastern Europe, the Counter-Reformation, the Seven Years' War, the breakup of the Holy Roman Empire in 1806, the battle of Königgrätz, and Nazi rule between 1938 and 1945? These questions have formed the core of the work of Austrian historians. The great differences in their answers are early evidence of the counterpressures which have marked Austro-German relations in the past.[2]

Counterpressures were inherent also in two other features of a cultural nation, a common ancestry and culture. During the interwar years it was quite clear, in the opinion of one prominent spokesman, that Austria was settled by Germans. "The Austrians of today are the descendants of Bavarians, Swabians, Franconians, and Saxons as a casual glance at any textbook of German and Austrian history will prove."[3] On the other hand, after 1945 the opposite conclusion was reached with similar ease: "We have attempted to show that almost all of today's Austria was settled, to varying degrees, by Slavs."[4] Similar disagreements exist on the issue of a distinct Austrian culture. In the field of musicology, for example, disagreement exists on whether the eighteenth-century Vienna school of music is stylistically distinct from the Mannheim school. Only since 1945 has the notion of an independent Austrian musical tradition received wider currency. An analogous discussion exists with regard to Austrian literature. In contrast to the interwar years, there is little disagreement today on the distinctly Austrian character of the *Biedermeier* culture in the early nineteenth century or of the *Caféhaus* culture in the early twentieth century. But it is considerably more difficult to decide to what extent this is a merely regional variation in German cultural history, as was argued after World War I, or an

---

2. See, for example, Alexander Novotny, "Austrian History from 1848 to 1938 as Seen by Austrian Historians since 1945," *Austrian History News Letters*, 4 (1963), pp. 18-50. Alphons Lhotsky, *Österreichische Historiographie* (Vienna: Verlag für Geschichte und Politik, 1962). Stanley Suval, "The Search for a Fatherland," *Austrian History Yearbook*, IV, 5 (1968-1969), pp. 275-299. Stanley Suval, *The Anschluss Question in the Weimar Era: A Study of Nationalism in Germany and Austria, 1918-1932* (Baltimore: Johns Hopkins University Press, 1974), pp. 55-71.
3. Friedrich F. G. Kleinwächter, "Der Deutsche Mensch im Grossdeutschen Raum," in Friedrich F. G. Kleinwächter and Heinz Paller (eds.), *Die Anschlussfrage in ihrer kulturellen, politischen, und wirtschaftlichen Bedeutung* (Vienna: Braumüller, 1930), p. 237.
4. Reginald Vospernik, "Reichtum der sprachlichen Vielfalt," in Albert Massiczek (ed.), *Die österreichische Nation: Zwischen zwei Nationalismen* (Vienna: Europa Verlag, 1967), pp. 201-202.

indication of a distinct Austrian cultural tradition, as is argued now.

Counterpressures between Austrian and German factors mark Austria's status as a political nation as well, as is shown in the political symbols the country commands to foster group cohesion: its name and its national anthem.

In the past 150 years the concept of Austria has been disturbingly ambiguous; its meaning has shifted several times. At the beginning of the nineteenth century "Austria" and "Germany" were still relatively undifferentiated concepts, a lack of differentiation that can be traced at least until the years 1866–1871. Then "Germany" was used at some times to describe the German Confederation (which included the German and Czech parts of the Austrian Monarchy), but at other times it referred to the geographical area to be united by the Second German Empire of 1871. At the same time there were additional ambiguities on whether "Austria" did or did not include the eastern half of the empire. Only in 1915, three years before the collapse of the monarchy, was the use of the term "Austria" for the western half of the empire officially sanctioned.[5]

Clemenceau's famous aphorism, "l'Autriche—c'est ce que reste," quashed Austrian hopes for unification with Weimar Germany in 1918–19. The victorious powers changed the name of the First Republic from "German-Austria" to "Austria." But throughout the 1920s "German-Austria" was a common and widely accepted term of self-reference indicating a mixture of a German cultural and an Austrian political nation. As between East and West Germany today, the slogan then was "two states but one nation." The concept of Austria became once again an object of political manipulation after the Anschluss of 1938. Eager to suppress all vestiges of previous Austrian independence or regional differentiation from Germany, the Nazis adopted a series of different provincial terms in an attempt to erase any

---

5. Erich Zöllner, "Formen und Wandlungen des Österreichbegriffs," in Hugo Hantsch, Eric Voegelin, and Franco Valsecchi (eds.), *Historica: Studien zum geschichtlichen Denken und Forschen* (Vienna: Herder, 1965), pp. 63-89. Theodor Schieder, *Das Deutsche Kaiserreich von 1871 als Nationalstaat* (Cologne: Westdeutscher Verlag, 1961), pp. 40-43.

notion of a distinct Austria. The return to the name "Austria" after 1945 was, therefore, not merely a matter of expediency but to many a symbolic reassertion of Austria's political independence and cultural identity.

The counterpressures between the Austrian and German components in Austria's political symbols stand out equally clearly in the country's national anthem. Ambiguity arose from the fact that the famous Haydn melody—composed in honor of the Austrian emperor in 1797—had become the unofficial national anthem of the Second German Reich. Throughout the second half of the nineteenth century, growing numbers of pan-German nationalists in Austria were thinking of Germany not Austria when listening to the monarchy's national anthem. This was even more true during the interwar years after the Weimar Republic had officially adopted the melody in 1922. Although a president of the First Republic, Karl Renner, had himself written the text for a new national anthem, it never became official and never achieved the popularity of the old anthem. Only in 1929 was a new national anthem, based on the old melody, adopted. But special mention was made of the fact that there would be no objection to the singing of the German national anthem at occasions that did not have an official character, and the school inspector of Vienna wrote in 1930, "As Austrians and as Germans we have every reason to teach our young generation the German national anthem."[6] Thus, during the interwar years the paradoxical situation arose in which playing the Austrian national anthem could well be regarded as a symbolic expression of the desire for union with Germany. It was only after 1945—and even then only against vigorous opposition—that the old Haydn melody was finally replaced by a Mozart tune, which no longer permitted the deliberate misuse or accidental misinterpretation that had occurred so frequently in the past.

Austrian historians and political analysts have viewed as mutually reinforcing the political and cultural forces shaping their country's history. Following World War I and World

---

6. Quoted in Franz Grasberger, *Die Hymnen Österreichs* (Tutzing: Schneider, 1968), p. 128.

War II, their analyses differed only with respect to the conclusion.[7] After 1918 these parallel moving factors, it was argued, had not only made Austria an integral part of the German cultural nation but also justified its aspiration to become a part of the German political nation. After 1945 the opposite view was expressed with equal conviction: Austria's distinct identity as a *Kulturnation*, so the argument ran, was as clearly established as its independence as a *Staatsnation*.

In the light of this illustrative evidence, it is a fundamental error to view as mutually reinforcing the political and cultural variables which shape autonomy, for the Austro-German case in particular as well as for relations of disjoined partnership in general. The data support, instead, an argument based on the contrary premise. Not copressures and integration but counterpressures and autonomy are the distinctive feature of relations among disjoined partners.

POLITICAL AUTONOMY: A TWO-DIMENSIONAL CONCEPT

Political integration and disintegration are ambiguous concepts which have been used to describe the presence or absence of institutions, interdependencies, and identifications.[8] In contrast, political integration and disintegration are understood here as different degrees of the purposeful coordination of political behavior in the achievement of common tasks. That coordination varies along two dimensions. The extent of political coordination measures the number of different purposes which are to be accomplished by a coordinated policy. The effectiveness of political coordination measures the probability of compliance with coordinated policies of the partners concerned. Table 1

---

7. Kleinwächter and Paller, *Die Anschlussfrage* and Massiczek, *Die österreichische Nation* are odd mixtures of polemical and serious writings illustrating a dramatic shift in Austria's intellectual climate. A recent analysis of the national integration of Austria agrees with the argument advanced here. See William T. Bluhm, *Building an Austrian Nation: The Political Integration of a Western State* (New Haven: Yale University Press, 1973).
8. The concept is discussed in J. S. Nye, *Peace in Parts: Integration and Conflict in Regional Organization* (Boston: Little, Brown, 1971), pp. 36-48.

TABLE 1. Two Dimensions Defining Different Degrees of Political Autonomy: The Austro-German Case (1815-1970)

Effectiveness of political coordination	Extent of Political Coordination		
	Single purpose	Multi-purpose	General purpose
Low	HH (1945-1970)	MH	M
Medium	MH (1870-1918)	M (1848-1870)	ML (1918-1938)
High	M (1815-1848)	ML	LL (1938-1945)

KEY: Political autonomy is:
HH = very high
MH = medium high
M = medium
ML = medium low
LL = very low

summarizes the changes along these two dimensions that have occurred in the Austro-German case since 1815.

The distribution of the six cases indicates that both the extent and the effectiveness of political coordination peaked only once, during the partially coerced unification of Austria with Germany between 1938 and 1945. During the other five periods different combinations of extent and effectiveness resulted in different outcomes with only one thing in common, the fact that they preserved for Austria significant amounts of political autonomy.

Changes in the extent and the effectiveness of political coordination are not peculiar to Austria and Germany with their cultural unity and political amity. They characterize also changes in the relationship between states such as the Soviet Union and the United States, which are cultural strangers and political rivals. Most often, though, the extent and the effectiveness of political coordination is higher between culturally homogeneous than heterogeneous states. What needs to be explained is why these partners stop short of unification. Disjoined partnership is, then, a descriptive summary for political relationships between culturally cohesive states that preserve signficant amounts of political autonomy.

To the question of why disjoined partnership obtains, a satisfactory answer rests on an analysis of two distinct sets of factors. On the one hand, we need to understand the nature of integration processes: What are the important economic, social, and cultural variables? How can these variables be summarized succinctly? And how can such a summary be used for purposes of explanation? On the other hand, we should analyze also the process of politics: How will political actors adjust to changing processes of integration? Will they respond by choosing political strategies of integration or autonomy?

This analysis is based on a detailed consideration of social and cultural interdependence on the one hand and economic and political rewards on the other. The balance between the two types of interdependence explains the waxing and waning of communities. The interrelation between the two types of rewards accounts for differences in political strategy. Counterpressures within and between these two clusters of variables help to explain the persistence of political autonomy.

SOCIETY, COMMUNITY, AND AUTONOMY

The distinction Austrians and Germans make between a cultural and a political nation points to the two main forces that shape political autonomy and disjoined partnership. But a satisfactory explanation of political autonomy fashioned from nonpolitical and political variables requires greater precision than these two concepts can provide. What is needed is a set of concepts that permits an accurate description and parsimonious explanation of the forces that shape political autonomy. These concepts are provided by the communications approach to the analysis of political integration which emerges from a tradition of research started by Karl W. Deutsch. Deutsch pioneered in the analysis of the interdependence between units—both peoples and states—as a precondition for the emergence of modern national states and, in some cases, for the transcendence of the national state by supranational regions.[9] This tradition of research suggests that political integration depends on five aspects of interdependence: its probability, magnitude, reward structure, symmetry, and leverage.

The *probability* distributions of interdependencies and political outcomes, it has been argued, correlate highly.[10] The *magnitude* of interdependence between societies, compared for example with the magnitude of interdependence within societies, has been viewed as an indicator of the distribution of potential economic and political power between groups, classes, and parties.[11] The balance between positive and negative *rewards*, both

9. Karl W. Deutsch, *Nationalism and Social Communication: An Inquiry into the Foundations of Nationality*, 2nd ed. (Cambridge, Mass.: M.I.T. Press, 1966); Karl W. Deutsch et al., *Political Community and the North Atlantic Area: International Organization in the Light of Historical Experience* (Princeton: Princeton University Press, 1957); Karl W. Deutsch, *Political Community at the International Level: Problems of Definition and Measurement* (Garden City: Doubleday, 1954). For interesting parallels see also Otto Bauer, *Die Nationalitätenfrage und die Sozialdemokratie* (Vienna: Brand, 1907).

10. The Relative Acceptance Indicator (R.A.) is a special statistic that measures these probabilities as differences between actually observed and statistically expected interdependence between pairs. These problems are discussed in the following works: I. Richard Savage and Karl W. Deutsch, "A Statistical Model of the Gross Analysis of Transaction Flows," *Econometrica* XXVIII, 3 (July 1960), pp. 551-572; Hayward Alker and Donald J. Puchala, "Trends in Economic Partnership: The North Atlantic Area, 1928-1963," in J. David Singer (ed.), *Quantitative International Politics: Insights and Evidence* (New York: Free Press, 1968), pp. 287-316; Richard W. Chadwick and Karl W. Deutsch, "International Trade and Economic Integration," *Comparative Political Studies*, VI, 1 (April 1973), pp. 84-109; Donald J. Puchala, "International Transactions and Regional Integration," *International Organization*, XXIV, 4 (autumn 1970), pp. 732-763; Bruce M. Russett, *Community and Contention: Britain and America in the Twentieth Century* (Cambridge, Mass.: M.I.T. Press, 1963); Cal Clark and Susan Welch, "Western European Trade as a Measure of Integration: Untangling the Interpretations," *Journal of Conflict Resolution*, XVI, 1 (September 1972), pp. 363-382. The R.A. is not used in this study of Austro-German relations because it can be calculated only on the basis of the worldwide total of different transaction and communication measures. For the nineteenth century these data do not exist.

11. Karl W. Deutsch and Alexander Eckstein, "National Industrialization and the Declining Share of the International Economic Sector, 1890-

objective and perceived, will lead to different political outcomes.[12] Different degrees of *symmetry* in the balance of initiative of, dependence on, and vulnerability to interdependencies could be expected to affect politics.[13] Finally, the critics more than the proponents of the communications approach have pointed to the *leverage* that crucial interdependencies may provide to key political actors at critical points in time.[14]

The major weakness of the communications approach to problems of national and supranational integration is its descriptive character. The five dimensions of communications lend themselves more easily to a description of the social and economic context of politics than to the explanation of different political outcomes. The existing literature shows its greatest strength in the generation and classification of large amounts of data which bear on one or several of the five aspects of interdependence. In contrast, the analysis offered here is based on the insight that the relationship between different types of interdependence is more important for purposes of explanation than is an analysis of any one of the other five aspects of interdependence. The tools the communications approach provides, but so

---

1950," *World Politics*, XIII, 2 (January 1961), pp. 270-271; Russett, *Community and Contention*, p. 52; Karl W. Deutsch, "Social Mobilization and Political Development," *American Political Science Review*, LV, 3 (September 1961), pp. 500-501.

12. Karl W. Deutsch, "Power and Communication in International Society," in A. V. S. de Reuck and Julie Knight (eds.), *Ciba Foundation Symposium on Conflict in Society* (London: Churchill Ltd., 1966), pp. 300-316. Donald J. Puchala, "The Pattern of Contemporary Regional Integration," *International Studies Quarterly*, XII, 1 (March 1968), p. 51. Karl W. Deutsch et al., *Political Community and the North Atlantic Area.*

13. Karl W. Deutsch, "Integration and Autonomy: Some Concepts and Data," *Ekistics*, 179 (October 1970), p. 327. Johan Galtung, "A Structural Theory of Imperialism," *Journal of Peace Research*, VIII, 2 (1971), pp. 81-118. Bruce M. Russett, "Transaction, Community and International Political Integration," *Journal of Common Market Studies*, IX, 3 (March 1971), p. 231.

14. Stanley H. Hoffmann, *Contemporary Theory in International Relations* (Englewood Cliffs, N. J.: Prentice-Hall, 1960), p. 45. Hedley Bull, "International Theory: The Case for a Classical Approach," *World Politics*, XVIII, 3 (April 1966), pp. 363-374.

far has neglected, can be used to analyze not the gradual transition but the asymmetric reordering of two different types of interdependence over time. That reordering, I shall propose, affects the balance between cultural standardization and social differentiation and through them the balance between political integration and autonomy.

Theories of national and supranational integration have analyzed processes of social mobilization, economic development, and political participation in providing different explanations of how political autonomy is achieved. Despite many differences, these theories share an underlying central premise: as the process of modernization transforms society, economy, and politics, the interdependence between individuals and systems increases. An explanation of the persistence of political autonomy in culturally cohesive areas can take its point of departure from an analogous central premise, the growth of interdependence in community and society.

The modernization process is often defined as the result of increases in two different types of interdependence. The first type derives from the growth of human knowledge and increases in the volume of information available and transmitted. The second type of interdependence arises from man's growing physical control over his environment. In the words of C. E. Black, " 'modernization' may be defined as the process by which historically evolved institutions are adapted to the rapidly changing functions that reflect the unprecedented increase in man's knowledge, permitting control over his environment, that accompanied the scientific revolution."[15] The first type of interdependence describes changes in mental forces, the sharing of meaning in community. The second type of interdependence describes changes in material forces, the division of labor in society. Crucial to the difference between these two types of interdependence is the medium which links individuals in community and society. Communications within community involve the transfer of messages (information) with their impact on the memories and habits of the

---

15. Cyril E. Black, *The Dynamics of Modernization* (New York: Harper and Row, 1966), p. 7.

recipient. In society, on the other hand, what counts principally is the transfer of goods and services (matter and energy). Community and society are interdependent. The story of the Tower of Babel illustrates that there can be no society (division of labor) without a modicum of community (shared memories and preferences) and, one may add, there can be no community without a modicum of society.[16]

Inequality in the growth rate of these two types of interdependence offers a partial explanation of changes in the political autonomy of culturally cohesive states. These two types of interdependence, to be sure, cannot be compared directly. Information flows measured in absolute numbers of messages exchanged and trade flows measured in monetary value, for example, are incommensurable. But changes in the growth rates of interdependence in community and society are comparable and afford one part of an explanation of political autonomy. Such a comparison schematically summarizes intellectual, social, and economic history into a convenient shorthand, "community" and "society." The impact of community and society on political autonomy rests on an assumption concerning the standardizing and differentiating effects of these two types of interdependence on culturally cohesive areas. Increases in standardization should diminish political autonomy and gains in differentiation should enhance political autonomy. What is of interest for culturally homogeneous areas in general and for the explanation of Austrian autonomy in particular is the balance between standardization and differentiation.

But how can one distinguish between standardization and differentiation? Adhering to an analysis which makes a sharp distinction between an ideal type of tradition and an ideal type of modernity, one might agree with Turgot that in the traditional

---

16. Deutsch, *Nationalism and Social Communication*, p. 95. For a very different analysis of problems of integration from the perspective of society and community (*Gesellschaft* and *Gemeinschaft*), see Paul Taylor, "The Concept of Community and the European Integration Process," *Journal of Common Market Studies*, VII, 2 (December 1968), pp. 83-101; Ronn D. Kaiser, "Toward the Copernican Phase of Regional Integration Theory," *Journal of Common Market Studies*, X, 3 (March 1972), pp. 207-232.

community the peasant's awareness of the world beyond his local village is minimal: "A French parish . . . is a congeries of huts and countryfolk as inert as their huts."[17] In culturally cohesive areas the accelerating flow of information between villages, regional centers, and the capital made the peasant increasingly conscious of his similarity to vast numbers of people of whose very existence he had not even been aware. The medium that accelerates the flow of information may vary over time. The development of an efficient, large-scale postal service in central Europe increased greatly the flow of information in the middle of the nineteenth century; modern communications technology—television, satellites, and computers—has the same effect in the middle of the twentieth century. But whatever the medium of the message, the effect on culturally homogeneous areas is the same. The sharing of meaning is not only a definition of interdependence in community. It also summarizes in a nutshell the impact of modernization on individuals and regions in culturally cohesive areas. Modernization and an increase of interdependence in community link up isolated fragments and thus reveal the unity inherent in these areas. The emergence of German nationalism in nineteenth-century Austria, for example, fits the notion of a community increasingly tightly knit through the flow of information and a simultaneous increase in the sharing of meaning. Modernization does not set people apart but unites them instead. It leads not to the divergence of regions and growing heterogeneity of individuals but to convergence and homogeneity.

In which way does a traditional community differ from a modern community in culturally cohesive areas? From Tönnies to Parsons, sociologists have largely agreed on a set of attributes that define a traditional community, including factors such as mutual sympathy, habitual compliance, kinship ties, and neighborhood relations. An increase in the quantity and changes in the quality of the flow of information in community accompany the modernization process. These changes affect individuals in two

---

17. Quoted in Alexis de Tocqueville, *The Old Régime and the French Revolution* (Garden City, N. Y.: Doubleday, 1955), p. 49.

different ways. They uproot individuals psychologically from their traditional identity and loyalty. And these changes also create an awareness of the existence of culturally alien communities which appear as threatening simply because they are different. The majority of the German-Austrians in the Austrian Empire, for instance, gradually became German nationalists in the nineteenth century due to both these changes. Identification with a national community became a cure for both anomie and enmity. The modern community differs from the traditional community not only in size but in the intensity of the psychological commitment of its members.[18] An acceleration of information flow in traditional communities of culturally homogeneous areas breaks down barriers between people and regions that had previously concealed the potential strength of underlying cultural cohesion.

The reverse process is observable for social interdependence defined in terms of the transactions of goods and services in society. The absence of a division of labor in traditional society, as Marx observed, makes the great mass of the peasants, a "simple addition of homologous magnitudes, much as potatoes in a sack form a sack of potatoes."[19] The growing division of labor in society in the modernization process leads to two mutually antagonistic changes. The first change points toward a strong differentiation of regions and of classes, the second toward a weaker standardization. The social mobilization of the peasants in the process of economic development starts a process of differentiation, geographically between different markets and socially between different classes. That process of differentiation eventually leads to a highly complex pattern which does not resemble the simple polarized structure of industrial society which Marx had envisaged. The division of labor, thus, is not only a definition of interdependence in society. It is also an apt summary of

18. Boyd C. Shafer, *Nationalism: Myth and Reality* (New York: Harcourt, Brace and World, 1955); Hans Kohn, *The Idea of Nationalism: A Study of Its Origins and Background* (New York: Collier Books, 1967).
19. Karl Marx, "The Eighteenth Brumaire of Louis Bonaparte." in Lewis S. Feuer (ed.), *Basic Writings on Politics and Philosophy: Karl Marx and Friedrich Engels* (Garden City, N. Y.: Doubleday, 1959), p. 338.

the impact of modernization on individuals and markets in culturally homogeneous regions. Modernization and the growth of interdependence in society transform an economically and socially relatively undifferentiated mass population into a highly differentiated one. Throughout the first half of the nineteenth century, for instance, the German-Austrians were largely undivided. But by the early 1880s the process of differentiation had progressed sufficiently for them to split into three different camps (*Lager*) comprised largely of different classes—peasants and small artisans, workers, and the middle class. Modernization does not unite people but sets them apart. It leads not to the convergence of markets and a growing homogeneity of individuals but to divergence and heterogeneity.

But at the same time there is a second, albeit weaker, tendency toward standardization and greater unity. Compared with traditional society, the growing specialization of production of different classes and regions leads to much greater joint economic rewards for parties linked together in complementary relationships. The logic of Adam Smith is, therefore, at work and that logic tends to unify classes and regions around enlarged economic benefits. But this unifying effect is relatively weak. Even though increasing, the material rewards resulting from the division of labor in society are limited. Whether left to the mechanism of the market or of government, the distribution of limited joint rewards among unequal partners may often lead to the formation of coalitions, countercoalitions, and factional conflict. In contrast, gains in the sharing of meaning in community center on the production and distribution of symbolic instead of material rewards. These symbolic rewards, typically, are less scarce in supply and more encompassing in their appeal than are material rewards.[20] The potentially unifying effect that derives from the production of joint economic rewards is more than offset by the divisive effect that derives from the distribution of these economic rewards. Compared with

---

20. Murray Edelman, *The Symbolic Uses of Politics* (Urbana: University of Illinois Press, 1964); Murray Edelman, *Politics as Symbolic Action: Mass Arousal and Quiescence* (Chicago: Markham, 1971).

the distribution of flexible symbolic rewards in community, the distribution of fixed material rewards in society produces differentiation. On balance, then, as the division of labor in society grows, divisive impacts could be expected to predominate over unifying ones. In culturally homogeneous areas material forces increase differentiation and only mental forces standardization.

An analysis of changes in the sharing of meaning in community and the division of labor in society offers not merely a descriptive summary of economic and social history but also a partial explanation of political autonomy in culturally cohesive areas. Changes in the interdependence in community and society lead to different political outcomes. The sharing of meaning in community draws people and regions together. It causes standardization and political integration. The division of labor sets people apart. It leads to differentiation and political autonomy.

This analysis of political autonomy is helpful only if there are some empirical measures of community and society. As such, two sets of behavioral and attitudinal indicators suggest themselves. In the study of culturally heterogeneous societies, rates of linguistic assimilation are an intuitively plausible and easily obtainable *behavioral indicator* of information transfer and of the waxing and waning of cultural communities. In culturally homogeneous areas, however, linguistic differentiation is often absent and one needs other indicators of information transfer and communications flow. The number of books, periodicals, letters, telegrams, and telephone calls exchanged can be thought of not merely as measures of changing interdependence in general but as indicators of information transfer and the changing strength of community in particular. Conversely, indicators of social transactions such as trade or the movement of capital and labor can be assumed to measure changes in the relative importance of Austro-German society over time.

Corresponding *attitudinal indicators* of community and society are also identifiable.[21] Three different features of the attitudinal

---

21. On this subject, see Richard L. Merritt, *Symbols of American Community, 1735-1775* (New Haven: Yale University Press, 1966); Gebhard L. Schweigler, *National Consciousness in Divided Germany* (Beverly Hills,

integration of people could be postulated: the attention people pay to one another; how much they like each other; and how much they identify with one another. It seems reasonable to expect that positive evaluations are measures of the attitudinal integration of society, as mutual identifications are measures of the attitudinal integration of community. We might think of this difference between evaluation and identification as analogous to the difference between anchoring a ship on the shifting sands of easily changed evaluations or on the hard rock of stable identifications.

Just as the sharing of meaning in community presupposes a minimum of social transactions, so attitudinal integration at the cultural level will require also a minimum amount of positive evaluation; but, generally speaking, changes in the degree of mutual identification are the distinctive characteristic of attitudinal integration at the cultural level. Conversely, just as the division of labor in society requires at least a minimum of communications, attitudinal integration at the social level will also require a minimum amount of mutual identification; but on the whole, changes in positive or negative evaluations are the most distinctive attribute of attitudinal integration at the social level.[22]

In summary, what matters for an explanation of the political autonomy of states in culturally homogeneous areas is the difference in the growth rate of standardizing and differentiating effects as measured by changes in community and society. If

---

California: Sage Publications, 1975); and Karl W. Deutsch and Richard L. Merritt, "Effects of Events on National and International Images," in Herbert C. Kelman (ed.), *International Behavior: A Social-Psychological Analysis* (New York: Holt, Rinehart and Winston, 1966), pp. 132-187.

22. One problem is not satisfactorily dealt with here. But in my opinion this does not seriously damage the validity of the analysis. The problem arises from the fact that transactions and communications are both cause and consequence of society and community. In the absence of better indicators for the analysis of the relation between society and community, there is no adequate way in which the cause-and-effect chain can be disaggregated. Crucial for the purpose of testing the explanation are changes in the trends of social transactions and cultural communications over time. Fortunately, these trends can be ascertained without establishing a clear-cut cause-and-effect relation between concept and indicator.

these growth rates are roughly equal, standardization and differentiation cancel each other out and leave unaffected existing levels of political autonomy. If standardizing experiences derived from the sharing of meaning in community grow faster than differentiating experiences in society, this cluster of variables points to losses of political autonomy as the expected outcome. If, on the other hand, differentiating experiences derived from the division of labor in society grow faster than standardizing experiences in community, these variables point to probable gains in political autonomy. If, finally, behavioral and attitudinal indicators of community or of society point in different directions, then there is no clear effect associated either with the sharing of meaning in community or with the division of labor in society. Counterpressures between standardization and differentiation should leave existing levels of political autonomy largely unchanged.

REWARDS AND AUTONOMY

Relying on nonpolitical variables, the persistence of political autonomy can be made partially intelligible. But the social, economic, and cultural variables from which the explanation was fashioned define only one set of forces shaping different levels of political autonomy. A consideration of the way in which the effect of nonpolitical variables is reinforced or counterbalanced by the political process itself is essential for a full understanding of the persistence of political autonomy. An analysis of the strategy of the actors should supplement an analysis of the structure of their relationships.

As the focus of analysis shifts toward domestic politics, the discussion will center on the concept of reward. For theoretical purposes the disaggregation of the reward concept by type is most useful. The structure of both economic and political rewards is important in prompting political strategies more or less favorable to the persistence of political autonomy. But the structure of political rewards alone points to a theoretical reason accounting for political autonomy.

Significant variations in the frequency and intensity of economic rewards associated with political strategies of integration or autonomy have been found in most instances of political unification and fragmentation analyzed to date.[23] The availability of sufficient material facilities and incentives associated with different strategies of political integration or autonomy could be expected to affect directly the political strategies fashioned by political coalitions in each of the partner countries. The economic rewards of the Austrian Empire, for example, were of great importance in convincing the Austrian elites to opt for relatively high degrees of political autonomy throughout the nineteenth century.

The challenging task of providing leadership in the economic unification of Germany met with two divergent responses from the Prussian and Austrian elites. One reason stands out clearly. The economic well-being of the German-Austrian aristocracy and bourgeoisie depended less on the economic unification of Germany than did that of their Prussian counterparts; the German-Austrians had options and alternatives which simply did not exist for the Prussians. The development of the commerce and industry of Prussia's far-flung and disconnected provinces depended vitally on the economic unification of Germany. The German-Austrians, on the other hand, occupied the commanding heights of a vast empire which offered to many of them channels of upward social mobility that even an enlarged and unified Germany under Austrian leadership did not seem to promise. Manifold and profitable careers in the imperial army and bureaucracy were the German-Austrians' prize for what they might well have called "carrying the empire's burden." Not industrialization but bureaucratization was their avenue to prosperity. One might almost say that the Prussians were industrial, not imperial, while the Austrians were imperial, not industrial.

The effects of economic rewards on political strategies are crucial. An analysis of the distribution of economic rewards that motivate political actors may be of great importance in each and every case in which the partial or total sacrifice of political autonomy is at stake. Such analysis differs from a description of

---

23. Deutsch et al., *Political Community and the North Atlantic Area*, pp. 46-50, 71.

transaction and communication flows in the different weights it assigns to different types of transactions and communications. Flows affecting directly the stature of economic rewards are weighted more heavily than those that do not because they are more likely to affect political strategies. Thus, the flows of trade and capital in particular take on a special importance in the study of integration no less than of imperialism. But the analysis of economic rewards shares with the previous investigation of society and community the underlying assumption that the behavior induced by the structure of economic rewards will pass through the filters of the political process without being deflected in any way. It is an apolitical explanation of politics in that the effects of economic rewards on politics are assumed, not analyzed.

This is an assumption worth testing. It is, after all, not intuitively plausible that the structure of economic rewards should be more important than the differential political payoffs accruing to different actors from competing political strategies of integration and autonomy. A focus on political rewards, then, necessarily leads to a distinction between different political actors. The question concerning the choices and constraints of political strategies favoring integration or autonomy remains to be answered.

Where the partial or total sacrifice of political autonomy abroad is a realistic option, a very high degree of interpenetration of domestic and foreign policy is a central political feature. This interpenetration has two distinct though related implications. First, domestic politics becomes foreign: political elites are compelled to adjust to the impingement of foreign political influences on their political position at home. Second, foreign policy becomes domestic: how much political autonomy will be sacrificed is a decision linked intimately to the actors' political position at home. Political strategies favoring different levels of political autonomy, therefore, become valuable resources in politics, domestic and foreign, on which certain actors in domestic politics draw to strengthen their position at the expense of others. Since strategies of integration and autonomy become hotly contested stakes, a lasting political coalition at home which backed unambiguously a strategy of political integration abroad would be the exception, not the rule.

Political elites controlling the foreign policy machinery, in particular, could be expected to pursue two objectives: to cut off foreign influences undermining their domestic position and to resort to strategies of political integration in response to domestic challenges to their established ranks. Political integration, thus, is likely to become a crisis strategy which promises high returns in the defense of established positions in domestic politics. But at the same time, and this is crucial, these same elites have an interest in pursuing a strategy of no more than partial integration. Political support from abroad is welcome but too much support would endanger the very object it was designed to defend, the citadel of domestic power. Political integration as a crisis strategy, thus, more likely than not will remain partial. In reaching too far, it would relinquish the bastions of political power not to the opposition at home but to allies abroad.

There exists, however, no reason why the adoption of political integration as a crisis strategy should be limited only to the established elites. Even though they are excluded from the formal foreign policy machinery, counterelites may operate under a similar logic. A strategy of integration can be a political resource desperately needed in an otherwise unpromising political conflict over the distribution of political power at home. In fact, as long as they do not share power to a significant degree at home, counterelites have little to lose from the adoption of an unconditional policy of integration abroad as is illustrated by the long history of unrestrained irredentist movements.

This political logic could be postulated as a characteristic feature of all political systems and processes of partial or total political integration. It is illustrated particularly clearly, however, by situations in which established political elites are challenged by counterelites newly mobilized in the process of modernization. The Austro-German case reveals with monotonous regularity how established elites resort to crisis strategies of partial integration when domestic opposition rises on the one hand, and how new groups and counterelites, in turn, seek political support abroad on the other. The years 1866-1871 marked a transition from an older to a newer pattern of partial political integration across the Austro-German political boundary. The very moment that saw the breakup of the traditional coalition between the Austrian and the Prussian aristocracies over the issue of leadership in Germany also witnessed the forging of links between Austria's new workers' movement and socialist organizations in Germany. The cross-national partnership of a preindustrial era gave way to a new coalition of the industrial age.

Political and economic rewards do not always point in the same direction. In the late nineteenth century, for instance, economic rewards dictated to many German-Austrians a strategy of autonomy from Germany, while political rewards made preferable a strategy of integration. Nothing can be said in the abstract about the distribution of economic rewards associated with alternative strategies of integration or autonomy. That distribution is revealed only by the study of concrete cases. The distribution of political rewards, on the other hand, puts elites and counterelites into a predicament for which there exists no clear-cut answer. Political elites will wholeheartedly support strategies of political integration only if they face certain elimination from the power they hold, and political counterelites will do the same only if they confront permanent separation from the power they want. Conversely, unequivocal support of full political autonomy is possible only for political elites securely entrenched in positions of domestic power and for counterelites irrevocably isolated from potential foreign allies. Such unambiguous situations are rare. Normally, elites and counterelites operate in situations which have costs as well as benefits associated with strategies of integration and autonomy. In these instances, partial political integration as a crisis measure is the most likely result. The analysis of the Austro-German case offers an abundance of evidence that supports this view.

The first nonpolitical explanation can, thus, be supplemented by a second political one, in which the notion of reward is central. The exclusive reliance on the concept of economic reward was unsatisfactory because resultant political rewards for political actors were assumed instead of analyzed. But an analysis of the prime political condition of situations in which the sacrifice of political autonomy becomes a real option, the interpenetration of domestic and foreign policy, reveals competing strategies of political integration and political autonomy as crucial to the distribution of power in domestic politics. In an attempt to improve their political position, political elites and counterelites could be expected to adopt conflict strategies of political integration and autonomy. Political integration, thus, becomes the foremost instrument of a political crisis strategy.

Granting that nonpolitical and political variables shape political autonomy, two questions still remain to be answered. What is the relation between both sets of factors and how should each of them be weighed? The analytical distinction here drawn between nonpolitical and political elements is overly sharp. Social transactions and economic rewards, for example, refer in part to identical aspects of reality, such as trade, and thus provide a link between both sets of variables. Any application of these theoretical arguments to empirical material thus will inevitably undermine the neat distinction.

Equally problematic is the question of how the two sets of factors should be weighed relative to one another. In the absence of more precise knowledge on this point, the two groups of variables are here considered as roughly equal in their impact on political autonomy. At its simplest, the argument we have developed points to the persistence of counterpressures as the critical reason for the persistence of political autonomy. In the second half of the nineteenth century, for example, these counterpressures were reflected in the divergent movements of different indicators of society and community. In the first half of the twentieth century on the other hand, these indicators pointed in the same direction, toward political integration during the interwar years and toward political autonomy since 1945. In these two periods the counterpressures that mattered occurred not within the first nonpolitical but in the second political cluster as well as between both clusters of variables. These counterpressures make the probability of the status quo in the relations between culturally cohesive states greater than the probability of structural change.

Central European thought on problems of nationalism has traditionally focused on the concepts of a cultural and a political nation. Illustrative evidence for the Austro-German case indicates that these nonpolitical and political variables were mutually opposed. Counterpressures within and between these two clusters of variables suggest the most promising explanation of the persistence of Austria's political autonomy since 1815. Throughout this chapter that explanation has been deliberately cast in probabilistic terms. There is no necessary relation between political autonomy and the balance between community and society, on the one hand, and the balance between economic and political rewards, on the other. Relative changes in political autonomy could be likened not to a ladder but to an assembly line, that is, not to a sequential process with a small number of predetermined outcomes, but to a probabilistic process with a large number of combinatorial ones. To validate this argument fully, nothing short of a large-scale comparative analysis of the political relationships between culturally homogeneous states would do; the appendix to this book is a first step in that direction. An intensive analysis of the Austrian half of the Austro-German case can serve only a paradigmatic purpose in illustrating how the persistence of political autonomy might be explained in other situations where states are culturally united and politically divided. But such an analysis will also help to clarify some aspects of central European politics. What were the conditions which made for different levels of political autonomy in the past? What are they today? What might they be in the future?

Traditional historiography has distinguished between three major phases in Austro-German relations since 1815. The strength of dynastic powers and diplomatic considerations in conjunction with the weakness of nationalism before 1848 made subnational-regional and supranational-confederal solutions viable political options. Between 1848 and 1918 Austrian politics in general and Austro-German relations in particular were defined by the nationality problem of the multinational empire. The fragmentation of the Austrian monarchy and the change of Europe's balance of power system in 1918, finally, put the Austro-German partnership on entirely different terms which pointed to a bilateral arrangement during the interwar period and to a multilateral one since 1945. Traditional historiography, however, is not the sole concern of this analysis. The persistence of Austria's political autonomy throughout the nineteenth and twentieth centuries is a central theme informing the periodization of Austro-German relations chosen here.

The chronology of the persistence of Austria's political autonomy since 1815 falls into six consecutive but distinct patterns which form a logical framework for analysis. An attempt to identify these six patterns by different labels can be undertaken only by escaping into metaphors. For easy identification, reference will be made to the six patterns in Austro-German relations since 1815 as aristocratic, conflictual, hierarchical, voluntaristic, structural, and pluralistic. The *aristocratic* pattern (1815–1848) was based on a political alliance across political boundaries which united the traditional centers of power in Austrian and German society in the accomplishment of one overriding purpose, the political suppression of liberal and national forces. In all other spheres of life Austria and Germany remained largely isolated from each other. The *conflict* pattern (1848–1870) represented just the opposite extreme. Partial cooperation occurred in the economic and social sector which greatly accelerated the growing interdependence between Austria and the German states. But in the political sphere the period was dominated by an intense conflict between Austria and Prussia over the position of leadership in Germany.

The *hierarchical* pattern (1870–1918) was marked by both imperialistic hierarchy and imperialistic defeat. In defense of their elite position within the Austrian Empire, the German-Austrians increasingly came to rely on the political support of the German Empire. The partial erosion of Austria's political autonomy resulted in an enlarged capability for conflict behavior at home and abroad which, in the end, led to total defeat on both fronts. The *voluntaristic* pattern (1918–1938) revealed a widespread desire in Austria for unification with Germany. It stood for integration by consent and in 1938, at least in part, by conquest. The *structural* pattern (1938–1945) assured the Austrians of a privileged, if subordinate, position in a second attempt to establish German (and Austrian) dominance over central and eastern Europe. But within a span of a few years, a disastrous defeat showed that the structural experiment had failed. Finally, the *pluralistic* pattern (1945–1970) has witnessed the emergence of an independent Austrian political community, tied to Germany by many links at the social and cultural level but sharing no longer any significant political concerns.

III

ARISTOCRATIC PATTERN
(1815-1848)

THE ARISTOCRATIC pattern predated the industrial revolution with its tremendous acceleration of economic growth, social mobilization, and, eventually, political participation. It is marked by a widespread discrepancy between the cosmopolitanism of international elites at the top of society and the segmentation of parochial populations at the bottom. The process of modernization was eventually to lead to a two-pronged attack on the parochialism of the many and the internationalism of the few in bringing about the convergence of both into a nationalism encompassing all classes.

The fundamental difference between the integration processes of traditional societies (with their extreme discrepancy between cosmopolitanism at the top and parochialism at the bottom of society) and of modern societies (with their smaller differentiation between nationalism at the national level and patriotism at the regional level) raises the question why one should analyze in depth a pattern seemingly unrelated to modern times. Why does this analysis of Austro-German relations start in 1815 rather than at some earlier date when the aristocratic pattern was first established or at some later point when it finally became obsolete?

Austro-German relations between the Congress of Vienna and the formation of the German Confederation under Austrian leadership (1815), on the one hand, and the Treaty of Versailles and the founding of the German Empire without Austrian participation (1871), on the other, could be likened to a thaw in many traditional patterns of behavior and attitudes in Austria and Germany. Political choices by the Austrian elite between 1815 and 1848 left a deep imprint in the muddy tracks; with these tracks gradually hardening, a change in direction became increasingly less probable with the passing of time. A break with Austria's eighteenth-century policy of isolation from Germany had to wait until the Revolution of 1848 brushed aside the Metternich regime. The aristocratic pattern of relations between Austria and Germany is a study of Austria's unwillingness and inability to develop and cultivate political capabilities for the building of a wider Austro-German community and society. In many ways this choice was to shape Austro-German relations for the rest of the nineteenth century.

Because of the relative absence of economic modernization and social mobilization throughout the years 1815–1848, a primary focus on community and society, as reflected in mass behavior and attitudes, is not helpful for an analysis of the Austro-German case. The nonexistence of reliable data on communications and transactions flows merely reflects this fact. Important to an analysis, however, are the economic and political rewards that the Austrian government attempted to secure through a double strategy of integration and isolation. The Austrian government favored a partial political integration of Austria and Germany in order to repress all liberal and national movements in central Europe. But swayed by economic and political rewards, the Austrian government adopted also a policy of isolating the Austrian community and society as much as possible from Germany. In the end, this double strategy failed because Austria simply lacked the required capabilities for its execution. The primacy of domestic politics and the persistence of political autonomy make the aristocratic pattern a good example of the relationship between disjoined partners.

POLITICAL COMMUNITY: CLASS COALITION ACROSS BORDERS

After a generation of bloody wars, the Congress of Vienna heralded a new era in European affairs. In organizing it, Metternich followed the dictates of Austrian domestic politics no less than the requirements of international diplomacy. In domestic politics Metternich's task was not to turn back or forward but simply to arrest the clock of change. In eighteenth-century Austria the major political battle had raged between representatives of an old and a new political order, between church and aristocracy speaking for local autonomy on the one hand and dynasty and bureaucracy favoring central authority on the other. In Austria, as in the rest of Europe, the battle had eventually ended with a victory for the proponents of a new order. The turbulent years of the Napoleonic wars at the outset of the nineteenth century pointed to the social class and political counterelite which, eventually, would challenge in the name of nationalism and liberalism the anational and conservative alliance between dynasty and bureaucracy. Metternich's task in domestic politics was to control both the spokesmen of the past and of the future, and to steer the empire between reaction and revolution on the unexciting but harsh course of restoration.

Metternich saw the strongest guarantee for the continued existence of the polyglot Austrian Empire in the establishment of an interstate system which rested on the principles of dynastic legitimacy at home and political stability abroad. The world that was restored[1] in 1815 required, then, both the suppression of movements of national liberation on the periphery and the quelling of liberal agitation in the center of Europe. The promise and the dilemma of the new international order were inextricably linked. The institutionalization of great power cooperation in a number of European congresses rested on the requirements of joint counterrevolutionary action; but the case of Greece proved

---

1. Henry A. Kissinger, *A World Restored: Metternich, Castlereagh, and Problems of Peace, 1812-1822* (Boston: Houghton Mifflin, 1957).

as early as the 1820s that the capability for joint action was insufficient to meet these challenges.

Austria's active commitment to the principles of legitimacy and stability extended not only to European but German affairs. This congruence of goals stood in sharp contrast to the traditional clash between the European and German political interests of the Habsburgs. From the fifteenth century onward Austria had been an instrument in the hands of the Catholic church, which used the empire to counter the growing power of absolutist France, to resist the Hussite insurrection in Bohemia, to combat the Protestant Reformation, and to man the defenses of Europe's eastern borders. This European orientation of Austrian foreign policy before 1815 is reflected in the military history of the country. France, Italy, and Turkey account for forty-one of the sixty-three wars Austria fought between the beginning of the sixteenth and the end of the nineteenth centuries and for 180 of the total of 259 years Austria was at war.[2]

It was, therefore, fitting that Austria's rise to the ranks of one of the foremost European powers was accompanied by a decline in the strength and vitality of the Holy Roman Empire. Two events illustrate how far this process of decline had advanced by the first decade of the nineteenth century. When the Austrian emperor, under strong indirect pressure from Napoleon, renounced his rights to the crown of the German Empire in 1806, the repercussions of this step were minimal. Popular response in Germany and Austria was a mixture of lukewarm nostalgia and outright indifference. Thus, the Austrian emperor was gravely mistaken when he opened his disastrous military campaign against Napoleon in 1809 with a proclamation which contained the passage: "Our cause is the cause of Germany. United with Austria, Germany was once independent and happy; only through Austria's support can Germany once again regain both."[3] The expected uprising of the German masses against the

---

2. Otto Berndt, *Die Zahl im Kriege: Statistische Daten aus der neueren Kriegsgeschichte in graphischer Darstellung* (Vienna: Freytag, 1897), p. 22.
3. Quoted in Hugo Hantsch, *Die Geschichte Österreichs* (Graz: Styria, 1953), II, 286.

yoke of the French occupation failed to materialize, and the German princes wavered between neutrality (Prussia) and alliance with Napoleon (Bavaria). In the absence of an Austro-German political community, the Austrian war effort against the French collapsed within a few weeks.

After 1815 Austria's interest in establishing a conservative political order extended to Germany as much as it did to the rest of Europe, but this interest was reflected only in part in newly created institutions. Different measures point to the weakness of the German Confederation. Sizable parts of the territories of the confederation's two largest members, Austria and Prussia, were not included, but membership was extended to Denmark, the Netherlands, and from 1837 onward to Great Britain to the extent that these states controlled parts of what was considered German territory. On the most important issues a unanimous vote was required. The General Assembly consisting of sixty-eight instructed delegates met only sixteen times between 1816 and 1866. The confederation's central staff never exceeded a total of twenty-seven officials. Contributions of member states were minimal. The number of individual petitions submitted to the Executive Council between 1816 and 1866 was small and varied only between 20 and 133 per year, the lowest number falling in the final year of the institution's existence; and making decisions was slow, often stretching over decades.[4] The measures of political coordination that were achieved—some like the Elbe, Weser, and Rhine conventions of 1821, 1823, and 1831 with Austrian participation, others like the German customs union without it—occurred outside the institutional structure of the German Confederation. The confederation simply was not designed to achieve extensive political coordination.

The German Confederation contributed only on the issue of internal subversion to the effective coordination of government

---

4. Karl Fischer, *Die Nation und der Bundestag: Ein Beitrag zur Deutschen Geschichte* (Leipzig: Fues, 1880), pp. 8-9, 11, 53-54, 60, 526-527. Carl von Kaltenborn, *Geschichte der Deutschen Bundesverhältnisse von 1806 bis 1856: Unter Berücksichtigung der Landesverfassungen* (Berlin: Heymann, 1857), I, 311-312.

policy, and even there it was only one of many instruments, bilateral and multilateral, by which its creators sought to defend the old order. Institutional activity peaked in the three crisis periods which marked the beginning, middle, and end of the years 1815–1848.[5] Austria activated the confederation in the defense of the old order whenever needed. In their fight against nationalism and liberalism the Austrian and German governments saw eye to eye. Their agreement is reflected in the intermittent crisis-oriented spurts of activity of the German Confederation.

The seeming weakness of the institutional linkage of Germany and Austria should be evaluated from the proper perspective. Compared with the Holy Roman Empire—whose shadow, long after its substance, had finally paled in 1806—the German Confederation provided a more effective institutionalization of the coalition of the Austrian and German governments across political boundaries. In the absence of economic, social, or cultural institutions linking Austria with Germany during the years 1815–1848, the degree of institutionalization achieved in the sphere of politics stands in striking contrast.

The strength of the Austro-German political linkage stands out as clearly in the political interactions that took place outside the German Confederation. The German states played a prominent part in Austria's foreign relations. Between 1815 and 1848 the proportion of bilateral Austro-German treaties signed and diplomatic personnel exchanged varied between one-third and one-half of the Austrian total. The increase from 47 to 55 percent in the number of direct bilateral agreements concluded in the years 1816–1829 and 1830–1847 indicates that political interdependence was evidently on the upswing.[6] At the same time,

---

5. The annual average number of executive council sessions for the crisis years 1816-1822, 1830-1834, and 1848 was 36, 46, and 70, respectively; during the quiet years 1823-1829 and 1835-1847 the corresponding figures were 25 and 28. Computed from data provided by Fischer, *Nation und Bundestag*, p. 508.
6. Calculations are based on Ludwig Bittner, *Chronologisches Verzeichnis der Österreichischen Staatsverträge: Die Österreichischen Staatsverträge von 1763 bis 1847* (Vienna: Holzhausen, 1909).

however, channels of political communications failed to expand at a similar rate. This is particularly clear in the number of German diplomats in Vienna, which declined from 46 percent in 1822 to 36 percent in 1846 of the total number of diplomats in Vienna. At the same time the number of Austrian diplomats in Germany remained unchanged, while expenditures on Austrian missions in Germany declined with a simultaneous expansion of Austrian representation abroad.[7] During the first half of the nineteenth century, the German states seemed to start turning inward, away from Austria, at the same time that Austria started to turn outward, away from Germany. Strong political ties seemed to be headed for a gradual decline.

Between 1815 and 1848 the coordination of Austrian and German policies served only one overriding purpose, the suppression of antidynastic, liberal, and national movements. The predictability of political behavior in Germany depended largely on policies formulated in Vienna. Their architect, Metternich, wrote in 1820: "The Austrian emperor is quite mistaken if he doubts being emperor of Germany as well."[8] On the single most important issue of the day, the Austrian emperor had succeeded in convincing the ruling groups in Germany of the necessity of effective cooperation in defense against a new political movement threatening to undermine the old social and political order. Austrian domination over vital aspects of the domestic politics of the German states was mostly uncontested. Fear of Jacobin agitation kindled by political unrest in the years after 1815 and the assassination of a Russian agent, the German poet Kotzebue, led to the Carlsbad Conference of 1819. Political radicalism among students, still confined to only four universities—Giessen, Jena, Würzburg, and Heidelberg—served as a pretext for initiating

---

7. Computed from *Hof- und Staats-Schematismus des Österreichischen Kaisertums, 1822*, Part I, pp. 211-226; *1846*, Part I, pp. 196-214. *Handbuch über den königlich Preussischen Hof und Staat für das Jahr 1828*, pp. 126-130; *1846*, pp. 213-218. Friedrich von Reden, *Allgemeine vergleichende Finanzstatistik: Vergleichende Darstellung des Haushalts, Abgabewesens und der Schulden Deutschlands und des übrigen Europas* (Darmstadt: Junghaus, 1853), II, Part I, pp. 434-436.
8. Quoted in Hantsch, *Geschichte Österreichs*, II, 311.

far-reaching political controls over the press and the universities everywhere in Germany. The extension of Austrian political practices to the rest of Germany—what 100 years later with reversed roles was to be called *Gleichschaltung*—was reinstituted in 1833 after a half-hearted and easily defeated attempt of student radicals to storm some army barracks in Frankfurt. The international class coalition among princes was highly effective.

SOCIETY: ECONOMIC REWARDS OF ISOLATION

The effective integration of Austrian and German political practices in the defense of the conservative political order points to the intimate, if limited, political connections between Austria and Germany between 1815 and 1848. A broadening of this base of integration through the gradual construction of networks of social, economic, and cultural institutions and communications would have required official encouragement of Austro-German contacts on a broad front. Instead, the Austrian government pursued a strict policy of isolation. A large number of political, social, and economic reforms implemented in the eighteenth century by Maria Theresa and Joseph II had been designed effectively to unify the lands under the rule of the Habsburgs. Between 1740 and 1790, far-reaching changes in the areas of administrative structure, education, health, transport, military organization, and internal tariff legislation assured Austria a measure of unity which antedated by several decades similar developments in Germany. After 1815, it appeared to Metternich and the men around him that to complete this task of Austrian integration at the elite level, under the leadership of the German-Austrians, was a more urgent task than to further the amalgamation of Austria's and Germany's social and economic structures. Austria's isolation from Germany was indicated by the small number of consulates which the two countries maintained with one another. In 1828, for example, only five of a total of seventy-one foreign consulates in Austria were German, as compared to thirty-two Italian ones. In the same year, of a total of seventy-eight Austrian consulates abroad, only four existed in Germany while twenty-four were located in Italy.[9]

---

9. *Hof- und Staats-Schematismus, 1828*, Part I, pp. 211-226.

Austria's policy of isolation was shaped by the large economic rewards which the effective unification of the Austrian Empire promised. These rewards were considerable. The peace settlement of 1815, for instance, had added northern Italy to the Austrian Empire. The rich provinces of Lombardy and Venetia promised ample returns by increasing Austrian tax revenues, offering large markets to the products of Austrian industry, and adding substantially to Austria's economic capacity. In 1841 one-third of the industrial output of the monarchy was produced by its Italian provinces.[10] Rewards of that magnitude were important in shaping the preferences of Austrian bureaucrats and industrialists. Austrian policy is best studied in those two issue areas that had the greatest impact on the social and economic amalgamation of Germany in the nineteenth century, the railways and the customs union.

Geography preconditioned the role of the Viennese basin as an intersection and turnstile of communications and transactions within the empire. For strategic reasons Austria's major roads were already developed by the beginning of the nineteenth century. The main flow of goods ran from the north, from Austria's border with Saxony and Prussia, to the port of Trieste in the south. Passenger traffic, on the other hand, was more evenly divided between the empire's north-south and east-west axes.[11] In the middle of the eighteenth century Vienna was linked by a weekly but slow coach service to Prague in the north, Trieste in the south, and Passau in the west. Compared to the biweekly departures of coaches from Prague to Leipzig and central Germany, Vienna's connection with the most developed regions of the empire was still tenuous. But by 1828 the situation had changed greatly, as the ratio between domestic and foreign coach service leaving Prague had changed from 0.5 to 3.5. At the same time the cost of travel per kilometer was about 60 percent higher for trips from Vienna to Bavaria or Saxony

---

10. Nachum T. Gross, "Industrialization in Austria in the Nineteenth Century" (unpub. diss., University of California, Berkeley, 1966), p. 107.
11. Ulrike Schielin, "Aussenhandel des Österreichischen Zollgebietes, 1815-1838" (unpub. diss., University of Vienna, 1968), I, 40-53.

than corresponding figures for domestic travel.[12] Within two or three generations, then, the consolidation of the Habsburg empire had led to a weakening of ties between Austria and Germany.

But transport and travel by road were slow and expensive. Compared to the natural communications grid which Germany's superb river system offered, the Austrian Empire had little to show; and for lack of capital none of the grandiose schemes of linking Austria to Germany's river system through a number of long canals was ever implemented. Thus, the potential advantages to be derived from the revolution in transportation which the railway age brought to all countries were perhaps greater in Austria than in Germany. Yet here, as in many areas requiring innovative policies, the overall impression is one of promises for Austrian industrialization that remained unfulfilled and of opportunities for Austro-German transactions that were missed in the crucial first decades. The Austrian response to the challenge of the new technology is summarized in the history of the first railway on the European continent, which opened between Linz and Budweis in 1828. In the absence of sufficient capital this project substituted the appearance of economic might for its reality, and it sacrificed substantial long-term economic growth for short-term profits.[13]

The expansion of Austria's railway system took place primarily along the crucial north-south axis of the empire, thus linking Vienna with the industrial centers of Bohemia and Moravia in the north and the port of Trieste in the south. But expansion was comparatively slow. In 1840 there were 473 kilometers of railway track in Austria and 549 in Germany; by 1850 Austria had almost trebled the length of its railways to 1,357 kilometers, but in Germany the increase had been elevenfold to 6,044 kilometers.[14]

12. Alex Sturm, "Die Geschichte des Postwesens in Österreich," in Peter Koncnik (ed.), *Programm des K. K. Staats-Gymnasiums in Cilli* (Cilli: Rakusch, 1892), pp. 34-37. Statistische Zentralkommission, *Tafeln zur Statistik der Österreichischen Monarchie*, I (1828), Table 34.
13. Gross, "Industrialization in Austria," pp. 15-17.
14. Iring Grailer, "Das Österreichische Verkehrswesen im Wandel eines Jahrhunderts," in Hans Mayer (ed.), *Hundert Jahre Österreichischer Wirt-*

Just as slow as the expansion of the Austrian railway system were the steps the Austrian government took to establish links between the Austrian and German railway nets. Berlin and Dresden had been linked by rail as early as 1841. Austria, on the other hand, was tardy in its attempt to establish railway connections with southern or central Germany. A government proposal of December 1841 spelled out in great detail plans for future development. But it did not mention a western railway, connecting Vienna with Bavaria, among the high-priority lines.[15] After years of negotiation the first railway link between Austria and Prussia was finally opened in 1849. In the next decade important connections between Prague and Bodenbach, Linz and Munich, Prague and Fuerth, and Reichenberg and Zittau were added; and toward the end of the century forty-four of Austria's seventy-seven railway junctions with adjacent countries had been established with Germany as compared to only twenty with Hungary.[16] But the great acceleration in later development merely underlines Austrian indifference to the forging of durable links with southern and central Germany at a time when it mattered most, during the early years of the railway age. The strong impact of the rewards of the Austrian Empire on Austrian policy affected political and economic elites alike. During the second third of the nineteenth century the institutional responsibility for the development of the empire's railway system shifted between the public and the private sector. But whether private, public, or mixed, the policy which, in the end, was pursued was marked by Austria's continued indifference toward Germany in those crucial decades. Preoccupation with the consolidation of the empire at home and indifference to the amalgamation of Germany abroad were intimately linked.

---

schaftsentwicklung, 1848-1948 (Vienna: Springer, 1949), pp. 548-551. Ernst Kühn, "Die historische Entwicklung des Deutschen und Deutsch-Österreichischen Eisenbahnnetzes vom Jahre 1838 bis 1881," in *Zeitschrift des königlich Preussischen statistischen Büro's*, XXII, Ergänzungsheft 12 (1882), p. 161.

15. Alois von Czedik, *Der Weg von und zu den Österreichischen Staatsbahnen 1824-1854/1858 und 1882-1910* (Vienna: Teschen, 1913), I, 37-39.
16. *Österreichische Eisenbahnstatistik für das Jahr 1912* (Vienna: Hof- und Staatsdruckerei, 1914), Part I, p. 662.

The strong influence of economic rewards on Austria's policy of isolation can also be traced in the second issue of crucial importance to the amalgamation of Germany's social and economic structures in the nineteenth century, the German customs union.[17] The peace settlement of 1815 extended the economic frontiers of the Austrian Empire to include the Tyrol and Vorarlberg in the west and Lombardy and Venetia in the south. Between 1817 and 1826 the Austrian economy was enlarged by these new markets, thus increasing further Austria's self-sufficiency. Even without the economic policy of the years 1815–1848, the effect of this change might have led to a weakening of the trade links between Austria and Germany. But Austria's policy of self-encapsulation after 1815 augmented further these developments.

During the first half of the nineteenth century, the Austrian response to various proposals favoring closer economic cooperation between some or all members of the German Confederation was consistently negative. In 1817, a time of severe economic crisis, the Austrian government left unanswered an urgent request by Württemberg asking all members of the German Confederation to extend mutual concessions in their trade in agricultural products. In 1830 Saxony's petition for minor Austrian tariff concessions to compensate for the mounting economic pressure that Prussia was putting on the Central German Customs Union was flatly rejected by the Austrian government. Two factors appear to have been important in shaping the Austrian decision at the time. In general, such a policy was thought to restrict unduly Austria's freedom of action in foreign affairs. But these tariff concessions, in particular, would have been aimed directly against Prussia, yet Prussia was vital to Metternich's coalition of powers against liberal agitation in Germany and Europe at large. In the eyes of Austrian decision makers, the pursuit of a well-defined and

---

17. William O. Henderson, *The Zollverein* (London: Cass, 1959). Arnold H. Price, *The Evolution of the Zollverein: A Study of the Ideas and Institutions Leading to German Economic Unification between 1815 and 1833* (Ann Arbor: University of Michigan Press, 1949).

highly valued antirevolutionary policy was more important than the adoption of a new, imprecise economic policy of questionable value. But, equally important, Austrian decision makers argued also that a change in Austria's fifty-year-old tariff system could not be undertaken without imposing a grave threat to Austria's national welfare and in particular to its small class of industrialists.[18]

The lack of responsiveness to the needs of the smaller German states which the Austrian government revealed on these two occasions, as well as its disinterest in the formation of the customs union, was in full agreement with business interests throughout the years 1815–1848. An opinion survey of business organizations undertaken in all Austrian provinces contiguous with a German state in 1830 revealed that the overwhelming majority supported the government's negative responses to proposals for the liberalization of Austrian tariffs. Neither outright amalgamation with the customs union nor the conclusion of bilateral trade agreements was favored by men fearful of German competition. As important as the negative reaction was the evident lack of attention which Austrian businessmen had paid to economic developments in Germany during the preceding fifteen years. There was a widespread dearth of information about the effect of German imports on Austrian business interests if some tariff cuts were made.[19]

Austria's isolation from Germany's economic amalgamation under Prussian leadership is reflected in the trade statistics of the time. Throughout the years 1815–1848, trade between Austria and Hungary was almost twice as large in absolute terms as trade between Austria-Hungary and Germany. More important, Austria-Hungary's trade with Germany stagnated in relative terms at the very time the customs union established a substan-

18. Adolf Beer, *Österreichische Handelspolitek im 19. Jahrhundert* (Vienna: Manz, 1891), pp. 59-61. Dwight C. Long, "Efforts to Secure an Austro-German Customs Union in the 19th Century," in A. E. R. Boak (ed.), *University of Michigan Historical Essays* (Ann Arbor: University of Michigan Press, 1937), p. 53. Vera Vomáčková, "Österreich und der Deutsche Zollverein," *Historica*, V (1963), p. 114.
19. Beer, *Österreichische Handelspolitik*, pp. 63-65.

tial measure of economic unification in the rest of Germany. The relative importance of trade between Austria and Hungary grew faster than trade between Austria-Hungary and Germany; between 1831 and 1846 the ratio of Hungarian over German trade rose from 1.15 to 1.63.[20] But dissimilar developments occurred in import and export trade. Compared with Germany, Austria's import dependence on Hungary stagnated at the same time the loss of traditional Austrian export markets in Germany increased the importance of Hungary as an outlet for Austrian products. Austria's policy of self-encapsulation not only cost it the loss of export markets in Germany; it also kept low the overall importance of Austria for Germany as a trade partner. According to one estimate, in the years 1846–1850 Austria-Hungary contributed only 14 percent to the foreign trade total of the German customs union.[21]

There existed one exception to the far-reaching isolation of Austrian society from Germany: the intimate contact at the level of elites. The cosmopolitanism of the old European order is reflected in the large volume of elite migration from Germany to Austria. The Austrian Empire acted like a magnet for many members of the German elite who escaped the confinement of the different principalities and the limited opportunities for their own social advancement by moving in large numbers to Vienna with its many careers open to talented and ambitious men.

The Counter-Reformation had led to the expulsion of most members of the indigenous aristocracy of the Alpine provinces. This purge opened careers to many foreigners: Frenchmen, Spaniards, Swiss, but foremost to Reich-Germans. Studies of the composition of the Austrian elite from the sixteenth century onward attest to the predominant influence of Reich-Germans not merely in comparison with other groups of foreigners but with domestic elites as well. In the eighteenth century, for

---

20. Calculated from data given by Rudolf Sieghart, *Zolltrennung und Zolleinheit: Die Geschichte der Österreichisch-Ungarischen Zwischenzoll-Linie* (Vienna: Manz, 1915), p. 380. Statistische Zentralkommission, *Tafeln*, IV (1831), Table 40; *Tafeln*, XIX (1845-1846), Part II, Table 5.
21. Friedrich-Wilhelm von Reden, *Erwerbs- und Verkehrs-Statistik des Königstaats Preussen: In vergleichender Darstellung* (Darmstadt: 1854), III, 2, 105.

example, the Austrian army was recruited throughout Germany and fully one-half of the field marshals were Reich-Germans.[22] The economists and technocrats who designed and propagandized the plans according to which the Austrian Empire was to be modernized in the eighteenth century—men like Becher, Hoernigk, and Schroeder—were Reich-Germans. The same pattern can be observed in business, the arts, and to a lesser extent the sciences.

In the nineteenth century many of the bureaucrats and politicians who ruled the empire had come from Germany. Names like Metternich, Gentz, Bruck, Biegeleben, Rechberg, Beust, and Schäffle, to name but a few from a long and distinguished list, give testimony to the vital importance of elite migration which continued to flow freely between 1815 and 1848. Table 2 shows that the relative influence of the Reich-Germans continued to increase in most of the top careers of the Austrian Empire throughout the first half of the nineteenth century.

TABLE 2. Elite Migration to Austria: Top-Level Decision Makers by Place of Family Origin (since 1740) (in percentages)

	Foreign Office			Central Administration			Defense		
	Aus.	Ger.	Rest	Aus.	Ger.	Rest	Aus.	Ger.	Rest
1804	16	24	60	45	9	46	0	47	53
1816	8	16	76	0	28	72	9	34	57
1829	7	28	65	13	23	64	12	46	42
1848	9	31	60	10	35	55	14	35	51
1859	0	34	66	9	26	65	15	52	33

Source: Nikolas von Preradovich, *Die Führungsschichten in Österreich und Preussen (1804-1918): Mit einem Ausblick bis zum Jahre 1945* (Wiesbaden: Franz Steiner, 1955), pp. 1-58.

22. Nikolaus von Preradovich, "Die politisch-militärische Elite in Österreich, 1526-1918," *Saeculum: Jahrbuch für Universalgeschichte*, XV (1964), p. 413.

The attraction of the Austrian Empire for all these men and the indifference which marked Austrian responses to moves toward German economic unification were a result of the economic and political conditions of the Austrian monarchy. In the eighteenth century complementary trade relations of increasing importance with the eastern parts of the empire, and beyond, had offered Austrian industry safe markets and high profits. From 1815 on, new territorial acquisitions, especially in northern Italy, promised additional protected outlets for Austrian products. As a result Austrian policymakers, bureaucrats, and industrialists regarded the economic unification of the empire as a more salient and more rewarding task than joining an emerging German economic union of seemingly dubious value to Austrian economic interests. At the time, "the governing idea in Vienna required foremost the attempt to forge the closest links possible among the different provinces of the empire."[23] The unification of the Austrian Empire, not the unification of Austria and Germany, was the central concern.

The negative response of the Austrian political and economic elites to the opportunities offered by the coming of the railway age and the formation of the German customs union was typical of the pattern of political behavior adopted over the whole range of social and economic issues which might have served as instruments for bringing about moves toward the amalgamation of Austria and Germany. The Austrian quest for isolation was a result of the economic opportunities the empire offered. A growing interdependence of Austria and Germany was not valued simply for reasons of economic gain. Self-imposed isolation at a time when traditional preferences for transaction behavior were beginning to change was an important political choice. That choice was reinforced by a corresponding policy of isolating the Austrian community.

COMMUNITY: POLITICAL REWARDS OF ISOLATION

Between 1815 and 1848 the partial political community between Austria and Germany served one political

---

23. Karl Hudeczek, *Österreichische Handelspolitik im Vormärz* (Vienna: Konegen, 1918), p. 32.

Aristocratic Pattern (1815-1848) 51

purpose only, the suppression of liberal and national opposition to the existing political order. The coordination of policies remained highly restricted simply because the Austrian government expected greater political rewards from a policy of isolation. To secure its own political position the Austrian government sought to weaken any potential opposition by imposing strict controls on all communications flows. Ideological contamination was to be stopped at Austria's border.

The seventeenth and eighteenth centuries had left to Austria and Germany a heritage of partial estrangement which Metternich sought to accentuate with his policy of isolation. In the sixteenth and seventeenth centuries Catholicism regarded Austria as the most important bastion of religious orthodoxy. This manifested itself not merely in the oppression and expulsion of Protestant communities living in Austria but in the attempted exclusion of all north German influence in Austrian life. The split between Austria and Germany over religion was largely the result of the intolerance and isolationism that dominated ecclesiastical, dynastic, and bureaucratic thinking. This split may have been strengthened during the Napoleonic wars by the brief government-inspired attempt to propagandize the notion of a distinct Austrian community.[24] During the first half of the nineteenth century Austrian policy attempted to maintain this separatist posture for political reasons. Even though not all aspects of intellectual life were subjected to strict supervision, the rigid control of public speech and printing which was characteristic of Austrian political and cultural life between 1815 and 1848 gave some credence to the charge of one contemporary critic who called Austria "the European China."[25]

The dogged attempt of the Austrian government to pursue its policy of isolation revealed itself most clearly in the self-con-

---

24. William T. Bluhm, *Building an Austrian Nation: The Political Integration of a Western State* (New Haven: Yale University Press, 1973), pp. 13-15.
25. Andrian-Werburg, *Österreich und dessen Zukunft* (Hamburg: Hoffman, 1843), p. 125. Robert A. Kann, *A Study in Austrian Intellectual History: From Late Baroque to Romanticism* (New York: Praeger, 1960), pp. 272-273. The study of Julius Marx does not contradict this argument; it simply points to the many inefficiencies of the system. See Julius Marx, *Die Österreichische Zensur im Vormärz* (Munich: Oldenbourg, 1959).

scious attempt to suppress or control communication between Austria and the outside world in general and between Austria and Germany in particular. Traditional counterintelligence served new counterrevolutionary aims. The government's objective was to isolate Austria from the contagious liberal, democratic, and national ideologies which received increasing currency in the outside world. The methods were heavy-handed bureaucratic supervision of and intervention in many aspects of Austrian life. At times it seemed to produce an intensification of the relative intellectual estrangement of Austria from Germany, which made a number of participants and observers agree with Goethe's observation that Austria had become *Geistiges Ausland,* an intellectually foreign country.[26]

In this policy of isolation the control of public opinion was the central concern of the Austrian government. As an astute and admiring observer of Napoleon's manipulation of the press, Metternich was acutely aware of the power over the public mind which this instrument promised to those willing and able to use it. He devised an intricate system of economic sanctions, legal restrictions, police pressure, and personal supervision which initially succeeded in severely limiting the sources, volume, and diversity of political news that reached Austria's attentive public.[27]

Only two political newspapers existed in Austria during the first half of the nineteenth century, and the government had effective control over both of them. One, the *Wiener Zeitung,* founded in 1703, is the oldest Austrian newspaper still published today. During the first half of the nineteenth century the owners of the paper paid a fee to the Austrian government for the right of publication. Informal contacts as well as the censorship system

26. Georg Franz, *Liberalismus: Die deutschliberale Bewegung in der Habsburgischen Monarchie* (Munich: Callwey, 1955), p. 18. Eduard Winter, *Romantismus, Restauration, und Frühliberalismus im Österreichischen Vormärz* (Vienna: Europa Verlag, 1968), p. 162.
27. On Metternich's press policy see Frithjof Kammerer, "Die Pressepolitik Metternichs: Versuch einer Gesamtdarstellung" (unpub. diss., University of Vienna, 1958). Dorothea Lapter, "Die Wiener politische Journalistik unter Metternich" (unpub. diss., University of Vienna, 1950).

ensured that the *Wiener Zeitung* expressed the officially sanctioned view on all important questions of the day. But the paper retained its characteristic style of stressing factual reporting over editorial comments, thus giving it an exemplary documentary character. Its competitor, the *Österreichischer Beobachter*, was the second political paper and, unlike its rival, was Metternich's preferred propaganda weapon which he used for engaging in running battles with the more liberal German press. The circulation of this elite paper was considerably smaller than that of the *Wiener Zeitung*, but the *Österreichischer Beobachter* was held in very high esteem at home and abroad simply because people knew that it was Metternich's private news organ.

If undertaken over longer periods of time, a study of changes in the distribution of attention in these two papers is helpful in tracing the waxing and waning of one dimension of Austro-German community. The results of a content analysis of both papers for the years 1816–1849 are given in Table 3.[28]

The distribution of Austrian attention remained remarkably stable between 1816 and 1849. Notable, though, are the increases in attention accorded to northern and western Europe and a simultaneous decline in the relative importance of Germany. With the exception of two years, 1819 and 1849—the years of the Carlsbad Conference and the aftermath of the Revolution of 1848 under a new Austrian government—the

---

28. To reduce this task to manageable proportions, only every third year from 1816 on was chosen for analysis. Independent samples of four and twelve issues per year were drawn from both sets of papers for eleven different years. These samples were compared statistically using the "Mann-Whitney U Test." In all eleven cases the tests indicated no significant differences between the two samples (at the .05 level of significance for a two-tailed test). Intercoder reliability was above .80 for all pairs of coders using a simple percentage agreement index. For any given year Austrian attention to events taking place in Austria, Germany, or elsewhere was inferred from the relative volume of news coverage in the two papers. The triennial figures, aggregated into longer time periods, are presented as average percentage figures for both papers combined. The literature on content analysis has recently been summarized in Ole R. Holsti, *Content Analysis for the Social Sciences and Humanities* (Reading: Addison-Wesley, 1969).

TABLE 3. Relative Distribution of Austrian Attention: Average Foreign News Coverage in Two Austrian Papers, 1816-1849 (in percentages)

	1816-1831	1834-1849	Net change
Germany	18	13	−5
Northern Europe[a]	23	26	+3
Western Europe[b]	21	31	+10
Eastern Europe[c]	8	4	−4
Southern Europe[d]	15	17	+2
Southeast Europe[e]	5	2	−3
Rest of world	10	7	−3

Sources: *Wiener Zeitung; Österreichischer Beobachter.*
[a]Scandinavia and Britain
[b]France, Benelux, and Switzerland
[c]Russia and Poland
[d]Spain, Portugal, Italy, and Greece
[e]European parts of the Ottoman Empire

coverage Austria accorded to Germany hovered around 10 to 15 percent. This was less than the attention Austria paid to events in southern Europe.

This finding needs to be interpreted with great caution. Schopenhauer reportedly said that "newspapers are the second hands of history . . . they rarely give the right time."[29] Although over longer periods of time and with a relatively free press it appears reasonable to assume that published opinion reflects changes in public opinion, this assumption is patently absurd in a situation like Metternich's Austria with its strict censorship system. With regard to the restriction of the press Metternich's guiding principle was "for domestic papers foreign news and for foreign papers domestic news."[30] The strict adher-

---

29. Quoted in Friedrich Fexer, "Die 'Neue Freie Presse' und die Österreichische Sozialdemokratie, 1867-1897" (unpub. diss., University of Vienna, 1948), p. 1.
30. Lapter, "Wiener Politische Journalistik," p. 90.

Aristocratic Pattern (1815-1848)

ence to this principle is faithfully reflected in the very low proportion of domestic news reported. In the years 1816–1849 domestic Austrian news accounted for only 26 percent of the total news printed in the *Wiener Zeitung* and only 14 percent of that in the *Österreichischer Beobachter*.

If seen in this light, the low volume of attention accorded to Germany between 1815 and 1849 should be interpreted in exact contradiction to the face value of the figures in Table 3. In excluding German together with Austrian news from the attention of the Austrian public, the Austrian censors displayed a negative attitude to both types of news. Instead they revealed a consuming interest in the affairs of other parts of the world since the curiosity of the reading public was to be fed on the peripheral, exotic, and apolitical. The low figures for Germany, thus, appear to reflect not indifference but high and negative salience which was politically induced.[31] This interpretation is strengthened by the fact that the peak values of Austrian attention to German affairs were reached in 1819 (just before censorship practices became highly oppressive in the wake of the Carlsbad Conference) and in 1849 (when the Vienna press was still comparatively free after the revolutionary outburst of the preceding year); in both years German news accounted for about one-half of Austria's total foreign attention. That figure points to Germany's prominent position in Austrian attention when government restrictions were less stringent.

Naturally there was a widespread distrust of what was printed in the press, and the Austrians preferred reading foreign newspapers whenever possible. Metternich encouraged the importing of some foreign newspapers, especially from Germany, as long as he could maintain indirect forms of control. Foreign newspapers, especially from Germany, played a substantial role in Austria between 1815 and 1848.[32]

---

31. Robert E. Mitchell, "The Use of Content Analysis for Explanatory Studies," *Public Opinion Quarterly*, XXXI (summer 1967), p. 235.
32. In 1831 the 1.1 million newspapers imported from Germany represented one-quarter of the total domestic circulation. Statistische Zentralkommission, *Tafeln*, IV (1831), Table 17.

Of the imported papers, the *Augsburger Zeitung* in particular became a semiofficial spokesman for the Austrian government—unbeknown to the Austrian public. Metternich, at times, preferred using it for expressing opinions which the Austrian government did not care to see published in the official Austrian press.[33] The mere fact that a story appeared not in an Austrian but in a German paper greatly enhanced its credibility in the eyes of the Austrian readers. But for the Austrian government some costs as well as gains were involved in this system of indirect control. Importing foreign newspapers inevitably undermined somewhat the Austrian censorship system since, at times, news was printed that otherwise might have been suppressed altogether. Complete isolation, though desirable, did not prove to be feasible.

The Austrian government pursued a similar policy of isolation in other areas of Austro-German communications such as the flow of mail. Judging from the existing spotty evidence, Vienna was in particularly close contact with the states of southern Germany during the eighteenth century. This was reflected not merely in the relative frequency of mail service but also in the lower rates which letters sent to Germany enjoyed compared with rates charged for mail to other foreign countries. This special relation ceased to exist. The new postal rates of 1817 classified the German states together with all other states as foreign.[34] Whether it was for political or fiscal reasons, this change was symbolic of Austria's policy of self-encapsulation.

Here, too, Metternich was keenly aware of the political advantages to be derived from the direct control of communications. Censorship at home was widespread. Even the correspondence of the emperor's wife and of Metternich's closest associates did not escape scrutiny. Potential critics of the government were supervised carefully in their domestic and foreign correspondence.

---

33. Ignaz Beidtel, *Geschichte der Österreichischen Staatsverwaltung, 1740-1848* (Innsbruck: Wagner, 1898), II, 316.
34. Eduard Effenberger, *Geschichte der Österreichischen Post: Nach amtlichen Quellen* (Vienna: Spies, 1913), pp. 108-111. Eduard Effenberger, *Die Österreichische Post und ihre Reformen unter Kaiserin Maria Theresia und Kaiser Josef II* (Vienna: Spies, 1916), pp. 55-59.

Aristocratic Pattern (1815-1848)

Furthermore, Metternich pursued a similar policy abroad. He was successful in reaching agreements with many foreign governments which ensured that a large number of foreign diplomatic mail routes crossed Austrian territory and that many of these governments entrusted their diplomatic mail to an established, well-functioning Austrian messenger service abroad—as well as to Austria's secret service and its superb skill in breaking codes and decoding messages.[35] The obvious advantage of an effective surveillance system of this type to Metternich was his increased ability to assess the effects of his policy and to second-guess the reactions of his domestic and foreign opponents.

The universities provided the potentially strongest political challenge to the old order which Metternich had succeeded in restoring in 1815. Fraternities founded in Germany in the last years of the Napoleonic wars were deemed subversive; and the scope, size, and significance of these student movements were purposefully exaggerated by the Austrian government so as to justify the adoption of more repressive policies. The isolation of Austrian universities within society as well as from foreign influences was a crucial objective of Metternich's attempt to stop liberal and national ideologies at Austria's border. All foreign students, including those from Germany, were barred from Austrian universities in 1825, and in 1829 all Austrian students were prohibited from going to Germany or other countries for the purpose of study.[36] It was in those years, incidentally, that it became customary in Germany to study outside of one's own state for at least two out of eight semesters.

Written communications between Austrian and German universities ceased for all practical purposes, and with it the exchange of new ideas and scientific findings. It was rare for a German scholar to be called to teach at an Austrian university and even rarer for an Austrian scholar to receive a teaching position in Germany. Scientific congresses were held only

---

35. Karl Josef Mayr, *Metternichs geheimer Briefdienst, Postlogen und Postkurse* (Vienna: Holzhausen, 1935).
36. Karl Gebhart, "Die Reformen im Hochschulwesen in der Zeit von 1860-1905/1906" (unpub. diss., University of Vienna, 1953), p. 45.

infrequently in Austria. The German Conference of Scientists and Doctors, for example, founded in 1822, convened twenty-five times between 1822 and 1848; only three of its meetings were held in Austria. The German Conference of Classical Philologists, Secondary Schoolmasters, and Orientalists, founded in 1838, met ten times before 1848, but not one of these ten meetings was held in Austria.[37] In the eyes of an occasional visitor from Germany, the downgraded, parochial, and traditional ways of the Austrian university made it look, in comparison to the thoroughly modernized educational system of Prussia, like a country which "in terms of culture was foreign to Germany."[38]

The cumulative effect of these policies favoring Austria's intellectual self-encapsulation was a partial intensification of the intellectual estrangement of Austria from Germany. Austria's experience with the Age of Enlightenment, as typified by the *Josefinismus,* had been a distinct one not matched in Germany. Similarly contrasting was the tacit, if limited, coalition between dynasty and the Catholic church which resulted, for example, in the expulsion of Protestants from western Austria in 1837, almost a century after that particular policy of intolerance had been discontinued even in Austria. Austria's distinctiveness was mirrored also in the *Biedermeier* culture which differed in important ways from German Romanticism. It brought an intensely private atmosphere to Austria with its characteristic mixture of lightheartedness and skepticism. Later attempts to characterize these years as the Augustan age of Austrian national culture presided over by Austria's national poet, Grillparzer, although one-sided, contain an important grain of truth.[39] Even though

---

37. R. Hinton Thomas, *Liberalism, Nationalism, and the German Intellectuals (1822-1847): An Analysis of the Academic and Scientific Conferences of the Period* (Cambridge: Heffer, 1951), p. 139.
38. Quoted in Alphons Lhotsky, *Österreichische Historiographie* (Vienna: Verlag für Geschiche und Politik, 1962), p. 137.
39. Fritz Valjavec, *Der Josephinismus: Zur geistigen Entwicklung Österreichs im 18. und 19. Jahrhundert* (Vienna: Verlag für Geschichte und Politik, 1945), pp. 13, 69, 88-89. Winter, *Romantismus,* pp. 104-109. William M. Johnston, *The Austrian Mind: An Intellectual and Social History, 1848-1938* (Berkeley: University of California Press, 1972), pp. 20-23.

he may have overstated his case, a letter Friedrich Schlegel wrote to his wife in 1819 is still instructive: "How can you make the strange error of believing that Vienna is located in Germany or that it has the least to do with Germany? They are separated by entire continents, and one could hardly think of more polar opposites."[40]

POLICY OF ISOLATION: RACE BETWEEN CAPABILITIES AND LOADS

The aristocratic pattern as the product of a preindustrial age featured a large discrepancy between the cosmopolitanism of international elites at the top of society and the segmentation of parochial mass publics at the bottom. This asymmetry revealed itself primarily in the difference between an overarching, if limited, Austro-German political community on the one hand, and a far-reaching isolation of Austrian society and community from Germany on the other.

The aristocratic pattern was distinguished by political controls imposed on a traditional society and community. One crucial query still to be answered is why the policy of isolation did not succeed in effecting a lasting differentiation of Austria from Germany, why it failed to create a permanent sense of estrangement. Why did a policy of isolation in the Austro-German case in the first half of the nineteenth century not result in an approximation of the outcome of a similar policy in the East German–West German case in the second half of the twentieth? The answer to this question must be sought in two asymmetric developments, in the decrease in the capacity for political control and the simultaneous gradual modernization of Austrian society. At the very moment at which the capabilities of the Austrian government declined, Austrian society imposed increasing loads on it.

Austria's growing political weakness had institutional roots. The conservative predilections and policies of Metternich and Emperor Francis I were reinforced by a permanent bureaucratic stalemate. Coordination between domestic and foreign affairs

---

40. Quoted in Winter, *Romantismus*, p. 111.

had often been inadequate even between 1815 and 1830. But from the early 1830s on, the personal incompatibility of Metternich and Kolowrat, respectively the main architects of Austria's foreign and domestic policies, prevented any coherent formation of policy. This rivalry became permanently institutionalized in the State Council, created to ensure a semblance of political authority after the imbecile Ferdinand had succeeded Francis I on the Habsburg throne. A cumbersome bureaucratic machinery made an effective formulation and execution of policy increasingly difficult. This structural condition for immobility was duplicated by a universal fragmentation of power everywhere in the bureaucracy, and it was reinforced also by a deliberate delay of policy decisions. A pervasive attitude of "distrustful indecision" characterized Austrian policymaking throughout the years 1815–1848.[41] But only the blundering and incompetence of the Austrian bureaucracy in the face of a severe economic crisis in the 1840s fully justified the evaluation of Austria's political system before 1848 by a nineteenth-century Austrian historian as "a machine which turns with great noise yet which never can move."[42]

The crisis of Austrian bureaucracy was compounded by government insolvency. In 1811 the Austrian currency was devalued by 80 percent and a second devaluation in 1816 was barely avoided. Many pressing economic, social, and political problems could not be dealt with simply because the Austrian government lacked the financial resources to do so. Budget deficits were permanent and high, and the Austrian government depended on the assistance of a handful of wealthy and powerful bankers to get its deficits financed. In 1823 the most powerful of them all, Salomon Rothschild, almost single-handedly, settled Austria's main foreign debt by persuading the British government to renounce the greater part of it and by financing the

---

41. Anton Springer, *Geschichte Österreichs seit dem Wiener Frieden, 1809* (Leipzig: Hirzel, 1863), I, 112. See also Friedrich Walter, *Die Österreichische Zentralverwaltung: Die Zeit Franz II und Ferdinand I (1792-1848)* (Vienna: Selbstverlag des Haus-, Hof- und Staatsarchives, 1935), p. 13. Beidtel, *Geschichte der Staatsverwaltung*, II, 259-262, 346-352.
42. Springer, *Geschichte Österreichs*, I, 120.

Aristocratic Pattern (1815-1848)

remaining sum himself.[43] Investment in the government debt promised high and secure profits to the bankers. But in the Austrian budget, debt service accounted for a high proportion—between 9 and 24 percent during the years 1815-1848—which reduced the government's capability for action in other areas.[44] It also undermined the prospects for long-term growth. Capital badly needed in the Austrian economy was siphoned off instead, thus effectively retarding Austria's industrialization. The discrepancy between the semblance and the reality of Austria's economic and political power increased throughout the first half of the nineteenth century.

The declining political capabilities of the Austrian government can be traced in many aspects of the policy of isolation. In 1811, before the adoption of the harsh policy of repression, 10,000 informers were working for the Austrian government.[45] It seems reasonable to assume that this number increased substantially after 1819. The entire system of denunciation and suspicion probably magnified the image of government supervision beyond all realistic proportions. But this system of surveillance, impressive though it may have looked at the time, was still small if compared with the size of either the total population or the potential liberal and democratic counterelites. In 1848, for example, a total of only 15,000 letters were opened by Austrian censors, roughly 0.50 percent of Austria's foreign correspondence and only 0.08 percent of the domestic mail. This is little compared with the 96 to 120 million letters and postcards inspected per year by Austrian censors between 1916 and 1918, roughly 25 percent of Austria's foreign and about 10 percent of its domestic mail.[46] In other words, in this area the capacity for

---

43. Karl F. Helleiner, *The Imperial Loans: A Study in Financial and Diplomatic History* (Oxford: Clarendon, 1965).
44. C. A. Macartney, *The Habsburg Empire, 1790-1918* (New York: Macmillan, 1969), pp. 205-206.
45. Oscar Jaszi, *The Dissolution of the Habsburg Monarchy* (Chicago: University of Chicago Press, 1929), p. 77. The figure seems high and may include part-time personnel such as hotel owners, janitors, or domestics.
46. Mayr, *Metternichs geheimer Briefdienst*, pp. 21-22. The figure in 1848 was probably abnormally low; even so, my conclusion would still stand had it been two, three, or four times higher in the 1820s and 1830s.

political control increased by a factor of 50 to 100 between 1850 and the years 1916-1918, even though the Austrian war government was by no means a model of bureaucratic efficiency or totalitarian control. This comparatively small capability for control explains why the record of the Austrian surveillance system was so spotty; the Galician uprising of 1846, for example, planned months ahead, remained unnoticed by the Austrian informers and caught the Austrian government by complete surprise.[47]

Limitations in the capacity for control were manifest also in other parts of the policy of isolation. Austria's protectionist trade policy made the smuggling of manufactured goods from Britain and Germany a profitable and widespread enterprise. Although no reliable estimates of the volume of this illegal trade exist, most students of Austrian economic history agree that it must have been sizable. The low probability of success and the fruitlessness of the entire policy of isolation in a world of a gradually accelerating rate of change was revealed in the tenacious diplomatic battle over the transportation (and interception) of foreign diplomatic mail. The Austrian system lost much of its effectiveness with the passing of time. Other states, notably Austria's rivals in Germany and Italy, Prussia and Piedmont, gradually succeeded in attracting an increasing share of foreign diplomatic mail to cross their own territories. But the deathblow to Austria's policy was the coming of the railway age which made the old messenger service for diplomatic mail increasingly irrelevant; Austria's policy of espionage simply became technologically obsolete.[48]

This decline in capabilities should be contrasted with a growing volume in the loads which a gradually modernizing society imposed on the Austrian government. Economic develop-

---

The figures for 1916-1918 are given in Peter Hanak, "Die Volksmeinung während des letzten Kriegsjahres in Österreich-Ungarn," in Richard Plaschka and Karlheinz Mack (eds.), *Die Auflösung des Habsburgerreiches: Zusammenbruch und Neuorientierung im Donauraum* (Vienna: Verlag für Geschichte und Politik, 1970), p. 59.

47. Mayr, *Metternichs geheimer Briefdienst*, p. 125.
48. *Ibid.*, pp. 124-125.

Aristocratic Pattern (1815-1848)

ment and social mobilization were slow in the years 1815–1848, but they occurred nonetheless. The conflict between a modernizing society and an ossified state was reflected in the halting growth of a small Austrian middle class which began to challenge cautiously the political rule of the bureaucracy, aristocracy, and dynasty. In the 1840s this new class, weak though it was, founded its own organizations (such as the *Nieder-Österreichische Gewerbeverein* of 1839) and pleaded, unsuccessfully, for reforms of the autocratic system of government and authoritarian bureaucratic practices.[49]

A number of persecuted or frustrated intellectuals and members of the middle class moved to more liberal German states and proceeded to criticize Austrian affairs caustically in political pamphlets which were smuggled in large numbers across the border and apparently were read widely. Books with a liberal or democratic flavor, published by the Reclam Publishing House in Leipzig, enjoyed a wide if somewhat furtive circulation in Austria. To many of these Austrian authors and readers Germany became a model for imitation, and they became somewhat ashamed to be called Austrian.[50]

Austria's growing link with Germany is revealed in the increasing volume of communications. Between 1831 and 1846 the German share in the total number of letters Austria received from abroad increased from 41 to 49 percent, while the corresponding figures for Austrian mail sent to Germany rose from 41 to 58 percent.[51] The informal penetration of Austria from Germany was perhaps nowhere so obvious as in the universities, where the policy of isolation had seemingly been most successful. Yet, the students of the University of Vienna remained potential radicals. The strength of their national, liberal, and democratic

---

49. Eduard Winter, *Frühliberalismus in der Donaumonarchie: Religiöse, nationale, und wissenschaftliche Strömungen von 1790-1868* (Berlin: Akademie Verlag, 1968), pp. 129, 180-181.
50. Andrian-Werburg, *Österreich und dessen Zukunft*, I, 127. Also Beidtel, *Geschichte der Staatsverwaltung*, II, 234, 387-388. Winter, *Frühliberalismus*, pp. 114, 179, 182.
51. Statistische Zentralkommission, *Tafeln*, IV (1831), Table 17; and *Tafeln*, XIX (1845-1846), Part I, Table 17.

convictions in 1848 points to the most conspicuous failure of the previous generation's policy of isolation.

Changes in political autonomy can be accounted for by nonpolitical and political explanations. In the analysis of the aristocratic pattern the distinction between standardization and differentiation, between community and society, was not of central importance simply because the Austrian public was still largely untouched by the process of modernization. What did seem to matter and help explain the mix between partial integration and partial autonomy of political behavior was the impact of economic and political rewards on the strategies pursued by Austria's economic and political elites.

These rewards motivated the Austrian decision to cling in the nineteenth century to a set of policies adequate only in the eighteenth. In adhering to the time-honored political practices of the collection of taxes, the maintenance of a large army, the staffing of a sizable bureaucracy, and the financing of a splendid court, Austrian elites squandered the country's scarce capital resources and—unlike Prussia—retarded its industrialization. These policies were a recipe for economic stagnation, as the Austrians seemed to gamble on the Industrial Revolution—and with it modernity—going out of fashion. Monopolistic gains from the political control of culturally alien taxpayers and markets were valued more highly than a sacrifice of autarchy for the opportunity to participate in the economic unification of Germany.

Austrian policymakers valued political autonomy as highly as economic isolation. The overriding problem was how to minimize foreign influences—national, liberal, and democratic—threatening to undermine the established political order in Austria. The Austrian political elite responded with a double strategy of political integration and isolation. On the one hand, Austria was willing to coordinate its policies with other governments in a crisis strategy which implemented repressive practices throughout Austria and Germany. On the other hand, Austria also developed a policy of isolating Austrian society and com-

Aristocratic Pattern (1815-1848)

munity by controlling foreign transactions and communications at all points of entry and exit.

With their preference for policies suited more to the eighteenth than the nineteenth century, Austrian policymakers may have reacted pathologically to the one-sided race between declining political capabilities for control and increasing social loads. The outcome, in 1848, was a violent revolution which pulverized the old crust and revealed an entirely new pattern marked not by isolation from Germany but interdependence with it. But as long as the aristocratic pattern lasted, its most characteristic feature was the asymmetry between the effectiveness of Austro-German coordination on the issue of political repression and the absence of any significant political steps toward the amalgamation of social, economic, and cultural structures. The aristocratic pattern was marked by factors prominent in the eighteenth century whose relative weight was bound to decline in the process of modernization. The Austro-German case might have become a clear-cut case of disintegration if the policy of isolation had totally succeeded; it might have become a clear-cut case of integration of the policy had totally failed. But complete success and complete failure if that policy describe accurately only the very early and the very late stages of the race between capabilities and loads. For most years in between, the aristocratic pattern, like those to follow, made Austria and Germany disjoined partners.

IV

CONFLICT PATTERN
(1848-1870)

THE SLOW modernization of Austrian society in the course of the nineteenth century effected a gradual change in two distinctive features of the preindustrial order. During the middle of the nineteenth century the internationalism of elites and the parochialism of publics became of minor importance. Conflict rather than cooperation at the top and interdependence rather than isolation at the bottom of society were the distinctive features of the conflict pattern of Austro-German relations.

This chapter will trace the political and nonpolitical explanation of autonomy at the level of the elites and the general public. Austria's government obeyed the imperatives of the empire's domestic politics when it attempted to impose Austrian domination over Prussia, the rest of Germany, and all of central Europe. In the wake of the national rebellion of Slavs, Italians, and Hungarians, the political offensive the Austrian government started in Germany after 1848 was designed to achieve one end: an increase in the political weight of the German-Austrians as a necessary precondition for the consolidation of the unity of a centrally run Austrian Empire. Although still powerless until 1860, the German-Austrian middle class saw its economic and political position at the empire's center served by that policy. As had been true of the aristocratic pattern, partial integration of

Austria and Germany was a crisis strategy motivated by considerations of domestic politics; but in contrast to the earlier pattern of Austro-German relations this strategy coincided with an increase in the interdependence of Austria and Germany at the mass level.

These gains in interdependence did not point toward political integration. In the relation between standardization and differentiation, between cultural communications and social transactions, counterpressures dominated copressures. Behavioral and attitudinal indicators of community and society suggest that these counterpressures left the balance between standardization and differentiation largely unaffected. Mass and middle-class behavior and attitudes thus complemented elite strategies in making autonomy a highly probable outcome.

ELITES, COUNTERELITES, AND REWARDS

In order to accomplish successfully the task of restoratin during the aristocratic pattern, the coalition between dynasty and bureaucracy had steered a delicate course between its opponents of the past (the church and the aristocracy) and its opponents of the future (the industrial elites of the middle class). The growing disparity between political capabilities and social loads had pointed to the increasingly tenuous position of the Metternich regime long before the Revolution of 1848 brushed aside its three characteristic features: dynastic incompetence, bureaucratic intransigence, and political indifference.

The 1848 Revolution prompted dynasty and bureaucracy no less than church and aristocracy to forget old quarrels and to close ranks against the national, liberal, and democratic opposition which had struck so forcefully at the empire's very foundation. From the component parts of this new coalition the top policy-makers were recruited after 1848. The young emperor relied heavily on the advice of his new chancellor, von Schwarzenberg, an aristocrat born into one of the most distinguished families of the empire; on men like Bach and Bruck, representing the imperial bureaucracy; and on Bishop Rauscher, a respected and powerful spokesman for the Catholic church.

The reassertion of the political influence of the Catholic church after 1849 was one of the most visible signs of Austria's new political order. Throughout the first half of the nineteenth century, the church had attempted in vain to loosen the grip of the Austrian state over church affairs. Drastic changes in the composition and ideological outlook of the ruling political coalition made success more probable after 1849. In Austria's regeneration after 1848/49 the emperor had no choice but to draw on all existing sources of authority. On the issue of church-state relations the dictates of political prudence accorded with his ideological commitments. The April decrees of 1850 restricted state control over church affairs and pointed to the far-reaching concessions ratified by the Concordat of 1855. In many vital spheres such as jurisdictional powers over internal church affairs, relations between Austrian bishops and the Vatican, and marriage legislation, the Austrian government returned a degree of autonomy to the church which the church did not enjoy anywhere else in Europe. The emperor thus created himself a powerful ally in domestic affairs. On the future relations between Austria and the German states the views of these new allies were also in full agreement. Both favored an eventual unification of most of the German states under Austrian auspices. But the coalition between state and church in the Austrian Empire hardly helped that overall objective. Although it was undoubtedly welcomed by segments of the Catholic public in Germany, the alliance was, at the same time, viewed with profound alarm in Protestant and liberal circles.[1]

The new coalition of political forces was joined by the only institution of the empire whose stature had been enhanced by the events of 1848. In its hour of greatest need the Habsburg dynasty had found one reliable ally at home, the army. It had

---

1. Erika Weinzierl-Fischer, *Die Österreichischen Konkordate von 1855 und 1933* (Vienna: Verlag für Geschichte und Politik, 1960). Friedrich Engel-Janosi, *Österreich und der Vatikan, 1846-1918* (Graz: Verlag Styria, 1958), I, 66-69. Josef Wodka, *Kirche in Österreich: Wegweiser durch ihre Geschichte* (Vienna: Herder, 1959), pp. 317-328. Franz Riedl, "Die Deutschen Katholikentage zwischen 1848 und 1867 und Österreich," in *Katholischer Glaube und Deutsches Volkstum in Österreich* (Salzburg: Anton Pustet, 1933), pp. 160-176.

crushed the social revolution in Vienna as effectively as the national revolutions in Bohemia, Italy, and with Russian help in Hungary. It was, therefore, only natural that after 1848 political power should be shared with the military. Chancellor Schwarzenberg was its choice as much as the emperor's. Within a short span of years, during the reconstruction of the empire, the number of Austrian generals doubled even though there was no corresponding expansion in the size of the Austrian army.[2]

The reform program of the new regime reflected the divergent interests of the different partners of the ruling coalition. Government compensation for abolishing the last vestiges of serfdom provided landowners, in particular large aristocratic ones, with funds sufficient to permit not only the modernization of agricultural production on large estates but to furnish speculative capital invested partly in the empire's rapidly growing banking sector in the 1850s. The reform of Austria's education system after 1848 reflected the successful bid of the Catholic church to reclaim from the dynasty in the nineteenth century privileges and prerogatives which it had relinquished in the eighteenth. Since it was free to impose new policies throughout the empire, the bureaucracy, finally, enlarged its power together with the scope of its activity. The centralizing and Germanizing of political practices throughout the Austrian monarchy was to restore cohesion, especially in those parts where national agitations had been strongest in 1848. The empire's central bureaucracy, largely staffed and dominated by German-Austrians, acted as an agent of national repression. The peculiar combination of modernity and tradition which marked the policies adopted after 1848 was symbolized by the young Emperor Franz-Joseph himself, named after both Austria's greatest reformer, Joseph II, and Austria's archconservative, Francis II.

But the Revolution of 1848 had scared the advocates of a new order no less than the spokesmen for the old. The revolution's national character in the empire's periphery had alarmed all German-Austrians; its liberal aspects had frightened the middle

---

2. Viktor Bibl, *Der Zerfall Österreichs: Von Revolution zu Revolution* (Vienna: Rikola, 1924), II, 232.

class in the German-Austrian provinces; and its democratic features had intimidated the German-Austrian middle class in the capital. When the national revolution of Slavs, Hungarians, and Italians was defeated in 1848, the Austrian poet Grillparzer spoke for the large majority of the German-Austrian middle class in his immediately popular poem, dedicated to the aging archconservative military hero of the time, Field marshal Radetzky:

> Good speed, my general, strike the blow
> Not only for the splendor of glory,
> In thy camp is Austria,
> We others are only isolated ruins.[3]

In the camp of the military stood Austria and, one might add, the greater part of the German-Austrian bourgeoisie.

The limited appeal the revolution had for the German-Austrians was striking. While Hungarian, Italian, and Czech national demands set ablaze the whole structure of the empire, among the German-Austrians the revolution was largely confined to Vienna. In May 1848 the emperor and his court fled to Innsbruck, rightly assuming that the towns in the German provinces were unshaken and firm in their dynastic loyalties.[4] The German flag which the revolutionaries had hoisted on top of the Stephansdom and the Hofburg in Vienna was not typical of the sentiment of the majority of German-Austrians.

This was reflected in the political preferences of the German-Austrian delegates elected to the Frankfurt Assembly. Only the democrats from Vienna favored a strong central authority in Frankfurt. The representatives from the provinces, on the other hand, were not willing to relinquish Austria's independence and

---

3. The translation is taken from Oscar Jaszi, *The Dissolution of the Habsburg Monarchy* (Chicago: University of Chicago Press, 1929), p. 90.
4. Veit Valentin, *Geschichte der Deutschen Revolution von 1848-1849* (Berlin: Ullstein, 1930-1931), I, 555; II, 9, 81. C. A. Macartney, *The Habsburg Empire, 1790-1918* (New York: Macmillan, 1969), p. 361. The Austrian poet Bauernfeld was so agitated by the events in Vienna that he retired to Graz, one of the few provincial towns that experienced a moderate measure of unrest, "for rest and recreation." Heinrich Friedjung, *Österreich von 1848 bis 1860* (Stuttgart: Cotta, 1912), II, 351.

thought of the assembly as adding political weight to the German element in Austrian politics in general and to the German-Austrian middle class in particular. In October 1848 the Frankfurt Assembly voted on the dissolution of the existing structure of Austria-Hungary and the incorporation of its German parts into a newly unified German state. Only 42 of Austria's 115 delegates voted for it, nine of them with the caveat that they expected Austria's special conditions to be taken into account.[5] At the outbreak of the civil war with Hungary, when the future of the empire still seemed to be very much in doubt, two-thirds of the German-Austrian delegates preferred Austria to a unified Germany.

When the successes of the counterrevolutionary campaigns of the Austrian army became increasingly clear, most of Austria's hard-core German nationalists who had favored the dissolution of the empire in October 1848 changed their minds. As the issue of a great German (*Grossdeutsch*) or a small German (*Kleindeutsch*) solution to the problem of unification became the central concern of the Frankfurt Assembly, the Austrian delegates disregarded their political differences and formed an Austrian caucus which tried to counter the influence of the proponents of German unification without Austrian participation. In marked contrast to the first vote, all but two Austrians voted against the proposal requiring the dissolution of the empire when the issue came up for a second time in March 1849. The view of the German-Austrian middle class was well expressed in the parting speech of one of its delegates: "the Germans in Austria will be friends of Germany, will support it, will be Germans, as long as you do not expect of them not to be Austrians."[6]

Political demands of the liberal German-Austrian middle class had triggered the revolution in the center of the empire. But the national revolutions that subsequently exploded on the empire's

---

5. Wilhelm Schüssler, *Die nationale Politik der Österreichischen Abgeordneten im Frankfurter Parlament* (Berlin: Rothschild, 1913), p. 36. Only 79 Austrian delegates were present, but most of those absent were probably adherents of the Great German solution.
6. Quoted in Schüssler, *Nationale Politik*, p. 66.

periphery were, in the eyes of the German-Austrian middle class, a far greater danger than the dynastic repression against which the initial protest was directed. Even though after 1848 the middle class was excluded from the levers of power, on the nationality question of the monarchy it saw eye to eye with the new governing coalition; after the national insurrections of the years 1848–1849, only an autocratic, centralized system of government, run by German-Austrians, could keep the empire together.

Large economic rewards attached the German-Austrians still closer to the ruling coalition which, after 1849, they supported quietly for reasons of political fear. The privileged position of the German-Austrians in the empire dates back at least to the unification of the Austrian monarchy as a centralized state under German leadership in the eighteenth century; that German became the empire's official language in 1784 was symbolic. The German-Austrians lived in the richest provinces; and even though German-Austrians constituted only 35 percent of the Austrian population in 1850, the provinces where they formed large majorities produced two-thirds of Austria's industrial output. Minimum wages were considerably higher in the Alpine provinces than in the rest of the empire, with the exception of the Littoral and Dalmatia. The same was true in cultural affairs. In 1852 three-quarters of Austria's periodical press appeared in the German language; twenty years later the figure had dropped only six percentage points. Three-quarters of Austria's total budget for higher education was allocated to the University of Vienna in 1867, and in the same year 60 percent of its students were German-Austrians. Between 1860 and 1875 the German-Austrians were the only ethnic group that was significantly overrepresented among university students (46 percent) compared to the proportion in the total population (35 percent). Discrimination in favor of the German-Austrians was noticeable also in the empire's system of elementary education. In 1847, 58 percent of all elementary schools were German, and in 1871 the same proportion of all Austrian school books was printed in German. The calm reaction of the German-Austrians to the exclusion of Austria from German affairs in 1866 was consistent with the rewarding opportunities for individual and collective advancement which the empire had offered them in the past and promised for the future.[7]

The empire's economic rewards attracted the German-Austrians in general. These rewards were particularly potent, though, for the counterelite still formally excluded from the empire's politics after 1848, the middle class. This was true for areas where dynastic and middle-class interests were conflicting no less than where they were complementary. For the industrialists of middle-class origin, ample opportunities beckoned even in the darkest hour of dynastic defeat. In 1866 the Austrian government drew the funds necessary for the payment of the Prussian war indemnification from large banks and the open market at high interest rates, thereby enabling a sizable number of German-Austrians to make a good profit on this investment. Furthermore, the defeat of 1866 prompted the Austrian military to reequip the Austrian army from scratch; large orders were placed with domestic producers, most of them German-Austrians.[8]

The divergence between middle-class and dynastic interest was less noticeable in other areas, such as policy implementation.

---

7. Nachum T. Gross, "Industrialization in Austria in the Nineteenth Century" (unpub. diss., University of California, Berkeley, 1966), p. 107. Jerome Blum, *Noble Landowners and Agriculture in Austria, 1815-1848: A Study in the Origins of the Peasant Emancipation of 1848* (Baltimore: Johns Hopkins University Press, 1948), pp. 188-189. Johann Winckler, *Die periodische Presse Österreichs: Eine historisch-statistische Studie* (Vienna: Sommer, 1875), pp. 8-9. Rudolf Wurzer, "Die Stellung der Technischen Hochschule Wien im Ablauf ihrer Geschichte," in Heinrich Sequenz (ed.), *150 Jahre Technische Hochschule Wien, 1815-1965* (Vienna: Unterrichtsministerium, 1965), I, 44. *Statistisches Jahrbuch der Österreichischen Monarchie*, V (1867), pp. 268-271. F. Juraschek, "Der Besuch der Österreichischen Universitäten in den Jahren 1861-1875," *Statistische Monatsschrift*, II (1876), p. 317. Bundesministerium für Unterricht (ed.), *200 Jahre Österreichische Bildung und Erziehung* (Vienna: Österreichischer Bundesverlag, 1960), pp. 8-9.
8. Franz M. Mayer, Raimund F. Kaindl, Hans Pirchegger, Anton A. Klein, *Geschichte und Kulturleben Österreichs: Von 1792 bis zum Staatsvertrag von 1955*, 5th ed. (Vienna: Braumüller, 1965), III, 216, fn. 8. Ferdinand Tremel, *Wirtschafts- und Sozialgeschichte Österreichs* (Vienna: Deuticke, 1969), p. 353.

Dominion over the empire's administration and politics offered the German-Austrians, and in particular their middle class, splendid opportunities for upward social mobility. The proportion of representatives of the middle class in the higher echelons of the Austrian civil service was 0 in 1804, 27 percent in 1829, 35 percent in 1859, and 55 percent in 1878. In the diplomatic corps the increase was less substantial; still, by 1850, about one-half of Austria's career diplomats were drawn from the bourgeoisie.[9] The economic interests of the middle class were served well by the existing political structure of the empire.

These economic rewards were the result not so much of differences in the rates of economic development and social mobilization preordained by the impartial reason of History as of political decisions that affected the distribution of resources in the past. In these decisions the convergence of dynastic and middle-class interests stands out quite clearly. The case of the Italian provinces is only one example among many. The incorporation of Lombardy and Venetia into the Austrian Empire after 1815 promised new rich markets to Austria's industry. More important still, these provinces helped to replenish the empty coffers of the Austrian treasury. The Italian provinces carried a tax burden second only to that of Lower Austria. There occurred a transfer of resources from the empire's peripheries to its center. In 1844 Lower Austria, including Vienna, registered a net tax inflow of 2.52 florins per capita at the same time at which the net tax outflow of funds from Lombardy-Venetia amounted to as much as 2.21 florins per capita.[10] The great splendor of Viennese architecture, arts, and sciences (not to mention the power of the dynasty, army, and bureaucracy) was financed by people with little influence over the empire's politics. The German-Austrians had no reason to leave the empire.

9. Nikolaus von Preradovich, *Die Führungsschichten in Österreich und Preussen (1804-1918): Mit einem Ausblick bis zum Jahre 1945* (Wiesbaden: Steiner, 1955), pp. 24, 39-40.
10. Calculated from data provided by Robert Meyer, "Zur Geschichte der Finanzstatistik in Österreich," *Statistische Monatsschrift*, XXXIX (August-September 1913), p. 23. Thomas Banfield, *The Austrian Empire: Her Population and Resources* (London: Taylor, 1842), Appendix I, Table 1.

Conflict Pattern (1848-1870)

In the economic exploitation of Hungary, finally, the economic interests of the dynasty and the middle class dovetailed neatly. Since the proud Hungarian Estates refused to tax themselves for the greater glory of the dynasty, the Austrian emperor retained the import duties levied on goods coming from Hungary into the rest of Austria when he implemented the economic unification of the Austrian Empire in the late eighteenth century. He so sought to raise indirectly through tariffs the taxes he had been denied in direct payment. Discriminatory assessments of goods crossing Austria's eastern border increased the prices of Hungary's agricultural exports to Austria while leaving unaffected the prices of Austria's industrial exports to Hungary. Until 1849 trade relations between Austria and Hungary were, thus, a one-sided preferential trade system which favored Austrian industry and, to a lesser extent, protected Austrian agriculture. In an attempt to consolidate the empire after 1848, these internal tariff barriers were abolished and Hungary was incorporated into the Austrian market. The effect was a further increase in the sales of Austria's industrial products in Hungary. On the other hand, the unrestricted import of agricultural goods lowered food prices in Austria and with it wages and production costs.[11] Because of these two changes the profit margins of Austria's industrial producers—most of them members of the German-Austrian middle class—increased. To reap a maximum long-term advantage from the incorporation of Hungary into the Austrian market, Austria invested heavily in the development of Hungary's railway system and raw materials and exported primarily consumer goods rather than capital goods. These trade and investment patterns helped slow down the growth of the productive capacity of Hungarian industry. As a result, between 1846 and the end of the century, the composition of trade between Austria and Hungary remained virtually unchanged.[12]

11. Krisztina M. Fink, *Die Österreichisch-Ungarische Monarchie als Wirtschaftsgemeinschaft: Ein historischer Beitrag zu aktuellen Integrationsproblemen* (Munich: Trofenik, 1968), pp. 11-12, 25-29.
12. Considerable shifts reflecting the growing strength of Hungarian industry are, however, observable from 1900 on. See Iván T. Berend and György Ránki, "Ungarns wirtschaftliche Entwicklung, 1849-1918," in

It is, therefore, understandable that the German-Austrian industrialists defended the trade system set up in 1849. They attempted with great regularity to maintain the protection of their profitable domestic market, while the Hungarian agricultural producers pleaded repeatedly for a low tariff which would have reduced the domestic price of industrial products and enlarged the export markets for Hungary's agricultural goods. Austrian industry remained adamant in its opposition to the government's attempt to join the German customs union. A majority of the members of the Austrian Association of Industrialists voted against joining the customs union in 1862. A survey of Austria's chambers of commerce undertaken in 1863 revealed that their position had remained substantially unchanged for a generation. In the words of the prestigious chamber of Lower Austria, it was inadvisable to sacrifice the interests of Austrian industry "for the sake of maintaining a political position in Germany with uncertain prospects which could outweigh the economic sacrifices for the forseeable future."[13] For the German-Austrians the economic rewards of the empire acted like a magnet. Compared with all other national groups, the German-Austrians derived the greatest economic benefits from their central position in the monarchy. More specifically, the German-Austrian middle class as a potential counterelite to the ruling coalition had the highest economic stakes in the empire. It was, therefore, only natural that this middle class cherished highly Austria's political autonomy.

GROWING EXTENT AND DECLINING EFFECTIVENESS OF POLITICAL COORDINATION BETWEEN AUSTRIA AND GERMANY

For the political elite and counterelite alike, considerations of domestic politics pointed to the need for a new approach to Austro-German relations. The centralization of the

---

Alois Brusatti (ed.), *Die Habsburgermonarchie, 1848-1918 (I): Die Wirtschaftliche Entwicklung* (Vienna: Verlag der Österreichischen Akademie der Wissenschaften, 1973), pp. 462-527.

13. Quoted in Heinrich Benedikt, "Die Casa d'Austria, das Reich und Europa," in Otto Schulmeister (ed.), *Spectrum Austriae* (Vienna: Herder, 1957), p. 144.

Austrian Empire under German-Austrian leadership required, at the minimum, an increase in the political weight of the German-Austrians through intense political involvement in German affairs and, at the maximum, an increase in German-Austrian numerical strength through a restructuring of the German Confederation. The increasing coordination of Austro-German political behavior points to the success of the first strategy, the declining effectiveness to the failure of the second strategy. The coincidence of both developments left Austria's political autonomy largely unimpaired.

Judging by most indicators, the extent of Austro-German policy coordination increased. Table 4 illustrates that the new interest the Austrian government took in Germany coincided with its diplomatic offensive in Germany. But when, together with Bismarck's ascendancy in Prussia, the Austro-Prussian conflict intensified, attention dropped slightly. In the 1860s, though, the interest in German events was probably still well above the level of the 1830s and 1840s.

The growing extent of political coordination was reflected also in increases in institutionalized political contacts. The German share in the total bilateral treaties entered into by Austria rose from 55 percent for the years 1830–1847 to 64 percent for the years 1848–1865. The relative number of Austrian diplomats stationed in Germany—a constant 31 percent throughout the first half of the nineteenth century—rose to 39 percent by 1866. An increase in the activity of the German Confederation also showed Austria's renewed interest in German affairs. The average number of sessions per year rose from twenty-eight for the period 1835–1847 to thirty-nine for the years 1860–1866, and the volume of protocols and recommendations increased by roughly a third during the same period.[14]

The increased importance of Germany was reflected as well in

14. Ludwig Bittner, *Chronologisches Verzeichnis der Österreichischen Staatsverträge: Die Staatsverträge des Kaisertums Österreich und der Österreichisch-Ungarischen Monarchie von 1848 bis 1911* (Vienna: Holzhausen, 1914). *Hof- und Staats-Handbuch des Kaiserthumes Österreich für das Jahr 1866* (Vienna: Manz 1866), pp. 130-140. Karl Fischer, *Die Nation und der Bundestag: Ein Beitrag zur Deutschen Geschichte* (Leipzig: Fues, 1880), p. 508.

TABLE 4. Relative Distribution of Austrian Attention: Average Foreign News Coverage in Two Austrian Papers, 1831-1870 (in percentages)[a]

	(1) 1831-1846	(2) 1849-1861	(3) 1864-1870	(4) Net Change 1849/1861-1864/1870
Germany	13	32	26	−6
Northern Europe[b]	26	15	16	+1
Western Europe[c]	31	24	29	+5
Eastern Europe[d]	4	8	6	−2
Southern Europe[e]	17	10	12	+2
Southeast Europe[f]	2	3	1	−2
Rest of world	7	7	9	+2

Sources: *Wiener Zeitung; Presse; Neue Freie Presse; Österreichischer Beobachter.*

[a]The method of calculation is explained in Chapter III, fn. 28. Because of rounding off, percentages do not always add to 100.
[b]Scandinavia and Britain
[c]France, Benelux, and Switzerland
[d]Russia and Poland
[e]Spain, Portugal, Italy, and Greece
[f]European parts of the Ottoman Empire

the substance of Austria's foreign policy. The old policy of isolation was all but abandoned. Instead, the Austrian government sought to extend political coordination through functional integration and cooperation with the German states. On some issues Austria and most of the German states succeeded in reaching agreement despite the Austro-Prussion rivalry. The Austro-German Monetary Convention of 1857, for example, reduced the heterogeneity of different currency systems and thus helped facilitate commercial relations. Another significant advance was the codification of an Austro-German commercial law in the early 1860s, a task that had been started some forty years earlier.[15]

15. Reinhard Kamitz, "Die Österreichische Geld- und Währungspolitik von 1848 bis 1948," in Hans Mayer (ed.), *Hundert Jahre Österreichische*

The extension of coordination of Austro-German policies is shown also in the flow of communications. Fearful of the erosion of the Austrian position in Germany, Metternich had seized on the idea of a German postal union as an inexpensive but effective way of involving Austria more actively in German affairs. Despite Prussia's original opposition, the Austrian government succeeded in concluding a series of bilateral agreements with Bavaria, Baden, Saxony, the postal service of the family of Thurn and Taxis, and, finally, with Prussia itself. In these treaties a rough standardization of rates and administrative practices was achieved. A conference of all German states in 1847 laid the foundation for the German Postal Union established finally under Austrian leadership in 1850. It unified and reduced postal rates of all member states. Functional cooperation centering around the unification of the Austrian and German postal systems would be sufficient, or so Austrian officials hoped, to counter Prussia's growing influence in Germany.[16] Cooperation in this area led to a great expansion in Austro-German communications. Between 1846 and 1867 the German share in the total number of letters received from abroad increased from 49 to 72 percent, while the corresponding figures for Austrian letters sent to Germany rose from 58 to 73 percent.[17]

The Austro-German Telegraph Union, also organized in 1850, illustrates why Austria's political expectations were unfounded. Like the Postal Union, the Telegraph Union helped expand Austro-German communications by unifying administrative practices and by reducing rates. But the thrust of this technological innovation provided strong incentives for expanding functional cooperation beyond the Austro-German level. Nothing short of a standardized treatment of transit telegrams in

---

Wirtschaftsentwicklung, 1848-1948 (Vienna: Springer, 1949), p. 215, fn. 14. Fischer, *Nation und Bundestag*, pp. 86-88.

16. Josef K. Mayr, *Metternichs geheimer Briefdienst: Postlogen und Postkurse* (Vienna: Holzhausen, 1935), p. 116.
17. Statistische Zentralkommission, *Tafeln zur Statistik der Österreichischen Monarchie*, XIX (1845-1846), Part I, Table 17. *Das Österreichische Post- und Telegraphenwesen in den im Reichsrathe vertretenen Königreichen und Ländern mit Schluss des Jahres 1868* (Vienna: Staatsdruckerei, 1869).

all countries was required if the benefits of quick communications were to be shared by all. By 1869 an international organization with virtually universal membership had been created, the International Telegraph Union, superseding its Austro-German forerunner. Corresponding developments in mail communications took only a little longer. The Universal Postal Union was founded in 1874. The logic of the technological revolution in communications made the extension of bilateral political coordination a transient phase.

Disappointed by the internationalization of bilateral functional cooperation, Austrian hopes for political payoffs from a strategy of integration on the issue of mass communication were further doomed for a second reason. As long as patronage is not involved, the extension of political coordination in the area of communication has fewer and less significant political effects than in the area of trade. Groups do not easily organize on issues such as the cost or speed of mass communication, especially where illiteracy runs high. Politicization of Austro-German relations was, therefore, an improbable outcome on this issue.

Further coordination of policies proved to be impossible. No agreements were reached on many other issues under consideration—naturalization laws, copyright, patent rights, and the standardization of weights and measures, to name but a few.[18] Most importantly, the intensification of the Austro-Prussian conflict abroad and, later, political opposition at home prevented the extension of political coordination to the one area that mattered most, Austria's relations with the German customs union.

The economic program of Austria's trade minister, von Bruck, reflected the domestic political aspirations and economic objectives of the new government. Bruck energetically advocated the unification of the German customs union with the Austro-Hungarian trade bloc. The establishment of a common market encompassing the sixty-five millions then living in central Europe would have greatly enhanced the political weight of the German-Austrians in Austria-Hungary for reasons of numerical strength alone. But Bruck's plan expressed also the economic

---

18. Fischer, *Nation und Bundestag*, pp. 80-86, 96-99, 129-131.

interests of the large agricultural producers. The landed aristocracy regarded the customs union as an attractive market in which German agricultural producers could be easily outsold. Still excluded from the governing coalition and apprehensive of German imports, Austrian industrialists had not yet acquired the political power to veto the reductions in Austrian import tariffs which Bruck proposed.

In an attempt to demonstrate goodwill toward the German customs union, Austria-Hungary modified but did not abandon its protectionist trade policy. The assimilation of Austria-Hungary's tariff structure with that of the *Zollverein* stopped far short of lowering tariffs sufficiently to enable Austria-Hungary to join on the terms of the customs union. This left the Austrian government with only two choices. It could attempt to form a customs union with the states of southern Germany and with Saxony in order to compete with a North German customs union dominated by Prussia. Or it could settle for a compromise with Prussia, short of a full merger, yet assuring Austria-Hungary of a special status in the Zollverein's trade relations with the rest of the world.[19]

Adopting the second course of action, the government concluded a trade treaty with the Zollverein which lowered Austro-Hungarian tariffs substantially in exchange for granting Austria-Hungary a most-favored-nation clause in the custom's union trade relations with other countries. One part of the treaty stipulated that the issue of Austria-Hungary's joining the customs union should be renegotiated after a certain number of years. But Prussia's determined opposition stifled the reopening of such negotiations throughout the 1850s. The empire's strategy of biding time was unsuccessful, and Trade Minister von Bruck was sadly mistaken in writing, after the conclusion of the trade agreement of 1853, "time which heals everything will do

---

19. Adolf Beer, *Die Österreichische Handelspolitik im 19. Jahrhundert* (Vienna: Manz, 1891), pp. 84-87, 206-309. Helmut Böhme, *Deutschlands Weg zur Grossmacht: Studien zum Verhältnis von Wirtschaft und Staat während der Reichsgründungszeit, 1848-1881* (Cologne: Kiepenheuer, 1966), pp. 2-41.

so in this case too."[20] Within a decade, the Prussian government had succeeded in excluding Austria-Hungary from German economic unification once and for all.

The failure of Austrian policy was not merely due to determined Prussian resistance abroad. It reflected also a gradual shift of power toward Austria's industrialists at home prior to the formal inclusion of the middle class in the ruling coalition in 1860. The sharp pinch of Zollverein imports on Austrian markets after the onset of the economic depression of 1857 made Austria's industrialists press hard for a revision in government policy. By 1859, Austrian business organizations had assured themselves of a veto power over any future changes in trade policy.[21] The only avenue Austria had toward joining the Zollverein, tariff reductions, was thus blocked.

Although Austrian economic strength and political skill were insufficient to grant full success to the new policy, the reduction of Austro-Hungarian tariffs stimulated a moderate expansion in trade with Germany after 1852. While imports from Germany increased from 17 percent in 1851 to 34 percent in 1864, exports to Germany rose only slightly, from 29 to 32 percent.[22] The expansion of trade, thus, seems to have been a belated reaction in the middle of the nineteenth century to Austria's earlier policy of isolation.

The struggle for supremacy in Germany[23] was the fourth and

---

20. Beer, *Österreichische Handelspolitik*, p. 161.
21. Karl H. Werner, "Österreichs Industrie- und Aussenhandelspolitik 1848 bis 1948," in Mayer, *Hundert Jahre Österreichischer Wirtschaftsentwicklung,* pp. 380-381.
22. *Jahrbuch für Volkswirtschaft und Statistik,* II (1854), p. 321. A. Bienengräber, *Statistik des Verkehrs und Verbrauchs im Zollverein für die Jahre 1842-1864* (Berlin: Duncker, 1868), p. 460.
23. This is the title of a famous book. See Heinrich Friedjung, *Der Kampf um die Vorherrschaft in Deutschland, 1859 bis 1866* (Stuttgart: Cotta, 1904). Other surveys include Macartney, *Habsburg Empire,* pp. 426-494. Heinrich von Srbik, *Deutsche Einheit: Idee und Wirklichkeit vom heiligen Reich bis Königgrätz,* 2nd ed. (Munich: Bruckmann, 1936-1942). Richard Charmatz, *Geschichte der auswärtigen Politik Österreichs im 19. Jahrhundert* (Leipzig: Teubner, 1918), II.

final stage in the flow of events which had occurred since the middle of the eighteenth century. After the dynastic wars of the eighteenth century, limited and belated cooperation in the conflict with Napoleon, and joint counterrevolutionary action between 1815 and 1848, Austria in the years from 1849 to 1871 suffered the completion of a prolonged process of role reversal in Germany, in which Austria saw its position changed from leader to led, from *Führungsmacht* to *Gefolgsmacht*. The solution the new Austrian leadership offered for the German problem was neither *Kleindeutsch* (Germany without Austria) nor *Grossdeutsch* (Germany with the Austrian provinces that had been part of the German Confederation)—the two solutions that had polarized the debates of the Frankfurt Assembly of 1848–1849—but *Grossösterreichisch* (Germany incorporated into Austria-Hungary). The unification of central Europe and Germany was to occur not under Prussian or German leadership, as later plans for a unified *Mitteleuropa* envisaged, but under Austrian guidance. Only that political solution, it was thought, would create a political framework in which the government could hope to deal successfully with the political demands of the non-German nationalities.

In March 1849 the new Austrian government published a plan for the reorganization of the German Confederation which suited equally well the task of reasserting power at home and abroad. Prussia responded by founding the German Federation as a rival organization of the German Confederation. These two organizations soon clashed over the right to intervene in the constitutional affairs of the small duchy of Hesse. Despite a few diplomatic victories of the Austrian government, the stalemate reached by the end of 1850 suggested only one compromise solution, the reconstitution of the German Confederation in its old form.

But that organization became an increasingly less valuable instrument for controlling sensitive aspects of Austrian and German politics. After 1848, to be sure, ten German states were advised to delete some of the liberal clauses that had been included in their constitutions as a result of the Revolution of

1848, but this occurred as much at the insistence of Prussia as of Austria. Moreover, some of the harsher measures of political repression, passed at Austrian insistence during the first half of the nineteenth century and declared illegal at the height of the Revolution, were never renewed. The political conflict between Austria and Prussia, which on the Austrian side was grounded deeply in the empire's domestic politics, made the counterrevolutionary class coalition after 1849 a mere shadow of its former substance.

The low effectiveness of policy coordination between Austria and Prussia was readily apparent during the Austro-Italian War of 1859. In the hour of greatest need, Austrian calls for assistance from Germany evoked strong popular support in southern Germany. Prussia's political leadership, on the other hand, was willing to support Austria only if it were to make considerable concessions to Prussian demands for a position of parity in the German Confederation. Since Austria was unwilling to pay that price, Prussian neutrality contributed to Austria's quick defeat in Italy.

Bismarck's rise to power in 1862 initiated the next phase of the Austro-Prussian conflict, which climaxed in the defeat of Austria's armies in Bohemia in 1866. The conflict centered again around competing conceptions of how to reorganize the German Confederation. Austria's call for a "summit" meeting of all German states in Frankfurt in 1863 was boycotted by Prussia and, thus, achieved nothing. On the other hand, Bismarck proposed the election of a German parliament in 1866 because he knew the proposal would be unacceptable to the Austrians. Even the temporary cooperation of Austria and Prussia on the question of Schleswig-Holstein and during the German-Danish War of 1864 intensified the underlying conflict. By 1865, Austria and Prussia were on the brink of war over the issue for which they had fought side by side a year earlier; an interim agreement was worked out only at the very last moment. When war finally came in 1866, it was mercifully short. Austria ceded Venetia to the French almost without a fight in the south and was badly beaten by Prussian armies in the north. Within the span of a few weeks,

Austria had lost the two spheres of influence it had cherished the most.

It took another five years before the last doubts about Austria's exclusion from German unification were eliminated. The appointment of one of Bismarck's archenemies, Beust, as chancellor of Austria in 1867 reflected the revisionist political program of the dynasty, army, aristocracy, and bureaucracy.[24] Beust himself, however, viewed the matter more prudently. Compelling considerations of foreign policy spoke for an alliance between Austria and France directed against Prussia and Russia, the two states Austria feared most. But such an alliance would have greatly enhanced the chance of another war with Prussia, which neither the German-Austrians nor the Hungarians wanted. The two dominant ethnic groups in the empire's domestic politics, thus, forced Beust to tread lightly in the conduct of foreign affairs. At the outbreak of the Franco-Prussian war of 1870, the representatives of the old political order—the military and the aristocracy—favored Austria's intervention on the side of the French. But the quick succession of Prussian military victories made such plans idle speculation within a matter of weeks. In November 1871, a mere nine months after the German Empire had been proclaimed in Versailles, Beust, a symbol of revisionism in the public eye, was dismissed, and Austro-German relations proceeded quickly to take a turn for the better.

Considerations of domestic politics—the unity of the Austrian Empire and the strength of the German-Austrian position within it—prompted the Austrian government after 1849 to seek to enlarge both the extent and the effectiveness of Austro-German political coordination. Since Prussia was not to be eliminated as a contender for the leadership role in Germany, the persistence of Austria's political autonomy in the conflict pattern of Austro-German relations resulted from the combination of increasing extent and decreasing effectiveness of political coordination.

---

24. Victor-L. Tapié, "Autour d'une tentative d'Alliance entre la France et l'Autriche, 1867-1870," in Österreichische Akademie der Wissenschaften, *Sitzungsberichte*, 274 (5) (Vienna: Böhlaus, 1971).

POLICY OF INTEGRATION:
RACE BETWEEN CAPABILITIES AND LOADS

The primacy of the empire's domestic politics explains why the Austrian government adopted a strategy of partial integration as a crisis measure. It does not explain, however, why that strategy failed. The aristocratic pattern broke down in 1848 because the Austrian government lacked the capabilities necessary to maintain direct political controls on a gradually modernizing society at home. The conflict pattern ended in 1870 because the Austrian government lacked the requisite capabilities to reassert its power abroad. Revolution at home and defeat abroad were not inevitable outcomes. More perceptive governments might have tried harder to cultivate their political capabilities or to reshape their political objectives. In the case of Austria, however, the combination of declining capabilities and unchanged objectives pointed toward ultimate defeat.

Austria's relative weakness can be traced to its comparatively slow rate of industrialization in general and in particular to the ineffectiveness of the government in many areas of policymaking. Compared with the rest of western Europe, as Nachum Gross has shown, Austria's position at the outset of the nineteenth century was one of relative economic backwardness, and it failed to close the gap with the passing of time. If compared with Germany, however, the Austrian position was not uniformly disadvantageous at the end of the Napoleonic wars.[25] But as Table 5 illustrates, Austria lagged behind Prussia in the development of economic and military capabilities essential to its political objectives. In light of these data the conflict strategy that Austria's political elite adopted after 1848 was a risky gamble, and the defeats of 1859 and 1866 showed that the gamble did not pay off.

Throughout the aristocratic pattern of Austro-German relations, the insolvency of the Austrian government had been

25. Gross, "Industrialization in Austria," pp. 3-37. See also N. T. Gross, "The Industrial Revolution in the Habsburg Monarchy, 1750-1914," in Carlo M. Cipolla (ed.), *The Fontana Economic History of Europe: The Emergence of Industrial Societies*, IV, Pt. I (London: Collins, 1973), pp. 228-278.

TABLE 5. Five Indicators of Capability: Ratio of Austria-Hungary/Prussia, 1840 and 1860

		1840	1860
(1)	Troops under arms	1.64	1.31
(2)	Population	2.33	1.80
(3)	International status	1.03	0.94
(4)	Pig iron production[a]	0.61	0.43
(5)	Capacity of steam engines	0.50	0.39

Sources:
Row (1): Wolfgang Zapf, "Indikatoren des sozialen Wandels, 1760-1960: Vergleichende Übersichten" (unpublished paper, Cambridge, Mass., 1967), Table 36.
Row (2): Adna Ferrin Weber, *The Growth of Cities in the Nineteenth Century: A Study in Statistics* (Ithaca: Cornell University Press, 1965), p. 95. Michael G. Mulhall, *The Dictionary of Statistics* (London: George Routledge, 1899), p. 447.
Row (3): J. David Singer and Melvin Small, "The Composition and Status Ordering of the International System, 1815-1940," *World Politics*, XVIII, 2 (January 1966), pp. 466, 468.
Row (4): Nachum T. Gross, "Industrialization in Austria in the Nineteenth Century" (unpub. diss., University of California, Berkeley, 1966), Table 13, p. 79. Gerhard Bondi, *Deutschlands Aussenhandel, 1815-1870* (Berlin: Akademie Verlag, 1958), p. 101.
Row (5): Mulhall, *The Dictionary of Statistics*, p. 545.
[a]Data refer to Austria only, which produced the overwhelming share of Austria-Hungary's pig iron.

chronic, its dependence on a small coterie of bankers conspicuous. After 1848 the Austrian government stayed at the brink of bankruptcy. Between 1848 and 1866 the national debt trebled and most of it was raised in foreign money markets, in Paris, London, and Frankfurt.[26] To finance a policy of armed neutrality during the Crimean War, the Austrian government was forced to sell the entire Austrian railway system at disadvantageous prices to foreign bankers, most of them French. State finances collapsed

26. Alois Gratz, "Die Österreichische Finanzpolitik von 1848 bis 1948," in Mayer, *Hundert Jahre Wirtschaftsentwicklung*, p. 304. Herbert Matis, *Österreichs Wirtschaft, 1848-1913: Konjunkturelle Dynamik und gesellschaftlicher Wandel im Zeitalter Franz Josefs I* (Berlin: Duncker und Humblot, 1972), pp. 60-63.

completely when the government tried to raise funds for the war with Piedmont in 1859. Only one-half of a war bond issue was subscribed and even that small fraction only at a very substantial discount. In the eyes of the Austrian financiers and bourgeoisie the government was no longer a going concern. To avoid bankruptcy, the Austrian government was forced to share political control with the one social class that could return the Austrian Empire to a state of financial solvency, the German-Austrian bourgeoisie. The first hesitant move toward a limited form of constitutional government in 1860 and 1861 was nothing but capitulation at home after military defeat abroad.

Even though it reduced Austrian capabilities further, a strictly deflationary policy was adopted between 1860 and 1865 to restore some order to government finances. But in 1865 when war with Prussia became ever more probable, it was still next to impossible to float a loan in international money markets; and in 1866 Austrian bonds were traded at a discount of 45 percent below parity, an all-time low.[27] In this desperate financial situation there seemed to be no hope. In fact, some of Austria's top-ranking officials regarded war as the optimal solution since it promised certainty at last: in victory, indemnification; in defeat, bankruptcy.[28] Ill-equipped for the conflict strategy it had followed since 1848, Austria's political elite, in the end, regarded foreign policy simply as a game of roulette.

Unfortunately for the Austrians, the odds of the game were not even. The gap between aspirations and performance was most conspicuous in the area of military defense. Before the Austro-Italian War of 1859, military expenditures declined by 12 percent between 1856 and 1858, and after the defeat of 1859 expenditures declined by 34 percent between 1860 and 1863.[29]

---

27. Gratz, "Österreichische Finanzpolitik," p. 250. Srbik, *Deutsche Einheit*, IV, 298-299.
28. Georg Franz, *Liberalismus: Die deutschliberale Bewegung in der Habsburgischen Monarchie* (Munich, Callwey, 1955), p. 299.
29. Macartney, *Habsburg Empire*, pp. 492, 534. On the other hand, Prussian military expenditures increased by about two-thirds between 1849 and 1865. See Wilhelm Gerloff, "Der Staatshaushalt und das Finanzsystem Deutschlands," in Wilhelm Gerloff and Franz Meisel (eds.),

Expenditure cuts of this magnitude meant that Austria could not keep abreast of advances in military technology made during the 1850s and 1860s. Because of the failure to reequip its armies with rapid-fire rifles, Austria sustained heavy casualties in the fighting in 1866. On the northern front, Austrian war dead exceeded Prussian casualties by a factor of three.[30]

But the Austrian problem was not simply one of financial weakness. Government inefficiency also played an important role. In 1854 Austria's army was about 1.37 percent of its total population, while the corresponding ratio for Prussia was only 0.77 percent. On the other hand, Prussia spent almost twice as much as Austria on each man under arms, 209 thalers compared to Austria's 109. Yet, at the same time Prussia was able to mobilize a much larger proportion of its total population. Its wartime army numbered 428,000 men, or 2.59 percent of the total population, and additional trained reserves were available which would have brought that figure up to about 800,000. Compared with Prussia, Austria was using a larger proportion of its resources for military purposes in peacetime, but was capable of mobilizing a smaller proportion in the event of war.[31]

Financial weakness and government inefficiency diminished the potential success of Austrian policy. In the light of the professed aims of Austrian diplomacy in Germany after 1849, for example, it comes as a surprise that a direct rail link between Vienna and the states of southern Germany was opened as late as 1860, only six years before Austria's defeat in the battle of Königgrätz. Economic factors played a large role in this. The Austrian government lacked the funds to speed up railway construction, and private investors were attracted primarily to the

---

Handbuch der Finanzwissenschaften (Tübingen: J. C. B. Mohr [Paul Siebeck], 1929), III, 6.

30. Otto Berndt, *Die Zahl im Kriege: Statistische Daten aus der neueren Kriegsgeschichte in graphischer Darstellung* (Vienna: Freytag, 1897), p. 92.

31. Friedrich Wilhelm von Reden, *Deutschland und das übrige Europa: Handbuch der Boden-, Bevölkerungs-, Erwerbs- und Verkehrsstatistik; des Staatshaushalts und der Streitmacht. In vergleichender Darstellung* (Wiesbaden: Kreidel, 1854), pp. 1,010-1,011. Karl W. Deutsch et al., "Background for Community" (MS, Cambridge, Mass., n.d.), p. 418.

southern and northern railways which promised higher economic returns. Austria simply failed to commit sufficient resources for the fulfillment of its political interest in an alliance with the states of southern Germany against Prussia.

Besides the late opening of the western railway, Austrian weakness is illustrated by a second example. Under enormous difficulties and expense, a railway across the Semmering pass to the south of Vienna was completed in 1854. Yet Austria's bureaucrats never seriously considered the potential economic and political advantages Austria might have gained from making Bohemia's rich coal deposits available to southern Germany. The cost of Austrian coal was only half that of the Prussian shipments.[32] It would only have been necessary to construct a railroad from Bohemia to eastern Bavaria across a mountain range considerably less formidable than the Semmering pass. Clearly, the barriers the Austrian bureaucrats faced were not geographic but cognitive.

The mixture of Austrian impotence and indifference limited not only the extent but the effectiveness of policy coordination. In 1851 the Austrian War Ministry circulated within the government a secret memorandum which specified the railway lines most important to the country's military security. Of all the lines named, the western railway and the connection between Bohemia and Bavaria commanded top priority.[33] Even so, the completion of the western railway was another nine years off, and the line between Bohemia and Bavaria had to wait still longer. The elite that had seized power in Austria in 1848 lacked the perceptiveness to recognize change and the willingness to adjust to it.

After 1849 Austrian foreign policy toward Germany was motivated by one consideration, the consolidation of the monarchy. The reassertion of Austrian dominance in German affairs was an attempt to achieve that objective. Only an increase in the political power of the German-Austrians could have ensured the

---

32. P. F. Kupka, *Die Eisenbahnen Österreich-Ungarns: 1822-1867* (Leipzig: Duncker, 1888), pp. 51, 126.
33. *Ibid.*, p. 169.

Conflict Pattern (1848-1870)

unity of the empire. It was not for lack of desire but for want of economic resources and political skills that the Austrian plan failed to materialize. The Revolution of 1848 had illustrated the weakness of the aristocratic pattern because the government's capacity for political control at home had not kept pace with the growing burdens imposed on it. The military defeat of 1866 revealed that the pattern of conflict integration was about to change because the government's capacity for engaging in political conflict abroad had not kept pace with the growing power of its rival.

COMMUNITY AND SOCIETY:
ATTITUDINAL BASIS OF POLITICAL AUTONOMY

The foreign policy failures resulting from the widening gap between domestic capabilities and foreign loads shaped the response of the German-Austrian middle class and mass public to Austria's disastrous defeat in 1866. Compared with the beginning of the nineteenth century, the change in public sentiment was readily apparent. Upon his return to Vienna after a military defeat in 1809, the Austrian emperor had been greeted like a victor; two generations later, in the face of a military calamity of similar magnitude, the Austrian public greeted the emperor with a mixture of indifference and hostility.[34] In the era of elite politics, mass attitudes had been weak and undifferentiated. At the outset of the era of mass politics, public sentiment took a more distinct shape along two dimensions, the social and the cultural.

At the outbreak of the Austro-Prussian war of 1866, public hostility toward Prussia appeared to be well entrenched among the German-Austrian middle class and mass public. Both regarded the imminent conflict as a just and defensive war against an overbearing and aggressive enemy, a war that undoubtedly would end in Austrian victory. The negative evaluation was complemented by a self-perception as "Great German"

---

34. Franz Burtik, "Die Volksstimmung in Österreich nach der Katastrophe bei Königgrätz" (unpub. diss., University of Vienna, 1926), pp. 64, 89.

in the sense of 1848—that is, as an integral part of the Austrian Empire but with political ties to Germany.[35]

The Austrian conservatives—aristocracy, church, and army—differed in their reaction to the escalating crisis. Hostile to Austria's bourgeoisie, which had reached the levers of political power as late as 1860, the conservatives counseled moderation. With a deep admiration of Prussia, they continued to hope for a renewal of the old class coalition with Prussia's conservatives to contain the political advance of the middle class. Austria's conservatives differed from the middle class not only in their positive evaluation of Prussia but in a remarkably weak German national consciousness. The conservatives identified solely with the House of Habsburg. In their view national agitations, including "Great German" sentiments, could only weaken or destroy the delicate multinational structure of the Austrian Empire.[36] But by 1866 the conservatives in Austria had suffered a considerable weakening of their political stature, and they watched helplessly as the old order they cherished collapsed.

The asymmetry between the liberal and conservative evaluation of Prussia persisted after 1866 but in reverse order. Now Austria's middle class and mass public came to evaluate Prussia positively, while the conservatives argued for revanche instead. Public response to the swift military defeat of the Austrian armies was disconcerting. Cheerfulness rather than dejection characterized the atmosphere of the day. In Vienna the pace of life did not change despite the rapid advance of the Prussian troops toward the city. The evening after the defeat of the Austrian army in the battle of Königgrätz a fancy-dress ball was held. "People sing and dance in the pubs; theater shows are well

---

35. Friederike Steininger, "Die Entwicklung der Deutschen Frage in den Jahren 1864-1866 und die Presse in Österreich" (unpub. diss., University of Vienna, 1934), pp. 12, 84, 107, 137, 145-180. Margaretha Vollenhofer, "Der Österreichisch-Preussische Krieg 1866 im Spiegel der Wiener Presse" (unpub. diss., University of Vienna, 1936), pp. 36, 78-79.
36. Walter Lott, "Der Kampf um die Führung in Deutschland und die konservative Presse Österreichs von 1860 bis 1866" (unpub. diss., University of Vienna, 1935), pp. 49, 77, 91, 140-153.

attended. Similar things are reported from Graz."[37] The stock market soared. Only 3,000 citizens volunteered for Vienna's civil defense corps designed to accommodate 200,000.[38] The Viennese refused to build fortifications against an imminent Prussian attack. "Many of them declared: If the Prussians march on Vienna, they would rather move out to greet them; they would prefer to become Prussian rather than to remain Austrians."[39]

In contrast to the widespread hatred of Prussia before 1866, public sentiment after the war changed abruptly. Prussian occupation of Vienna had been feared by many, but the occupation was short—it lasted less than two months—and the behavior of troops and officers was meticulously correct. By the time they left, the Prussian troops appeared to have found favor with the local population.[40] This shift in public sentiment was very much in evidence in the partisan feelings evoked by the Franco-Prussian conflict between 1866 and 1871. By 1868 the German-Austrian middle class had followed the mass public in adopting a favorable attitude toward Prussia. At the outbreak of the Franco-Prussian war of 1870 a large majority of the German-Austrian public backed Prussia against France, as did large segments of the German-Austrian middle class.[41]

The reaction of Austria's conservatives, now strengthened by the court circles and parts of the bureaucracy, was different. They were not yet prepared to concede that Austria's loss of influence

---

37. Quoted in Friedrich Cornelius, *Der Friede von Nikolsburg und die öffentliche Meinung in Österreich: Eine Studie zur Völkerpsychologie* (Munich: Reinhardt, 1927), pp. 28-29.
38. Bibl, *Zerfall Österreichs*, II, 298.
39. This is a police report quoted in Burtik, "Volksstimmung in Österreich," pp. 68-69.
40. Othmar Tuider and Johannes Rüling, "Die Preussen in Niederösterreich 1866," in *Militärhistorische Schriftenreihe*, IV (Vienna: Österreichischer Bundesverlag, 1966).
41. Burtik, "Volksstimmung in Österreich," p. 134. Oskar Wiktora, "Die politische Haltung der 'Neuen Freien Presse' in der liberalen Ära" (unpub. diss., University of Vienna, 1948), p. 100. Saul Goldschlag, "Die Wiener führende Presse und der Deutsch-Französische Krieg, 1870-1871" (unpub. diss., University of Vienna, 1930), pp. 43, 47, 114-115. Ingrid Walter, "Moritz Benedikt und die 'Neue Freie Presse'" (unpub. diss., University of Vienna, 1950), p. 63.

in Germany was permanent.[42] Many members of these groups hoped for a French victory, some of them to the extent of speaking for active intervention on the side of Napoleon III in 1870. But the constraints of domestic politics and the rapid succession of German military victories made any such plans illusory. After the formation of the Second German Empire in 1871, Austria's conservative political elite gradually followed the path taken earlier by mass and middle-class opinion. The Three-Emperor-League of 1872 and the Dual Alliance of 1879 marked the completion at the level of diplomacy of a process started years earlier at the level of mass attitudes. An old enemy, Prussia, had been forgotten; a new ally, Germany, had been gained.

Although historically specific factors may have played a part, the asymmetric attitude changes of Austria's liberals and conservatives in 1866 reflect the difference between attitudinal measures of society and community, between evaluation and identification. This analysis confirms the expectation that cultural identification is less easily changed than social evaluation. Before and after the war of 1866, the conservatives identified solely with the House of Habsburg; but a change in political circumstances made it easy for them to switch from a positive to a negative evaluation of Prussia. The Austrian middle class and mass public, on the other hand, remained unshaken in their self-identification as (Great) German, which facilitated their change from a negative to a positive evaluation of Prussia. In neither case did the war of 1866 alter the mode of self-identification even though it affected drastically the patterns of evaluation. The change in evaluations that occurred after 1866 obliterated the inconsistencies in the attitudes of the conservatives no less than in those of the middle class and the mass public.

This analysis supports a second conclusion. The rapid change in the evaluation of Prussia by the German-Austrian public was facilitated by a persistent self-identification as Great German as defined in 1848. In sharp contrast to later periods, such as the

---

42. See, for example, Stephan Verosta, *Theorie und Realität von Bündnissen: Heinrich Lammasch, Karl Renner und der Zweibund (1897-1914)* (Vienna: Europa Verlag, 1971), p. 46.

1890s or the interwar period, no segment of the German-Austrians was yet willing to relinquish a self-conception in which Austrian elements still dominated. In the middle of the nineteenth century, mutual identification with Germany was still lacking, and the attitudinal integration of Austria with Germany was still weak.

The second pattern of Austro-German relations was a transition phase from the elite politics of the first part of the nineteenth century to the mass politics of the last part. Conflict instead of cooperation in politics, interdependence instead of isolation in the economy, society, and culture marked the change from the aristocratic to the conflict pattern. An increase in the extent of political coordination was offset by a decline in its effectiveness, thus leaving Austria's political autonomy substantially unimpaired for two different reasons.

Although still excluded from the political arena, changes in the behavior and attitudes of the German-Austrian middle class and mass public created a context conducive to the persistence of political autonomy. Since cultural communications (mail) increased much faster than social transactions (trade), the behavioral measures of society and community pointed to a process of relative integration of Austria and Germany. These advances were not matched by corresponding gains at the level of attitudes marked by the relative absence of mutual identification with Germany in the 1850s and 1860s. Counterpressures and political autonomy, not copressures and political integration, characterized the conflict pattern.

The ample rewards that the Austrian Empire offered to the German-Austrians, and in particular its middle class, enhanced further the probability of political autonomy. The division of labor prevailing in the Austro-Hungarian army was indicative of a more general pattern in the distribution of rewards: the Slavs served in the infantry, the Hungarians in the cavalry, the German-Austrians in the artillery. In the Austrian Empire the German-Austrians held better jobs, earned higher wages and profits, enjoyed positions of greater status, and received a better education than any other ethnic group. The German-Austrians simply lacked the incentive to bring about an effective political integration of Austria and Germany.

Most importantly, the conservative coalition and liberal opposition agreed on the political rewards of the empire and the desirability of one central objective: a continuation of the German character of the Austrian Empire. The policy of modernization, centralization, and repression adopted at home after 1849 was designed to achieve that overriding aim. This policy was backed by a political strategy in Germany. The Great German (*Grossdeutsch*) conception of the Austrian bourgeoisie in the Frankfurt Assembly and the Great Austrian (*Grossösterreichisch*) conception of the military-bureaucratic elite after 1849 were two similar attempts to mold the Austrian Empire permanently as a German centrally run political machine. A partial sacrifice of political autonomy was a price both elites were willing to pay for securing the political power of a greater number of Germans in the empire. The only difference was that the bourgeoisie favored increases in the effectiveness of Austro-German political coordination, while the military-bureaucratic elite worked for a growth in its extent. But the primacy of the empire's domestic politics meant also that neither group was willing to sacrifice autonomy by working for full political unification. In their reluctance to seek more than a partial integration of Austria and Germany, both elites, the old and the new, revealed a common preference for political autonomy, the trademark of a disjoined partnership.

V

HIERARCHICAL PATTERN
(1870-1918)

THE HIERARCHICAL pattern describes a political relationship between Austria and Germany in which Austria was no longer the dominating but the dependent partner. It witnessed the intensification of the national strife that marked the empire's domestic politics during the preceding decades. The strategy of partial integration with Germany, which the German-Austrians continued to favor until 1918, served to defend their position in the Austrian Empire against the political demands of the Slavs. This strategy brought about simultaneously the same two results that earlier had caused the breakdown of the first two patterns, revolution at home and defeat abroad.

Austria's political autonomy was preserved in the hierarchical pattern for three reasons. The balance between Austro-German community and society pointed toward autonomy, not integration. The economic rewards the Austrian Empire offered to the German-Austrians continued to be large. Finally, after the unification of Germany, a decrease in the extent of Austro-German political coordination without a simultaneous rise in its effectiveness made for the persistence of political autonomy.

COMMUNITY AND SOCIETY: COUNTERPRESSURES

The acceleration of economic modernization and social mobilization during the last third of the nineteenth century ushered in the age of mass politics. The context in which different actors were pursuing their political strategies was marked by opposing currents of integration and disintegration among Austrian and German mass publics which leveled off around the turn of the century. These counterpressures at the cultural and social levels were conducive to the persistence of political autonomy.

Behavioral Disintegration In the first decade and a half after 1848 trade between Austria-Hungary and Germany had shifted upward quite sharply. Between 1864 and 1900, on the other hand, the increase was much slower. After 1900, it halted altogether. But past growth had been important; between 1900 and 1912 Germany still accounted for about 40 percent of Austria-Hungary's total foreign trade. At the same time Austria-Hungary's relative share of Germany's foreign trade decreased from 15 to 8 percent on the import side and from 19 to 12 percent on the export side.[1] Thus, the relative asymmetry in the Dual Monarchy's trade dependence on Germany almost doubled, from two to one in 1864 to four to one, fifty years later. The composition of trade reflected this growing dependence as well. In 1900 three-quarters of Austro-Hungarian imports from Germany were manufactured goods, while the corresponding figure on the export side was less than one-half.[2]

Austrian dependence on Germany was also reflected in the exchange of capital. Austria suffered a traditional capital shortage. The interest rate paid by the Central Bank of the Dual Monarchy was consistently higher than the French or British and exceeded the German rate until the end of the nineteenth century. As a result more than one-third of common stocks and government bonds were owned in 1901 by foreigners. German banks started to invest heavily in Austria only after 1866. By the turn of the century the role of German capital in Austria and

---

1. *Statistik des auswärtigen Handels des Österreichisch-Ungarischen Zollgebietes im Jahre 1912* (Vienna: Hof- und Staatsdruckerei, 1913), I, 987, 991. *Statistisches Jahrbuch für das Deutsche Reich,* XXXIV (1913), pp. 241-242.
2. *Statistik des auswärtigen Handels im Jahre 1900,* I, 28-29.

Hungary was more important than that of any other country. Furthermore, 59 percent of German capital was concentrated in government securities, which combined high returns with political leverage and posed no threat of rivalry to German industry.[3]

Germany was not only a direct creditor of the Austrian government but an indirect owner of Austrian industry. Through control of Austria's largest bank, the *Creditanstalt,* as well as of numerous other banks, and through an increasing number of cartels, the German economy absorbed a large segment of Austrian industry. Cyclical and secular changes in Germany's economic activities determined economic developments in Austria.[4] When an acute capital shortage in Germany slowed the penetration of Austria by German capital, from 1900 on, Germany's preponderant influence had already been firmly established.

Throughout the second half of the nineteenth century, Austria exported labor at an ever-increasing rate. The annual average of intercontinental emigration rose from 2,900 for the decade 1851–1860, to 25,000 for the years 1881–1890, to over 100,000 for the years 1901–1910.[5] These estimates, however, do not include seasonal emigration to Germany, which was about four times as large as intercontinental emigration during the first decade of the twentieth century. The large flow of labor from Austria to Germany was primarily due to the underemployment of unskilled labor in the Austrian economy. The growing asym-

---

3. Juruij Křižek, "Beitrag zur Geschichte der Entstehung und des Einflusses des Finanzkapitals in der Habsburgermonarchie in den Jahren 1900-1914," in *Die Frage des Finanzkapitals in der Österreichisch-Ungarischen Monarchie, 1900-1918* (Bucharest: Verlag der Akademie der Sozialistischen Republik Rumänien, 1965), p. 24; Appendix, Table 17.
4. Křižek, "Finanzkapital in der Habsburgermonarchie," pp. 28-29, 54. Albert Trenkwalder, "Die Konjunktur in Österreich" (unpub. diss., University of Vienna, 1956), p. 83. Herbert Matis, *Österreichs Wirtschaft, 1848-1913: Konjunkturelle Dynamik und gesellschaftlicher Wandel im Zeitalter Franz Josephs I* (Berlin: Duncker, 1972). Eduard März, *Österreichs Industrie- und Bankenpolitik in der Zeit Franz Josephs I* (Vienna: Europa Verlag, 1968).
5. Felix Klezl, "Austria," in Walter F. Wilcox (ed.), *International Migrations: Interpretations* (New York: National Bureau of Economic Research, 1931), II, 398.

metry of this part of Austro-German relations is indicated by the increasing proportion of Austrians abroad who went to Germany (30 percent in 1869, 57 percent in 1910) and the declining proportion of Germans among the foreigners in Austria (31 percent in 1869 and 22 percent in 1910).[6]

A corresponding asymmetry is observable also at the elite level. The scarcity of jobs for highly skilled and educated labor led to a sizable migration from Austria to Germany. But at the same time the influx of Reich-Germans dwindled as the unification of Germany and the resultant great power status provided many of them the career opportunities at home which in earlier times they had found only in Austria. The proportion of Reich-Germans in Austria's diplomatic service declined from 34 percent in 1859 to 7 percent in 1908; the corresponding figures in the bureaucracy were 26 and 22 percent, and in the armed services 52 and 18 percent.[7]

Between 1870 and 1914 social transactions between Austria and Germany were complementary, with Austria playing the role of a dependent in a relationship of unequals. But two of the three indicators—the exchange of goods and the flow of capital—suggested that transaction flows leveled off at a high plateau around the turn of the century. The role reversal from a dominant to a dependent power, progressive from 1815, was substantially complete.

Social transactions lead to differentiation and only communications to standardization. Table 6 shows a gradual decline in Austrian attention accorded to Germany during the last third of the nineteenth century. As the transactions data also document, however, the attention figures remained stable after the turn of the century. The figures suggest that the decline in Austrian attention toward Germany was matched by the increasing importance of the non-European world. But Austro-German relations

---

6. *Österreichische Statistik*, Neue Folge, II, 2, pp. 6-7*. *Vierteljahreshefte zur Statistik des Deutschen Reiches*, XXV, 4 (Ergänzungsheft), p. 8*.
7. Nikolaus von Preradovich, *Die Führungsschichten in Österreich und Preussen (1804-1918): Mit einem Ausblick bis zum Jahre 1945* (Wiesbaden: Steiner, 1955), pp. 1-72.

TABLE 6. Relative Distribution of Austrian Attention: Average Foreign News Coverage in Two Austrian Papers, 1873-1912 (in percentages)[a]

	1873-1882	1885-1897	1900-1912	Net Change 1873/1882-1900/1912
Germany	26	21	20	−6
Northern Europe[b]	13	13	10	−3
Western Europe[c]	21	22	22	+1
Eastern Europe[d]	9	7	6	−3
Southern Europe[e]	12	19	13	+1
Southeast Europe[f]	13	7	14	+1
Rest of world	5	12	16	+11

Sources: *Wiener Zeitung; Neue Freie Presse*.
[a]The method of calculation is explained in Chapter III, fn. 28. Because of rounding off, percentages do not always add to 100.
[b]Scandinavia and Britain
[c]France, Benelux, and Switzerland
[d]Russia and Poland
[e]Portugal, Spain, Italy, and Greece
[f]European parts of the Ottoman Empire

were highly asymmetric here as well. The results of a content analysis of German papers suggest that Austria accorded about two to three times as much attention to Germany as did Germany to Austria; during World War I that difference increased to as much as ten to one.[8]

A long-term decline took place also in the volume of communications between Austria and Germany during the last third of the nineteenth century, but as in the previous instances the trend was arrested around the turn of the century. Personal mail (letters and postcards) received from Germany, for example,

8. Ithiel de Sola Pool, Harold D. Lasswell, and Daniel Lerner, *Symbols of Internationalism* (Stanford: Stanford University Press, 1951), p. 68. Their measure of attention is based on an analysis of editorials, not on the relative amount of space of news reports printed.

amounted to 72 percent of the foreign mail in 1867, 26 percent in 1900, and 23 percent in 1912; the corresponding figures for mail sent to Germany were 73, 39, and 40 percent. A similar decline is observable also in the number of telegrams sent and received, down from 68 and 66 percent respectively in 1867, to 40 and 41 percent in 1900, and 40 percent in 1912.[9]

The available data on other aspects of Austro-German communications confirm the conclusion of a declining trend, which halted toward the end of the nineteenth century, as well as a considerable asymmetry in the degree of mutual dependence of Austria and Germany. The value of Austria's exports of printed material to Germany, for example, declined from 76 to 66 percent between 1891 and 1912, while the import figure remained unchanged at about 92 percent; on the other hand, corresponding figures for Germany did not exceed the 25 percent level in those years.[10] As was true of the other indicators of transactions and communications flows, Austrian dependence on Germany was about three to four times greater than that of Germany on Austria.

Integration at the mass level depends on the relation between standardization and differentiation, between community and society. In the Austro-German case between 1871 and 1914 a long-term rise in transactions accompanied a simultaneous decline in communications. But the data also suggest that the behavioral disintegration that resulted was arrested around the turn of the century.

Attitudinal Integration The probability of political autonomy is affected also by a second, attitudinal, dimension. Evaluation and identification are measures of attitudinal integration at the social and cultural levels. The last chapter, using this distinc-

---

9. *Das Österreichische Post- und Telegraphenwesen in den im Reichsrathe vertretenen Königreiche und Länder mit Schluss des Jahres 1868* (Vienna: Staatsdruckerei, 1869), pp. 26-27; Union Postale Universelle, Le Bureau International, *Relevé des Tableaux Statistiques du Service Postal International (Expédition), 1900; 1912. Jahrbuch für die amtliche Statistik des Preussischen Staates*, III, (1869), p. 250. *Nachrichten über Industrie, Handel and Verkehr aus dem statistischen Department im K.K. Handels-Ministerium, 1900; 1912.*
10. *Statistik des auswärtigen Handels, 1891*, I, 764-765; *1912*, I, 412, 864.

tion, presented a qualitative analysis of attitude change; this section will measure attitude change quantitatively.

Two sets of documents designed to measure changes in Austrian evaluation of Germany were subjected to a content analysis. One set consisted of all the crown speeches of the Austrian emperor and the inaugural addresses of his prime ministers as well as those of the chancellors of the First and Second Republics. The second set of documents comprised 179 New Year's Eve editorials published between 1853 and 1969. The newspapers were chosen according to their political viewpoint and include the government press as well as organs of the liberal, socialist, Christian social, and German nationalist camps. Both sets of documents have the advantage of revealing evaluative judgments somewhat removed from the pressures of daily events. In addition they permit a comparison of the differences between the attitudes of the government and Austria's political elites.[11]

These speeches and editorials were read carefully, and the presence of a positive, neutral, or negative evaluation of Germany was coded. Not the frequency of evaluations but their presence or absence in each speech or editorial provides the basis for this analysis. The percentage figures quoted refer, therefore, to the relative number of speeches or editorials in which a positive, neutral, or negative evaluation of Germany was made during any given time period.

Table 7 summarizes the most important findings of this analysis. The emperor and his prime ministers, it turns out, rarely talked on the subject of Austro-German relations, since

---

11. The total number of speeches was 91, 37 for the years 1860 to 1911, 33 for the First Republic, and 21 for the Second Republic. The sample of newspapers was stratified by time periods, and within each period the sample was drawn nonrandomly to cover the maximum number of different dates per period. The selection and classification of the different papers were determined on the basis of the discussion of Kurt Paupié, *Handbuch der Österreichischen Pressegeschichte* (Vienna: Braumüller, 1960), I. The coding reliability was checked by pre- and post-analysis tests. Reliability was high, 0.90 or better, as measured by a simple percentage agreement index.

TABLE 7. Evaluation of Germany in Government Speeches and Newspaper Editorials in Austria, 1853-1918

	(1)	(2)	(3)			(4)	(5)	(6)		
	No. of Government Speeches	Government Evaltns.: Positive– Negative/ Positive+ Negative	Government Evaluations (in percent)			No. of Press Editorials	Press Evaltns.: Positive– Negative/ Positive+ Negative	Press Evaluations (in percent)		
			Pos.	Neu.	Neg.			Pos.	Neu.	Neg.
1853-1866	—	—	—	—	—	18	−0.09	36	29	43
1860-1866	8	1.0	50	—	—	—	—	—	—	—
1867-1879	12	1.0	8	—	—	20	−0.10	26	43	37
1880-1889	2	1.0	25	—	—	11	0.50	60	13	20
1890-1899	5	1.0	12	6	—	15	0.33	50	19	25
1900-1913	10	1.0	50	—	—	21	0.33	29	33	14
1914-1918	—	—	—	—	—	14	0.83	79	7	7

the conduct of foreign policy remained outside the bounds of parliamentary power until 1918. But the few times they did mention Germany, their evaluations were uniformly positive. More instructive, then, is the analysis of public opinion as reflected in newspaper editorials. As shown by the coefficient of net amity in column five of Table 7, the ambiguity in the evaluations of Germany disappeared only after diplomatic relations between the two countries had been cemented by the Dual Alliance of 1879. It is particularly significant in this context that the positive evaluations of Germany declined after 1880 and leveled off from the 1890s onward.

Column five, however, provides only an overall measure of net amity, which conceals variations in the relative importance of positive, neutral, and negative evaluations. A disaggregation of the figures in column six shows only one consistent trend, the decline of negative evaluations throughout the second half of the nineteenth century. Positive and neutral evaluations, on the other hand, were inversely related to one another. Reflecting the strength of the Austro-German alliance, the decline in net amity was the result of changes in the balance between positive and neutral evaluations. This greatly facilitated the closing of Austro-German ranks during World War I, when Austria's positive evaluations of Germany reached an all-time high.

The degree of mutual identification provides the attitudinal basis of community. During the last part of the nineteenth century, changes in the self-identification of the German-Austrians rested on multiple choices: between Austria or Germany as states; between monarchic or republican institutions; between the role as the empire's leading nationality or as members of a larger German nation; and lastly the choice between an "instrumental" mode of attachment to the larger whole—whether German or Austrian—based on economic well-being or a "sentimental" one based on psychological needs.[12]

12. See Herbert C. Kelman, "Patterns of Personal Involvement in the National System: A Social Psychological Analysis of Political Legitimacy," in James N. Rosenau (ed.), *International Politics and Foreign Policy: A Reader in Research and Theory*, rev. ed. (New York: The Free Press, 1969), pp. 280-281.

These multiple choices point to the dimensions along which changes in Austrian self-identification can be measured. Self-identification is a reflection of national consciousness, which Karl Deutsch defined as the "attachment of secondary symbols of nationality to primary items of information moving through channels of social communications or through the mind of an individual."[13] Even though changes in self-identification are not directly observable, variations in the usage of symbols of common identity can be assumed to be an indirect measure of underlying variations. The analysis will be applied to the same two sets of documents—government speeches and newspaper editorials—used for the analysis of changes in evaluations. As a method of empirical research, a content analysis of symbol usage requires the consistent application of a fixed set of categories. Table 8 depicts these categories as resulting from the dimensions of attitude change just postulated.[14] Figure 1 summarizes the important changes in the symbol usage of the Austrian government.

During the last third of the nineteenth century, symbol usage in government speeches had three notable features. Between 1860 and 1917 indirect Austrian symbols of identity never accounted for less than four-fifths of the total number of symbols used. Direct Austrian symbols were rare, and German symbols practically never appeared. The supranational orientation of the Austrian monarchy was thus shown in the heavy reliance on indirect symbols and an avoidance of the problem of a common identity in a community bitterly divided along ethnic lines. Secondly, the gradual shift away from symbols referring to the dynasty reflected the arrival of an era of mass politics. Lastly, in response to the empire's dismal defeats in 1859 and 1866, there occurred

13. Karl W. Deutsch, *Nationalism and Social Communication: An Inquiry into the Foundations of Nationality*, 2nd ed. (Cambridge, Mass.: M.I.T. Press, 1966), p. 172.
14. The categories of this content analysis are adapted from Richard L. Merritt, *Symbols of American Community, 1735-1775* (New Haven: Yale University Press, 1966); and Kelman, "Personal Involvement in the National System." Coding reliability, as checked by pre- and post-analysis tests, was never lower than 0.87 measured by a percentage agreement index.

TABLE 8. Categories for Symbols of Common Identity

Primary Identification	Secondary (Symbolic) Identification					
	Austrian		Austro-German		German	
	Direct	Indirect	Indirect		Indirect	Direct
Land or state:						
Instrumental	A. state	this country			this country	G. state
Sentimental	A. fatherland	homeland			homeland	G. fatherland
Dynasty:						
Instrumental	A. monarchy	our kingdom			our kingdom	G. monarchy
Sentimental	A.'s revered throne	our holy majesty			our holy majesty	G.'s revered throne
Population:						
Instrumental	A. citizens	population (Bevölkerung)			population (Bevölkerung)	G. citizens
Sentimental	A. people	people (Volk)			people (Volk)	G. people

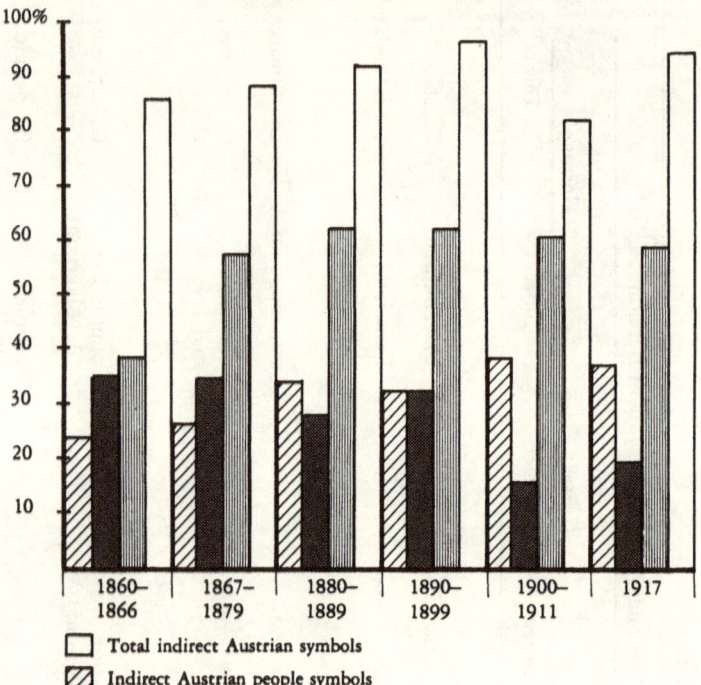

FIGURE 1. SYMBOLS OF COMMON IDENTITY IN AUSTRIAN GOVERNMENT SPEECHES, 1860–1917

a rapid change between 1860 and 1880 from sentimental to instrumental symbols.

An application of the same set of categories to the New Year's Eve editorials reflects attitude changes of the German-Austrian public at large. The central conclusion of this analysis is the decline in the relative number of Austrian symbols, illustrated in Table 9. But the decline halted around the turn of the century; and when the difference between Austrian and German symbols was smallest, during the years 1890-1899, the German-Austrians were still thinking of themselves in Austrian terms twice as often as they thought of themselves in German terms.[15]

A distinction between symbols referring to the land, the people, and the dynasty reveals that the two strongest trends were the decline of Austrian symbols referring to the land (from 67 percent in 1860–1866 to 40 percent in 1890–1899) and the increase in German symbols referring to the people (from 3 percent in 1860–1866 to 27 percent in 1890–1899). As had been true of other trends, however, these changes leveled off around 1900.

TABLE 9. Strength of Austrian Symbols of Common Identity as Measured by the Ratio of Direct Plus Indirect Austrian Symbols over Direct Plus Indirect German Symbols

	Austrian/German
1853-1866	15.5
1867-1879	6.4
1880-1889	2.1
1890-1899	1.9
1900-1913	2.6
1914-1918	3.1

15. This analysis, thus, contradicts Albert Fuchs's argument that a total vacuum existed in Austrian national consciousness and Austrian self-identification. See Albert Fuchs, *Geistige Strömungen in Österreich, 1867-1918* (Vienna: Globus Verlag, 1949), p. 171.

The main conclusion of this analysis is a halting of the growth of an Austro-German community around the turn of the century. The growing self-identification as a German people was, at least in part, a reaction to the intensification of the nationality conflict of the empire toward the end of the nineteenth century. But the political crisis which shook the empire to its foundation in 1897 on the issue of language policy ratified but did not create a change in public sentiments.

Behavior and Attitudes: Counterpressures This analysis of changes in the balance between standardization and differentiation, community and society, has led to two opposite conclusions. Since transactions increased at the same time that communications declined, the behavioral measures of community and society pointed to a process of relative disintegration of Austria and Germany. On the other hand, the decline in positive evaluations as indicators of society and the rise of mutual identifications as indicators of community pointed to a process of relative integration at the level of attitudes. Counterpressures existed not only between behavioral disintegration and attitudinal integration but also between behavioral and attitudinal measures of society and community. Social transactions increased at the same time that positive evaluations decreased, and cultural communications declined with a simultaneous growth of mutual identifications. These multiple counterpressures explain a feature common to all four measures of society and community, the deceleration of change around the turn of the century. This stabilization of countermoving processes of integration and disintegration occurred roughly a generation after the unification of Germany and signified the completion of a long-term process in which Austria had slipped from a position of dominator to that of dependent. The analysis of the hierarchical pattern points to counterpressures and political autonomy rather than copressures and political integration as the characteristic feature of the relations between society and community.

THE ECONOMIC REWARDS OF EMPIRE

Political autonomy is the most likely outcome as long as there are no overwhelming rewards associated with

Hierarchical Pattern (1870-1918)

strategies of integration. During the last part of the nineteenth century, the economic rewards that the empire held forth for all groups and classes of German-Austrians were comparable to those of Germany. More importantly, they were incomparably greater for the German-Austrians than for any other of the empire's many nationalities. These rewards were central to the bitter conflict between the different nationalities which marked the last five decades of the empire's existence. There was only one overriding issue: would the empire retain its predominantly German character? Disregarding the social problems dividing them, the great majority of German-Austrians felt that it should; the data suggest that it did. For the German-Austrians the rewards of empire did not lose their charm.

In the defense of their elite position the German-Austrians received indirect but powerful support from the institutions that seemed to symbolize the supranational character of the empire: the dynasty, the bureaucracy, and the army.[16] These pillars of the empire did not lose their German character. Although the dynasty was studiously supranational in its policies, it never ceased to be a latent symbol of German dominance. Of the 2,047 known ancestors of Francis Ferdinand, who was assassinated in Sarajevo in 1914, two-thirds were German or German-Austrian.[17]

The same was true of the bureaucracy. In 1914, 76 percent of the civil servants in the central ministries of the Austrian Empire were German, and in the joint ministries which linked the eastern and the western half of the Dual Monarchy, the corresponding figure was still as high as 56 percent; since the German-Austrians made up only one-third of the population of the western half of the empire, this was a sizable overrepresentation.[18] The predominance of the German-Austrians, further-

---

16. Andrew G. Whiteside, "The Germans as an Integrative Force in Imperial Austria: The Dilemma of Dominance," *Austrian History Yearbook*, III, Part 1 (1967), pp. 167-168.
17. Oscar Jaszi, *The Dissolution of the Habsburg Monarchy* (Chicago: University of Chicago Press, 1929), p. 136.
18. Karl Hugelmann, "Das Nationalitätenrecht nach der Verfassung von 1867; Der Kampf um ihre Geltung, Auslegung, und Fortbildung," in Karl Hugelmann (ed.), *Das Nationalitätenrecht des alten Österreich* (Vienna: Braumüller, 1934), p. 280.

more, increased in the top positions of each ministry, especially in Vienna. In 1910, for example, German-Austrians filled 81 percent of the 146 positions of the top six civil-service grades of the finance ministry, which was widely considered to be favorably disposed to candidates with other ethnic backgrounds. In the foreign ministry the figure was only 65 percent, still roughly twice as high as the German-Austrian proportion in the total population.[19]

The transfer of power from the aristocracy to the bourgeoisie, which had occurred during the first half of the nineteenth century, continued in the second half. The proportion of the middle class in top bureaucratic positions rose between 1859 and 1918 from 50 to 66 percent in the diplomatic service, from 50 to 58 percent in the internal affairs department, and from 10 to 75 percent in the armed services.[20] Undoubtedly the competition for administrative jobs increased between the German-Austrians and the other nationalities during the last third of the century, but for the German-Austrians the severity of the competition was lessened by the increase in the number of bureaucratic jobs available and by greater opportunities to move into top positions.

Another reputed pillar of imperial unity, the army, also retained its German character. In 1900 German-Austrians made up about two-thirds of the officer corps of the Austro-Hungarian army even though German-Austrians constituted only one-quarter of the total population of the Dual Monarchy. And in 1910 roughly 85 percent of the army's officer corps in the western half of the empire was German.[21] Like the dynasty and the bureaucracy, the army never ceased to be an institution with a predominantly German character.

19. Elizabeth Wiskemann, *Czechs and Germans: A Study of the Struggle in the Historic Provinces of Bohemia and Moravia* (London: Macmillan, 1967), p. 62. Erich Sieder, "Österreichs Botschafter und Gesandte zwischen Wiener Kongress und Erstem Weltkrieg: Versuch einer sozialhistorischen Bestandsaufnahme" (unpub. diss., University of Vienna, 1969), p. 62.
20. Preradovich, *Die Führungsschichten in Österreich und Preussen*, pp. 1-72.
21. Jaszi, *Dissolution of the Habsburg Monarchy*, p. 279. See also Ludwig Jedlicka, *Ein Heer im Schatten der Parteien* (Graz: Böhlaus, 1955), p. 4.

To a lesser extent the overrepresentation of German-Austrians in the institutions of the empire could also be found in the Austrian Parliament and Executive. In 1873, 66 percent of the members of Parliament were German-Austrians; in 1885, 52 percent; and in 1907, after the introduction of universal suffrage, still 44 percent.[22] These German-Austrians, to be sure, were split into numerous parties which did not always vote together along national lines. But their overrepresentation provided the German-Austrians with potential power which they used to great effect in the crisis decade of the 1890s.

The Austrian Executive was German as well. Between 1809 and 1918, 50 percent of Austria's chancellors and foreign ministers were German. Moreover, during the very decades in which the influence of the German-Austrians declined in Parliament, effective power shifted to the Executive, where German-Austrian influence still dominated. The proportion of civil servants appointed to serve in the cabinet increased from 72 percent in 1879 to 82 percent in 1911, and the overwhelming majority of top bureaucrats were German-Austrian.[23] Thus the Koerber cabinet of civil servants in 1900 returned political power to the German-Austrians from whose hands it had slipped in 1879.

This argument does not dispute the view that the Austrian civil service, like the dynasty and the army, may have sought to cultivate a "supranational" orientation and pressed for "anational" policies in times of increasing national strife. But it is important not to lose sight of two critical conditions. Until 1918 empire-wide institutions like the bureaucracy or the army continued to offer the German-Austrians opportunities for upward social mobility (especially at the center of the empire) which they could hardly expect to find in Germany. Furthermore, the German character of these institutions provided symbolic and

---

22. Hugelmann, "Das Nationalitätenrecht," p. 144. Stephan Verosta, *Theorie und Realität von Bündnissen: Heinrich Lammasch, Karl Renner und der Zweibund (1897-1914)* (Vienna: Europa Verlag, 1971), p. 250.
23. Sieder, "Österreichs Botschafter," p. 145. Peter Gerlich, "Austrian Political Elites, 1861-1970" (paper prepared for the Symposium on Legislative and Ministerial Decision-Makers in Parliamentary Regimes, Bellagio, August 23-29, 1970), p. 10.

actual reassurance and strengthened the sentimental commitment of the German-Austrians to the empire. From both an instrumental and a sentimental perspective, in the eyes of the German-Austrians the empire continued as a going concern; and when it finally collapsed under the cumulative impact of internal and external strains and stresses, the German-Austrians were the last ethnic group to abandon it.

Economic and social conditions in general continued to favor the German-Austrians' position in the empire. Most of Austria's industry remained concentrated in German areas, in the Alpine provinces and the Sudetenland. Between 1850 and 1890, industrial production in the Alpine provinces declined somewhat from 40 to 33 percent of total production, while the relative share of the Sudetenland increased from 46 to 59 percent. The relative share of all other provinces together declined from 14 to 8 percent, a fact that underlines the inability of the Austrian government and capitalists to diversify industrial production geographically.[24] At the beginning of the nineteenth century the Austrian government had outlawed industrial production for fear of creating an unruly proletariat; for fear of enhancing the power base of the non-German nationalities in the eastern parts of the empire, it did comparatively little to encourage the spread of industry at the end of the nineteenth century.[25]

Since the Sudetenland was ethnically mixed between German-Austrians and Czechs, it is not clear whether the increasing concentration of Austria's industrial power there benefited primarily German-Austrians or Czechs. But judging by the occupational census taken around the turn of the century, the German-Austrians, as a whole, were still enjoying a substantial lead. Only 34 percent of the German-Austrians were working in the

---

24. Franz M. Mayer, Raimund F. Kaindl, Hans Pirchegger, Anton A. Klein, *Geschichte und Kulturleben Österreichs: Von 1792 bis zum Staatsvertrag von 1955*, 5th ed. (Vienna: Braumüller, 1965), III, 277.
25. Johann Slokar, *Geschichte der Österreichischen Industrie und ihrer Förderung unter Kaiser Franz I: Mit besonderer Berücksichtigung der Grossindustrie und unter Benützung archivalischer Quellen* (Vienna: Tempsky, 1914), pp. 25-28. Kurt W. Rothschild, *Austria's Economic Development between the Two Wars* (London: Mueller, 1947), p. 10.

agricultural sector of the economy as opposed to 43 percent of the Czechs and a much higher proportion still of the other nationalities. This 9 percent difference was almost totally offset by the overrepresentation of the Germans in the tertiary sector, among civil servants, professionals, and self-employed.[26]

Even more important than industry location was industry control in support of the dominant role which the German-Austrians played in the empire. A very high degree of interlocking existed between the financial and the industrial sectors of the Austrian economy. Vienna remained the financial hub of the empire until 1918, even though its position gradually weakened. In 1900 fully 80 percent of the total Austrian share capital was controlled from Vienna and the Alpine provinces, and by 1914 the figure still stood at 67 percent.[27] The concentration of capital in the hands of German-Austrians had two effects. First, it discouraged active competition and favored instead the formation of cartels which, together with a high tariff policy, increased German-Austrian profits. Second, the pervasiveness of absentee capital throughout Austria created a considerable transfer of resources from the peripheries of the empire to its center. Compared with the 1840s the extractive mechanism had changed from government taxation to industrial profits, but the process was still the same.[28]

No reliable figures exist that measure the net effect of this transfer of resources. One estimate takes the net foreign indebtedness of the Austrian Republic at the end of World War I as a rough indicator of the annual minimum transfer of capital from the periphery to the center of the empire. The figure of 2.5

---

26. Otto Bauer, *Die Nationalitätenfrage und die Sozialdemokratie* (Vienna: Brand, 1907), p. 240.
27. Křížek, "Finanzkapital in der Habsburgermonarchie," p. 24.
28. *Ibid.*, pp. 27-37. Jaszi, *Dissolution of the Habsburg Monarchy*, pp. 203-207. Josef Wysocki rightly notes the difficulties that arise from interpreting budget figures without a consideration of not easily measured factors such as pricing policy or repatriation of profits. See his article, "Die Österreichische Finanzpolitik," in Alois Brusatti (ed.), *Die Habsburgermonarchie 1848-1918 (I): Die wirtschaftliche Entwicklung* (Vienna: Verlag der Österreichischen Akademie der Wissenschaften, 1973), p. 101.

billion kronen represents about three-quarters of the total Austrian budget of 1913.[29] National income estimates for 1910 tend to confirm this conclusion. Per capita income in the provinces that later became parts of the First Republic was about 150 percent above the empire-wide average and equal to the per capita income of the Reich-Germans.[30]

The elite position of the German-Austrians was reflected also at the level of mass culture. Between 1880 and 1910, to take one example, illiteracy in the Alpine provinces and the Sudetenland practically vanished even though it was extensive in the rest of the empire. In 1910 the periodical press published in the German language still amounted to about 55 percent of the Austrian total. At the turn of the century more than half of Austria's high schools were German, as were five of her eight universities.[31] There existed, then, a consistent and cumulative pattern of discrimination in favor of the German-Austrians in all political, economic, social, and cultural spheres.

Even though that discrimination weakened somewhat during the last two decades of the empire's existence, the favorable objective conditions continued to shape the reward perceptions of the German-Austrians. The relative strength of German-Austrian instrumental attachment, indicated by the ratio of instru-

---

29. Gustav Stolper, *Deutschösterreich als Sozial- und Wirtschaftsproblem* (Munich: Drei Masken Verlag, 1921), p. 116. The German-Austrians paid about two-thirds of the empire's direct taxes, twice as much as their relative share in the population. But not all of the excess payment was transferred from the center to the periphery of the empire. Furthermore, direct taxes accounted for only one-third of total taxes, and the regressive character of indirect taxation presumably worked against the poorer, that is Slavic, segments of the Austrian population. It is undoubtedly true that the economic centers of the empire supported the periphery by reallocating a major portion of the funds raised through direct taxation. But this was probably more than offset by the reverse flow of profit "repatriation" plus the effects of indirect taxation. For a different view, see Matis, *Österreichs Wirtschaft, 1848-1913*, pp. 392-398.
30. *Monatsperichte des Österreichischen Institutes für Wirtschaftsforschung*, 14. Sonderheft, *Österreichs Volkseinkommen 1913 bis 1963* (Vienna: Selbstverlag, 1965), pp. 4-5, 30-31.
31. *Österreichisches statistisches Handbuch für die im Reichsrathe vertretenen Königreiche und Länder*, XXXI (1912), p. 383. Jaszi, *Dissolution of the Habsburg Monarchy*, p. 278.

mental over sentimental symbol usage in newspaper editorials, increased from 1.2 in the years 1867–1879, to 2.8 in the last decade of the nineteenth century, to 3.7 during World War I. In the minds of most German-Austrians there was, then, little doubt about what was at the root of the empire's nationality strife. In the words of the *Neue Freie Presse,* organ of the liberal middle class, the Czech demands for more political power had a "class character; they are affected by something proletarian, the jealousy and envy which the poor harbor against the people better off than themselves."[32] The success of the German-Austrian defense of its elite position in the empire and the continued effectiveness of rewards and reward perceptions is illustrated dramatically in Table 10. These figures show that the

TABLE 10. Rank Order of Emigration and Casualty Figures for Different National Groups in Austria[a]

	(1) Specified National Stock Emigrating, 1901-1910		(2) Deaths per 1,000 of Population in World War I	
	%	rank	%	rank
Germans	0.22	4	29.1	1
Czechs/Slovaks	0.49	3	24.6	2
Croats/Slovenes	0.69	2	22.3	3
Poles	0.93	1	16.2	4

Sources: Column (1): Felix Klezl, "Austria," in Walter F. Wilcox (ed.), *International Migrations: Interpretations* (New York: National Bureau of Economic Research, 1931), II, 407.
Column (2): Wilhelm Winkler, *Die Totenverluste der Österreichisch-Ungarischen Monarchie nach Nationalitäten* (Vienna: Seidl, 1919), pp. 7-8.
[a]Computation by the author.

32. Quoted in Oskar Wiktora, "Die politische Haltung der 'Neuen Freien Presse' in der liberalen Ära" (unpub. diss., University of Vienna, 1948), p. 98.

German-Austrians were the least willing to leave the empire and the most willing to die for it. Judging by this evidence, the empire was truly theirs until the very end.

THE PRIMACY OF DOMESTIC POLITICS: PARTIAL POLITICAL INTEGRATION AS A CRISIS STRATEGY

The persistence of political autonomy is a result of the interplay of nonpolitical and political variables. In the hierarchical pattern of Austro-German relations, neither the balance between community and society nor the structure of economic rewards pointed to significant sacrifices of Austria's political autonomy. Most German-Austrians, however, favored a partial political integration of Austria with Germany as a crisis strategy in response to the political demands of the empire's non-German nationalities. The relative absence of Austro-German integration at the mass base was too strong and the economic rewards of empire were too large to make likely a serious erosion of autonomy. But the stabilization of opposing processes of integration and disintegration at the mass level at the turn of the century and the Slavs' attack on the unequal distribution of economic rewards created the conditions for a partial sacrifice of autonomy. As had been true for the transition from aristocratic to middle-class politics, the change from middle-class to mass politics was crucially affected by the delights and the dilemmas of the political position the German-Austrians enjoyed in Austria.

For the first time in the empire's history the coalition between the dynasty and the majority of the German-Austrians became tenuous during the last third of the nineteenth century. Not choice but the lack of alternative sources of political and financial support had compelled the dynasty to reach an agreement with the German-Austrian middle class in 1860. The divergent interests of these two partners were indicated by the contrasting strategies they advocated for dealing with the divisive effects of the process of modernization on the unity of Austria-Hungary.

Modernization produced a plethora of national conflicts between the two centers of the Dual Monarchy (Germans and Hungarians), between the centers and the peripheries (Germans and Czechs; Hungarians and Croats), and on the periphery itself (between Poles and Ruthenes; Serbs and Croats). The choice between the decentralization or centralization of the empire's politics was the very basis of the conflict between the dynasty and the middle class. The dynasty's main objective was the protection of its political power by maintaining the unity of the empire, be it centralized or decentralized. To the extent that the accommodation of some of the demands of the strongest non-German nationalities was in accord with that objective, the dynasty was willing to compromise. The German-Austrian middle class, on the other hand, was primarily concerned with defending the centralized structure of the empire and its position as the leading social class and national group within it. The fundamental conflict between these two positions showed up as early as 1867, when in the wake of the defeats by Prussia and Italy the dynasty made a quick political deal (the Compromise) with the Hungarians. In the colloquial Viennese language of the time, the Compromise was designed so that "they would keep down their barbarians and we ours." But the primary purpose was to shore up the shaky position of the dynasty. The German-Austrian middle class in particular was strongly opposed to the emperor's willingness to sacrifice its role as the empire's undisputed, leading group. On the related issue of the occupation of Bosnia-Herzegovina, the coalition between dynasty and middle class foundered in 1879. To the dynasty, counting the heads of its subjects, the occupation promised enhancement; to the middle class, counting the heads of Slavs, it meant erosion of power.

But with the advent of the age of mass politics, the relation between dynasty and middle class became increasingly irrelevant. In the 1890s the opposition of the great mass of German-Austrians to the policies of a government favoring the empire's Slavs grew so strong that by 1900 only a bureaucratic government, composed largely of German-Austrians and far removed from the tumultuous Austrian Parliament, seemed to offer political rule for a stalemated and conflict-ridden society.

In the insistence on a centralized empire and in defense of their elite position within it, all important German-Austrian political parties came to adopt, to different degrees, an explicitly German point of view. The decline of the old liberal party between 1873 and the end of the century was directly related to its inability to recognize the importance of the national question.[33] Only a disastrous electoral defeat in 1885 prompted concessions to the increasing tide of German nationalism. The old liberals agreed to abandon their designation as "Austrians" and answer to that of "German-Austrians" even though they continued to argue that the political interests of the German-Austrians and the dynasty were still identical. But whatever concessions the liberal party was willing to make to the growing wave of German nationalism, it was too little, too late. Only the three mass parties which were founded in the 1880s and 1890s provided a satisfactory answer to the political needs of the German-Austrians.

The publication of a political program of the national needs of the German-Austrians, the *Linzer Programm* of 1882, was the concerted effort of the leaders of three political camps (*Lager*) which have existed in Austria ever since: Schönerer and the German Nationalists, Lueger and the Christian Socials, and Adler and the Socialists.[34] The key demands of this program reveal that the German-Austrians were bent on securing their position in the empire. The non-German territories of the Austrian monarchy, the program demanded, were to be reduced in importance by granting a special status to Galicia and the Bukovina, by leaving the administration of Bosnia-Herzegovina to Hungary, and by cutting the existing ties with Hungary. But the program demanded also that the German character of what remained of the Austrian Empire be assured by centralized control. German was to become the only official language, and a close alliance with the German Reich was to ensure that all domestic antiGerman opposition would be crushed. Finally, Austria's expan-

---

33. Paul Molisch, *Geschichte der deutschnationalen Bewegung in Österreich von ihren Anfängen bis zum Zerfall der Monarchie* (Jena: Fischer, 1926), pp. 86-90.
34. Adam Wandruszka, "Österreichs politische Struktur: Die Entwicklung der Parteien und politischen Bewegungen," in Heinrich Benedikt (ed.), *Geschichte der Republik Österreich* (Munich: Oldenbourg, 1954), pp. 289-485. Klaus Berchtold, *Österreichische Parteiprogramme, 1868-1966* (Vienna: Verlag für Geschichte und Politik, 1967), pp. 198-203.

sion in the Balkans was encouraged to the extent that it did not weaken the domestic position of the German-Austrians by incorporating more Slavs into the empire. The *Linzer Programm* indicated the fundamental agreement which the founders of Austria's three mass parties shared on at least one point, the desirability of defending the privileged position of the German-Austrians in the empire.

The most vocal spokesmen for the national concerns of the German-Austrians were the nationalist parties. They had heterogeneous geographical, social, and ideological roots. These parties drew their strongest support from those of the empire's provinces that had German-Austrian minorities (Bohemia, Moravia, Silesia), from the middle class (including students and white-collar workers especially in provincial towns), and from a German ideology expressed by the democratic nationalists in 1848. Because of this heterogeneity there were six parties which competed with one another for electoral support.[35] Only two of these—the Pan-Germans and the German Radicals—favored the dissolution of the Austrian monarchy. The other four espoused different versions of a defensive nationalism which did not require the dissolution of the empire but asked for the political assistance of Germany in the stabilization of the position of the German-Austrians in Austria. The majority of the German nationalist parties were, then, not willing to abandon the empire but simply hoped to defend the German position within it.

Although the second mass party, the Christian Socials, professed to be supranational in its support of the empire, it was a thoroughly German party which enjoyed mass appeal only in the German provinces of Austria. As early as 1882 its members in Parliament stopped caucusing and sitting with Slavs of similar political convictions. Dynastic and clerical loyalties made the Christian Socials strong supporters of the dynasty but only under the condition that it supported the German-Austrians in their political conflict with the Slavs. The Christian Socials were a party supporting the empire as a German state.

35. Andrew G. Whiteside, *Austrian National Socialism before 1918* (The Hague: Nijhoff, 1962). Peter G. Pulzer, *The Rise of Political Anti-Semitism in Germany and Austria* (New York: Wiley, 1964).

To some extent the same could be said of the third mass party in Austrian politics, the Socialists.[36] For a long time the party's supranational class orientation and its practice of international socialism made it one of the strongest pillars of the empire's unity. But in the end the Socialist party, like the Christian Social party thirty years earlier, split in 1911 along ethnic lines chiefly because the German-Austrians continued to dominate the leadership of the party organization. The party's willingness to demand greater cultural autonomy for the empire's different nationalities, expressed in the Brunn Congress of 1899, left untouched the Slavs' insistence on the primacy of economic rather than cultural discrimination as the basis of the nationality conflict. What the German-Austrians really envisaged was a "socialized version of the Liberals' programme—a centralized Austria basically run by its Germans."[37] Despite the party's remarkable record in maintaining institutional unity within an empire undergoing an accelerating rate of fragmentation, the German-Austrian Socialists, in the end, could not escape the actuality that they served and advocated a state ruled by Germans. Alluding to the liberals' and Grillparzer's praise of the Austrian army in 1848, the founder of the Socialist party, Adler himself, said, "Austria lives in us alone if she can live. In our camp stands Austria today."[38]

Even though they pursued different strategies, Austria's three mass parties agreed on preserving the Austrian Empire as a German state. This became evident when on the issue of language policy the radicalization of these parties reached its height in the 1890s. With the exception of the Socialists and the Pan-German nationalists, in 1897 all German-Austrian parties formed a "German front" (*Deutsche Gemeinbürgschaft*). Its program centered on one demand, the explicit recognition of the special

36. Hans Mommsen, *Die Sozialdemokratie und die Nationalitätenfrage im Habsburgischen Vielvölkerstaat: Das Ringen um die Supranationale Integration der Zisleithanischen Arbeiterbewegung (1867-1907)* (Vienna: Europa Verlag, 1963). Herbert Steiner, *Die Arbeiterbewegung Österreichs, 1867-1889: Beiträge zu ihrer Geschichte von der Gründung des Wiener Arbeiterbildungvereines bis zum Einigungsparteitag in Hainfeld* (Vienna: Europa Verlag, 1964).
37. C. A. Macartney, *The Habsburg Empire, 1790-1918* (New York: Macmillan, 1969), p. 684.
38. Quoted in Mommsen, *Sozialdemokratie und Nationalitätenfrage*, p. 338.

status of the German-Austrians in the monarchy. This coalition was backed by a number of self-help organizations. The German School Club, for example, sought to protect the German position in ethnically mixed regions, especially on issues of language legislation, cultural affairs, and education. The Federation of Germans, a nonpartisan organization, counted about a half million members in 1910, 5 percent of the total number of German-Austrians in the Empire.[39] The increasing national concerns of the German-Austrians were reflected also in the growing share of votes cast for the parties of the national camp compared with the total polled by the other two parties. That ratio increased from .09 in 1891, to 0.13 in 1897, to 0.23 in 1901, and to 0.30 in 1911.[40] With 102 delegates, the German National party became the strongest party in the Austrian Parliament in 1911.

The crisis they faced in domestic politics pushed German-Austrians of all political persuasions toward the formulation of policies with which they attempted to defend their position in the empire. To accomplish that objective all of them also believed close relations with the German Reich abroad to be an indispensable political instrument.

As in the conflict pattern of Austro-German relations, Austria's political autonomy remained substantially unimpaired in the hierarchical pattern; but in contrast to its cause in the earlier period, autonomy resulted from a relative decline in extent and an unchanged effectiveness of political coordination. The declining extent of Austro-German political coordination is shown by a number of different indicators. The relative number of Austrian diplomats sent to Germany, for example, declined from 39 percent in 1866, to 20 percent in 1885, to 13 percent in 1912, with a corresponding decrease in the relative number of German diplomats from 31, to 15, to 12 percent. The relative number of diplomatic agreements concluded between Austria and Germany

---

39. Ernst Hoor, *Österreich, 1918-1938: Staat ohne Nation, Republik ohne Republikaner* (Vienna: Österreichischer Bundesverlag, 1966), p. 34.
40. Calculated from figures provided by *Österreichisches statistisches Handbuch* XVI (1897), pp. 332-336; XX (1901), pp. 404-408; XXVI (1907), pp. 466-469; XXX (1911), pp. 408-411.

decreased also, from 60 percent in the years 1851–1868, to 12 percent in 1869–1892, and to 9 percent in 1893–1912.[41] Although the declining trends between 1866 and 1885 are undoubtedly largely due to the unification of Germany, the continued decline until the eve of World War I points to another cause. That cause does not lie in the expansion of the international political system. A standardized measure of diplomatic representation which accounts for the increasing number of state actors also shows a decrease of more than 50 percent between 1866 and 1912. The reason for the decline thus is related to a change in the political relations between Austria and Germany. But despite this change, the relative number of agreements that Austria signed with Germany during the last two decades before World War I was still almost twice as high as with any other country.

Other evidence also suggests that the extent of Austro-German political coordination was not as high as it had been during the middle of the nineteenth century. An effective coordination of military planning, for example, was virtually absent until a few years before World War I, even though the Dual Alliance of 1879 was specifically designed for the purpose of military defense. On the issue of trade the Austrians rejected in the 1870s a German bid for the creation of a customs union. In short, political pressures for extensive coordination of Austrian and German policy remained small throughout the hierarchical pattern.

The effectiveness of political coordination, on the other hand, was relatively high. This was illustrated by the fact that defense installations at the Austro-German border were razed in the 1880s and 1890s, thus indicating that for the first time in the nineteenth century Austria and Germany had become a peace

41. *Hof- und Staats-Handbuch des Kaiserthumes Österreich für das Jahr 1866* (Vienna: Manz, 1866), pp. 130-140. *Hof- und Staats-Handbuch der Österreichisch-Ungarischen Monarchie für das Jahr 1885*, pp. 8-20; *1912*, pp. 277-294. The dates on diplomatic agreements are drawn from Ludwig Bittner, *Chronologisches Verzeichnis der Österreichischen Staatsverträge: Die Staatsverträge des Kaisertums Österreich und der Österreichisch-Ungarischen Monarchie von 1848 bis 1911* (Vienna: Holzhausen, 1914).

community. But it is important to distinguish the relations between the German and Austrian governments from the relations between the German government and the German-Austrians. Diplomatic relations between the two governments were most cordial as long as the German-Austrians held power in Austria, from 1871 to 1879 and from 1900 to 1918. In the intervening years, on the other hand, the convergence of the political objectives of the German-Austrians and the German government resulted in a joint, if limited, opposition to an Austrian government that attempted to meet some of the demands of the empire's Slavs.

On the subject of most importance to both the German-Austrians and the German government—the empire's nationality issue—the effectiveness of political coordination was striking. Effective coordination mattered to the German-Austrians because it seemed to ensure their elite position in the empire, and to the German government because it created a more dependable ally. German-Austrians of all political persuasions sought and welcomed the support of Germany as an indispensable resource in their political battles with the Slavs at home. German nationalists in the Reich took an active interest in the nationality problem of the Austrian Empire and supported the German-Austrians politically, propagandistically, and financially in the most difficult phase of the conflict during the 1890s.[42] The German government, on the other hand, was concerned with Austrian internal stability and perpetuation of an anti-Russian policy on the part of its most important ally, and deemed that stability and policy most assured as long as the German-Austrians were in a position to run the empire. The German government was willing to give informal support to the German-Austrians whenever the official policies of the Austrian government were at variance with the political preferences of the German-Austrians—as was true between 1879 and 1900.

The primacy of domestic politics for the German-Austrians

---

42. Wiskemann, *Czechs and Germans*, pp. 48-49. Bascan B. Hayes, "The German Reich and the 'Austrian Question,' 1871-1914" (unpub. diss., Yale University, 1963), pp. 316-317.

and its convergence with Germany's foreign policy interests can be traced from the very beginning of the hierarchical pattern to its very end. As early as 1871 the German government intervened in favor of the German-Austrians in Austrian domestic politics by letting the two top officials in charge of foreign policy—Beust and Andrassy—know how critically Berlin viewed the nationality policy of the new Austrian government which the emperor had appointed—and which he decided to dismiss soon thereafter.[43] At least in part, the Dual Alliance of 1879 was also designed to stabilize Austria's internal balance of power. Concluded in the year in which the dynasty transferred political power from the German-Austrian middle class to a coalition of conservative and clerical forces more favorably disposed toward the political demands of the Slavs, the Dual Alliance prevented a further decline in the political status of the German-Austrians.[44]

Throughout the 1880s the German Reich unofficially intervened with increasing frequency in support of the German-Austrians. But only the language conflict of the 1890s, which seriously threatened the position of the German-Austrians, prompted Germany's consistent and determined support of the German-Austrians.[45] Despite Germany's publicly proclaimed neutrality, the extent of its support is illustrated by a report which the German Chancellor Bülow sent to the German ambassador in Vienna: "The Emperor feels the time is favorable for the stimulation and encouragement of this process [of German national assertion in the Austrian monarchy]."[46] Berlin approved, therefore, the establishment of a consulate in Prague which was deemed necessary for the protection of German-Austrian interests in Bohemia. The determined opposition of the German-Austrians, backed by as potent an ally as the German government, left the Austrian emperor little room for maneuver. By 1900 he was compelled to appoint a cabinet favored by the German-Austrians and the German government alike, a central-

---

43. Verosta, *Theorie und Realität von Bündnissen*, p. 71.
44. Robert A. Kann, *Das Nationalitätenproblem der Habsburgermonarchie*, 2nd ed. (Graz: Böhlaus, 1964), I, 96-97.
45. Verosta, *Theorie und Realität von Bündnissen*, pp. 186-189.
46. Quoted in Hayes, "The German Reich," p. 340.

ized, autocratic government run by German bureaucrats and reminiscent of the political regime of the 1850s. Despite its many inadequacies, a government of that political composition remained in office until the very end of the monarchy.

World War I highlighted once more the divergent interests of the Austrian government and the German-Austrians in their relations with the government of imperial Germany. Conflict between the two governments was as consistent as it was muted. The Italian, Rumanian, and Polish questions and the issue of the economic union between the two countries provided a series of strains in mutual relations. The congruence of the political objectives of the German-Austrians and the German government, on the other hand, was never more obvious than between 1914 and 1918. The political objectives of the German-Austrians were expressed clearly by a wide-ranging coalition of parties. This coalition, the German National Union, officially included neither the Christian Social nor the Socialist parties but was probably backed by many of their supporters. The union demanded a new constitution firmly establishing Austria as a German state (by making German the only official language and by separating Galicia from the rest of the empire), tied closely to the German Reich. Thus, a significant number of German-Austrians regarded the war as an opportunity for securing their fragile position in central Europe. The plans the German government formulated in 1915 were entirely compatible with the proposals of the German National Union.[47] The German government, too, favored a reorganization of the Austrian Empire to stabilize the political position of the German-Austrians.

The strong political preference of all German-Austrians for close political relations with Germany demonstrates the great importance of the empire's domestic politics for the adoption of a strategy of partial political integration abroad. Although that

47. Joseph Redlich, *Austrian War Government* (New Haven: Yale University Press, 1929), p. 138. Fritz Fischer, *Griff nach der Weltmacht: Die Kriegszielpolitik des kaiserlichen Deutschlands, 1914-1918* (Dusseldorf: Droste, 1962), pp. 240-261. Henry C. Meyer, *Mitteleuropa: In German Thought and Action, 1815-1945* (The Hague: Nijhoff, 1955), p. 191.

strategy made Austria and Germany a peace community, it can be appreciated fully only if it is viewed as complementary to the strategy of conflict adopted against the Slavs at home and abroad. Only if the southern Slavs could be defeated in the Balkans, it was thought, could the Yugoslav irredenta be contained inside Austria.

Austria's occupation of Bosnia-Herzegovina in 1878–1879 led to the bitter resistance of the German-Austrian middle class, which prompted the Austrian emperor to replace the German-Austrian government with another more favorable to his own needs and the political demands of the Slavs. The southern Slavs, especially the Serbs, correctly interpreted Austria's new policy of expansion as an attempt to prevent the political unification of all southern Slavs. Over the next generation the record of the Austrian administration in Bosnia-Herzegovina did little to alleviate Yugoslav fear and hatred. Except for the construction of additional military installations, no significant investment occurred in the two provinces. The land-tenure and tax systems which had sparked the peasant revolt in 1875 remained unchanged. The efficiency in the system of tax collection was increased greatly; in all but two years between 1881 and 1913 Austria's effective income from the provinces exceeded its expenses. Corruption was widespread and barely concealed. Illiteracy among the peasants, after a generation of Austrian rule, remained constant at 88 percent.[48] These miserable conditions bred violence. The assassination of Archduke Ferdinand in Sarajevo in 1914 was not a random event planned by a handful of terrorists. Instead, it was the predictable result of an Austrian policy that had stretched over several decades. It was, in fact, the seventh attempt in four years to assassinate high Austrian

---

48. Peter F. Sugar, *Industrialization of Bosnia-Hercegovina, 1879-1918* (Seattle: University of Washington Press, 1963), pp. 32-36, 45, 48, 68, 94-95, Appendixes IV, VI. Adalbert Rom, "Der Bildungsgrad der Bevölkerung Österreichs und seine Entwicklung seit 1880, mit besonderer Berücksichtigung der Sudeten- und Karpathenländer," *Statistische Montasschrift*, N.F., XIX (1914), p. 591. Kurt Wesley, "Die wirtschaftliche Entwicklung von Bosnien-Herzegowina," in Brusatti, *Habsburgermonarchie, 1848-1918 (I)*, pp. 528-566.

officials who had come to visit the province.[49] The road to World War I was conspicuously well marked.

The domestic crisis the German-Austrians faced in the empire, once political power was returned to them in 1900, made them back an increasingly aggressive Austrian foreign policy in the Balkans.[50] Economic and political conflict with Serbia escalated, for the irredentist movement of the southern Slavs at home was thought to be manageable only if Serbia were crushed abroad. In 1909 the defensive character of the Dual Alliance of 1879 was sacrificed, with Germany backing unreservedly Austria's offensive plans in the Balkans. As had been true in the 1850s and 1860s Austria now adopted the strategy of a ruined gambler. With rapidly diminishing economic and political resources she wagered all in that last and most decisive bet. Sometime before 1914, war had become the most probable outcome of Austria's domestic troubles and the most valued course of action among the influential policymakers in Vienna. The monarchy's last foreign minister, Count Czernin, wrote, "We were compelled to die; we could only choose the manner of death, and we have chosen the most terrible one."[51]

Between 1871 and 1918 the German-Austrians faced one overriding problem, the defense of their political position within the empire. They responded in an unambiguous fashion, by increased reliance on the protection of their political interests by the German Reich. Partial political integration, adopted as a crisis strategy in order to contain the political pressure of the Slavs at home, was, however, no longer sufficient. The magnitude of the threat required an aggressive policy in the Balkans in

---

49. Jaszi, *Dissolution of the Habsburg Monarchy*, p. 414.
50. M. Constantinescu et al., "Zur nationalen Frage in Österreich-Ungarn (1900-1918)," in Peter Hanak and Zoltan Szasz (eds.), *Die nationale Frage in der Österreichisch-Ungarischen Monarchie, 1900-1918* (Budapest: Akademiai Kiado, 1966), pp. 47, 87. Jaszi, *Dissolution of the Habsburg Monarchy*, pp. 208-212, 416-417.
51. Quoted in Kurt Steiner, *Politics in Austria* (Boston: Little Brown, 1972), p. viii. See also K. B. Winogradow and J. A. Pissarew, "Die internationale Lage der Österreichisch-Ungarischen Monarchie in den Jahren 1900 bis 1918," in *Österreich-Ungarn in der Weltpolitik 1900 bis 1918* (Berlin: Akademie Verlag, 1965), pp. 32-33.

order also to shatter the Slavs' foreign political power base. The result of both policies pointed to World War I.

Political autonomy can be explained by nonpolitical and political variables. In contrast to the first two patterns, the hierarchical pattern witnessed the advent of mass politics. Explanations of autonomy focusing on preferences in mass behavior and attitudes gain, therefore, in plausibility. For the third pattern, behavioral and attitudinal indicators of community and society, of standardization and differentiation, pointed to multiple counterpressures and the flattening of all trend lines around 1900, which left the balance between them largely unaffected. This set of variables, thus, points to the persistence of political autonomy.

Economic rewards had similar results. The privileged position the German-Austrians enjoyed in the empire assured them of sizable, if politically contested, material benefits. These benefits were sufficiently large to deter all but the radical fringe of the Pan-German nationalists from advocating the dissolution of the Austrian monarchy and the incorporation of the German-Austrians into the German Reich. When the Austrian monarchy finally fragmented in 1918, the German-Austrians were the last to abandon it.

In the last third of the nineteenth century the German-Austrians faced two political crises, with the dynasty on the one hand and with the non-German nationalities on the other. These crises led to identical responses from the three mass parties; each sought political formulas that would preserve the German character of the Austrian Empire. On this crucial issue the political interests of the German-Austrians and the German Reich converged, but for different reasons. The German-Austrians looked to the powerful Reich as a highly valued ally to strengthen their position in domestic politics. Financial, propagandistic, and political support were sought—and obtained—in the 1890s in particular, when the nationality conflict of the empire reached its peak. The German government, on the other hand, was primarily interested in keeping Austria as its reliable ally. And that reliability was greatly enhanced as long as the German-Austrians dominated the empire's politics.

The hierarchical pattern, thus, witnessed the interpenetration of domestic and foreign policies characteristic of relations among disjoined partners. On the one hand, foreign policy became domestic: the German government sought to influence the course of events inside Austria. On the other hand, domestic politics became foreign: the German-Austrians adopted political integration as a crisis strategy to defend their position in Austrian politics. But the integration strategy of the German-Austrians remained partial. Autonomy, the trademark of disjoined partnership, was preserved.

VI

VOLUNTARISTIC PATTERN
(1918-1938)

AN ANALYSIS of the voluntaristic pattern must be cognizant of the dissimilarity between the small, poor, ethnically homogeneous First Republic of the interwar period and the large, prosperous, and ethnically divided Austrian Empire of the nineteenth century. But the same mode of analysis of political autonomy can be applied to the new Austria no less than to the old. The main feature of the fourth pattern was the interlocking of mutually reinforcing integration processes. For the first time since 1815 copressures rather than counterpressures created the conditions for an extensive and effective coordination of policies and a considerable erosion of Austria's political autonomy.

Austria and Germany stopped short of establishing a full-fledged political community, however, for two different reasons. During the interwar period the structure of the European state system simply did not permit it; French opposition to plans for Austria's unification with Germany never abated. More important for the purpose of this analysis, though, is a second factor. For the Christian Socials, who had managed to seize effective power in the First Republic from the early 1920s on, the political rewards pointed toward an independent Austria ruled by Christian Socials, not an Austria integrated with Germany and governed by a coalition in which, at best, they were to play a minor part. Although the integration of the Austrian and German mass publics, the structure of economic rewards, and the political strategies of the political opposition in Austria all pointed to integration, the charms of political autonomy were still not lost on the Austrian government.

COMMUNITY AND SOCIETY: COPRESSURES

In an age of mass politics, mass behavior and attitudes provide the context in which political actors pursue their conflicting strategies of autonomy and integration. The breakup of the Dual Monarchy greatly transformed the behavioral and attitudinal basis of Austro-German relations. Transactions and communications which had been domestic in the nineteenth century became foreign after 1918. Evaluations and identifications were affected by the transformation of Austrian politics no less than by changes in the European state system. The data demonstrate that these behavioral and attitudinal changes in the Austrian public moved along parallel lines and created copressures toward political integration characteristic of the voluntaristic pattern.

Behavioral Integration In contrast to the third pattern, Germany's capital shortage prohibited the export of large amounts of capital to Austria. Austria, therefore, became dependent on the international financial community. In the Austrian banking sector German capital played only a minor role. When Austria's largest bank, the *Creditanstalt,* closed its doors in 1931, only 7 percent of its total foreign debt was German, about one-tenth of the American and British sum combined. By 1937 the total of Austrian bank shares in German hands had hardly changed.[1]

---

1. Gottlieb Ladner, *Seipel als Überwinder der Staatskrise von Sommer 1922: Zur Geschichte der Entstehung der Genfer Protokolle vom 4. Oktober 1922* (Vienna: Stiasny, 1964), p. 94. Otto Bauer, *Die Österreichische Revolution* (Vienna: Volksbuchhandlung, 1923), pp. 144-145. M. Margaret Ball, *Post-War German-Austrian Relations: The Anschluss Movement 1918-1936* (Stanford: Stanford University Press, 1937), p. 142. Kurt W. Rothschild, *Austria's Economic Development between the Two Wars* (London: Mueller, 1947), p. 92, fn. 9.

Even though German capital played a somewhat larger role in some sectors of Austrian industry, its involvement in Austria remained quite minor, especially in comparison with the last decades of the nineteenth century.[2]

The same was true of Austro-German trade. Trade figures for the years 1924 and 1936 show that Austro-German imports and exports amounted to little more than approximately 15 percent of Austria's foreign trade total.[3] Even in 1930, at the height of the *Anschluss* movement and the year of the abortive Curtius-Schober agreement to establish an Austro-German customs union, Austria's trade with the five successor states of the Austrian Empire was about twice as important as her trade with Germany.

A third indicator also points to a decline of Austro-German transactions. Despite Austria's high unemployment rate, the migration of Austrian labor to Germany was small and diminished over time. In 1925 only 13 percent of the foreigners counted in Germany were Austrians as compared to 11 percent in 1933. The relative number of Germans in Austria hardly differed.[4] These data suggest that the flow of social transactions between Austria and Germany declined during the fourth pattern. Austro-German interdependence along this social dimension weakened.

Transactions lead to differentiation, communications to standardization. Table 11 illustrates that a first indicator of communications, attention, seems to have remained constant throughout the fourth pattern. The stabilization of Austrian attention toward Germany during the interwar years broke a long-term

2. The political implications of the role of German capital in Austria are analyzed in Rothschild, *Austria's Economic Development*, pp. 80-85, and in Oskar Grünwald and Ferdinand Lacina, *Auslandskapital in der Österreichischen Wirtschaft* (Vienna: Europa Verlag, 1971), pp. 40-41.
3. Statistisches Zentralamt (ed.), "Der Aussenhandel Österreichs in der Zeit zwischen den beiden Weltkriegen," *Beiträge zur Österreichischen Statistik*, I (1946), pp. 31-34.
4. Bundesamt für Statistik (ed.), "Die Ergebnisse der Österreichischen Volkszählung vom 22. März 1934. Bundesstaat. Tabellenteil." *Statistik des Bundesstaates Österreich*, II, 59. *Statistik des Deutschen Reiches*, vols. 401 (2), p. 629; 451 (4), p. 7.

TABLE 11. Relative Distribution of Austrian Attention: Average Foreign News Coverage in Two Austrian Papers, 1900-1938 (in percentages)[a]

	1900-1912	1915-1918	1921-1930	1933-1938
Germany	20	41	27	25
Northern Europe[b]	10	17	10	9
Western Europe[c]	22	15	17	15
Eastern Europe[d]	6	10	5	5
Southern Europe[e]	13	7	5	12
Southeast Europe[f]	14	3		
Successor states[g]			21	21
Rest of world	16	7	15	13

Sources: *Wiener Zeitung; Neue Freie Presse.*
[a]The method of calculation is explained in Chapter III, fn. 28. Because of rounding off, percentages do not always add to 100.
[b]Scandinavia and Britain
[c]France, Benelux, and Switzerland
[d]Soviet Union and Poland
[e]Portugal, Spain, Italy, and Greece
[f]European parts of the Ottoman Empire
[g]Czechoslovakia, Hungary, Roumania, Yugoslavia, Bulgaria, and Albania

decline noticeable throughout the second half of the nineteenth century. In contrast to transaction flows, throughout the fourth pattern Germany loomed larger in Austrian attention than all the successor states to the Dual Monarchy combined.

A consideration of the political conditions in Austria during the 1930s reconfirms this conclusion. In their conflict with the German Nazi regime, the authoritarian Dollfuss and Schuschnigg governments denied civil liberties and freedom of the press. The introduction of government censorship after 1932 makes it, therefore, inadvisable to interpret the figures for the years 1933–1938 at their face value.[5] The suppression of German news was

5. Wilhelm Döhne, "Presse- und Nachrichtenpolitik in Österreich von der Ersten zur Zweiten Republik, 1918-1946" (unpub. diss., University of

more evident in the government paper, the *Wiener Zeitung*, than in the *Neue Freie Presse*. For the years 1933–1938 the two papers show divergent trends. While the relative coverage of German news in the *Wiener Zeitung* decreased sharply from 29 to 22 percent, the corresponding figure for the less strictly regulated *Neue Freie Presse* rose from 24 to 28 percent. It is, then, highly probable that the actual level of attention to Germany was higher than the figures in Table 11 suggest for the years 1933–1938, and that Austria's attention to German affairs was rising over the entire interwar period. As had been true of the aristocratic pattern of Austro-German relations, censorship and the suppression of German news during the 1930s was an indication of high salience.

Increases in the flow of Austro-German communications are reflected also in a number of other indicators. Between 1924 and 1936 the German share in Austria's foreign trade in printed materials rose from 85 to 90 percent of imports and from 29 to 45 percent of exports. In 1934 Austria imported 45 percent of its movies from Germany.[6]

Student exchange between Austria and Germany is another indicator of community. Compared with the third pattern, the increases occurring during the fourth were particularly striking. In 1912 only 210 German students were enrolled in Austria's universities; by 1930 the figure had risen more than tenfold to about 2,500. The rise in relative numbers was as dramatic. German students accounted for 13 percent of the foreign total in 1913, 35 percent in 1926, 50 percent in 1930, 46 percent in 1933, and 20 percent in 1936.[7] The sharp drop in the absolute

---

Vienna, 1947). Walter Wisshaupt, "Das Wiener Pressewesen von Dollfuss bis zum Zusammenbruch (1933-1945)" (unpub. diss., University of Vienna, 1950).

6. *Statistik des auswärtigen Handels Österreichs im Jahre 1924*, pp. 10-12. *Monatshefte der Statistik des Aussenhandels Österreichs* (December 1936), pp. 167-168. Bundesministerium für Handel und Verkehr (ed.), *Aufklärungsdienst*, 35 (January 1, 1936), p. 4. Austrian film exports were highly dependent on the German market as well. See Rothschild, *Austria's Economic Development*, p. 84.

7. *Österreichische Statistik*, N.F., XI (3), pp. 3-8. *Statistisches Handbuch für die Republik Österreich*, IX (1928), p. 170; XII (1931), p. 182; XVI (1935), p. 208; XVII (1937), pp. 179-180.

and relative numbers of German students in Austria after 1933 was the result of a deliberate policy of the German Nazi government. Despite the economic depression, the relative number of German students in Austria hardly decreased before 1933. Thus, had it not been for that policy, there is little reason to believe that this communications indicator would have declined after 1933.

Changes in a fourth indicator of communications, the sum of personal mail, telegrams, and telephone calls, point to the economic depression rather than political repression as an effective barrier to a further expansion of Austro-German communications in the 1930s. In the 1920s the growth of Austro-German communications had been rapid especially in the technologically more advanced channels. Between 1924 and 1930, for example, the relative share of Germany in Austria's total foreign telephone communications increased from 25 to 30 percent.[8] It was only with the Great Depression that Austro-German communications experienced a period of decline. Between 1924 and 1936 Germany's share in the total number of Austrian messages received declined from 25 to 22 percent and in the total number of Austrian messages sent from 38 to 28 percent.[9] The fact that virtually the entire decline occurred in the 1930s points to the decisive impact of the Depression in a country which was impoverished in comparison to the prewar era.

Political autonomy is affected by the balance between community and society, between standardization and differentiation. Since the massive influence of economic and political factors disrupted the normal flow of transactions and communications between Austria and Germany, the figures do not suggest an unambiguous conclusion for the years 1930–1938. But for the greater part of the voluntaristic pattern of Austro-German relations, the 1920s, the data point to relative increases in standardization and, thus toward a probable erosion of political autonomy.

---

8. Österreichisches Bundesministerium für Handel und Verkehr, *Geschäftsbericht 1924* and *1930*.
9. Bundesministerium für Handel und Verkehr, *Geschäftsbericht 1924* and *1936*. Union Postale Universelle, Bureau Internationale, *Relevé des Tableaux Statistiques du Service Postal International (Expédition)*, 1925 and 1934.

Attitudinal Integration Corresponding processes can be traced in the realm of attitudes. Social integration is measured by changes in evaluations, cultural integration by changes in identifications. Table 12 summarizes the most important features of a content analysis of Austria's changing evaluation of Germany as indicated by government speeches and New Years' Eve editorials.

Throughout the interwar period, positive evaluations of Germany by the Austrian government declined (column two). This decline was the result of a U-shaped trend in positive and an upward trend in negative evaluations (column three). Although not quite as clearly, a downward trend over the entire period is observable also in the newspaper editorials (columns five and six). The voluntaristic pattern was, thus, marked by a consistent decline in Austria's positive evaluation of Germany.

Mutual identification provides the attitudinal basis of community. As had been true of the third pattern, Austrians continued to be exposed in the fourth to different types of counterpressures: between an Austrian and a German mode of self-identification; between symbols of common identity referring to land and people; and between a sentimental and an instrumental manner of attachment to the collective group.

Figure 2 depicts the most important changes. As long as the French did not veto the unification of Austria with Germany during the immediate postwar period, government speeches relied largely on German symbols of community. Direct Austrian symbols, for example, were outnumbered by a ratio of four to one. Between 1920 and 1932, however, the political stipulations of the Allies and the political preferences of the Christian Social chancellors of the First Republic reinforced one another in leading to virtual suppression of all German symbols. But direct self-references as Austrian remained relatively infrequent until after 1933, when Austria's new authoritarian regime sought to instil in the Austrian people some measure of patriotism in an effort to counter the growing ideological appeal of the Nazis. But that effort was futile. The most consistent trend from 1920 on was the decline in self-references as Austrian people. Independent Austrian political institutions, imposed from abroad, were

TABLE 12. Evaluation of Germany in Government Speeches and Newspaper Editorials in Austria, 1918-1938[a]

	(1) No. of Government Speeches	(2) Government Evaltns.: Positive−Negative/Positive+Negative	(3) Government Evaluations (in percent)			(4) No. of Press Editorials	(5) Press Evaltns.: Positive−Negative/Positive+Negative	(6) Press Evaluations (in percent)		
			Pos.	Neu.	Neg.			Pos.	Neu.	Neg.
1918[b]	7	1.00	86	43	—	14	0.54	71	29	21
1920-27	14	0.78	57	14	7	8	0.10	73	38	63
1928-32[c]	8	0.71	75	50	13	11	0.27	64	46	36
1933-38[d]	4	0.50	75	50	25	8	0.33	50	38	25

[a]The method of calculation is explained in Chapter V, fn. 11.
[b]1919-1922 for columns (5) and (6)
[c]1928-1933 for columns (5) and (6)
[d]1934-1938 for columns (5) and (6)

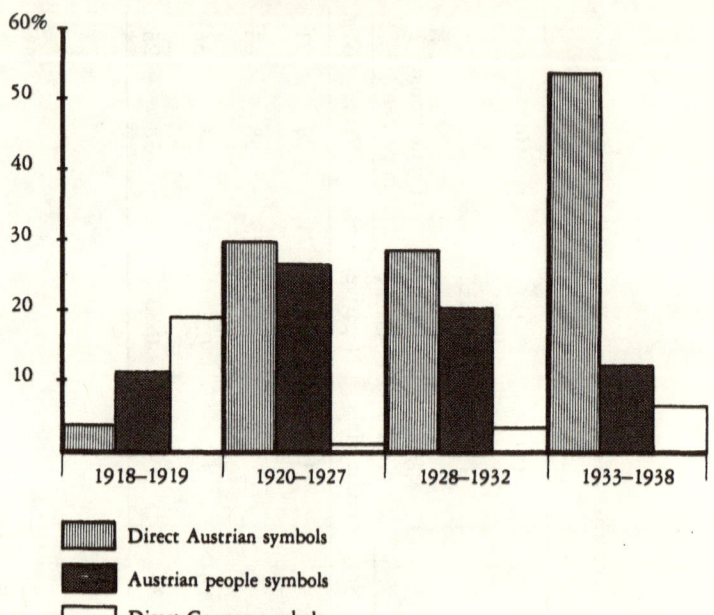

FIGURE 2. SYMBOLS OF COMMON IDENTITY IN AUSTRIAN GOVERNMENT SPEECHES, 1919–1938

gradually accepted. But the notion of Austrians forming a community weakened.

Since the Austrian government was watched closely by distrustful eyes from abroad, symbol usage in newspaper editorials reflects more accurately Austria's public opinion. In contrast to their government, the Austrian people were more willing to accept the political institutions of an independent Austria during the early years of the First Republic. Austrian symbols of the land were four times as frequent as German symbols. But this was not true of self-references as an Austrian people. Here the data point to the years 1923–1927 as a crucial period during which an Austrian consciousness briefly appeared. The Geneva Protocol of 1922 and its reaffirmation of the prohibition of the Anschluss for the foreseeable future diminished sharply the relative number of self-references as a German people. But even before the economic depression aggravated further Austria's serious economic problems, the psychological climate had shifted again toward a German pattern of self-reference. Between 1928 and 1933 German symbols outranked Austrian symbols along this particular dimension by a ratio of three to two. Only government censorship imposed after 1932 stopped further expression of the growth in these sentiments. These trends are summarized in Figure 3.

Between the two world wars, the experiment of creating an independent Austria endowed with its own psychological magnetism failed. This conclusion is opposed to the commonly held view that the experiment never took place. Many Austrian historians have deplored the absence of an Austrian consciousness during the First Republic as one of the important causes of the First Republic's drift toward civil war first and Anschluss later.[10] My data offer an important qualification to this view. At least for a few brief years during the mid-1920s, there was a chance of making the First Republic a viable and going concern in the eyes

---

10. Jörg Grosseweischeda, "Die parteitheoretischen Zeitschriften Österreichs als Mittler zur Bildung eines Österreichischen Staatsbewusstseins" (unpub. diss., University of Vienna, 1968), p. 205. Anton Pelinka and Manfried Welan, *Demokratie und Verfassung in Österreich* (Vienna: Europa Verlag, 1971), p. 32.

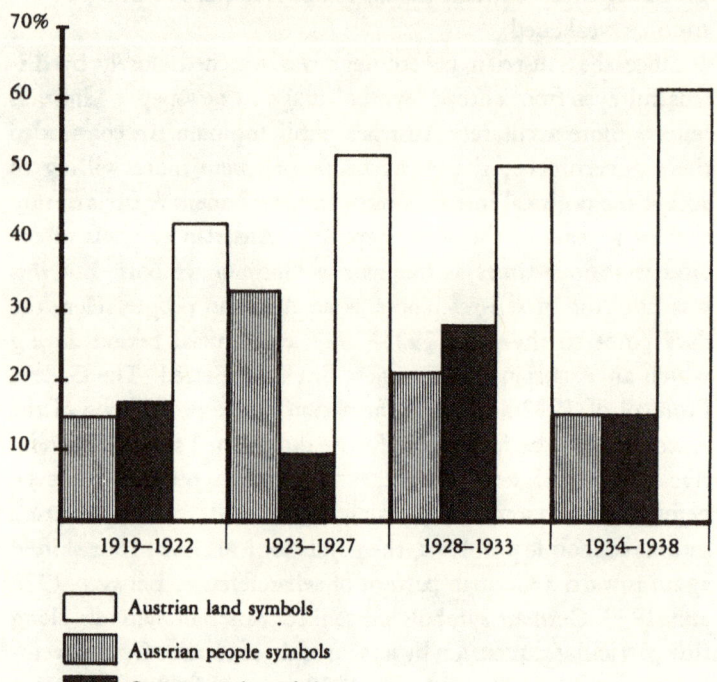

FIGURE 3. SYMBOLS OF COMMON IDENTITY IN AUSTRIAN NEWSPAPER EDITORIALS, 1919–1938

of its citizens.[11] Economic depression and the Anschluss movement prompted the Austrians to take up again a pattern of self-identification as a German people which they had adhered to in the immediate aftermath of the breakup of the empire. The data suggest, then, that with the exception of a few years during the mid-1920s the attitudinal integration of Austria and Germany along the cultural dimension increased in the voluntaristic pattern.

Behavior and Attitudes: Copressures Community and society affect the probability of political autonomy. The analysis of the voluntaristic pattern of Austro-German relations has led to two mutually consistent conclusions. In the 1920s Austro-German transactions stagnated in comparison to increases in communications; mass behavior pointed toward relative gains in Austro-German integration. The same was true of attitudes, as positive evaluations of Germany decreased with a simultaneous rise in mutual identification. Multiple interlocking copressures toward the integration of Austrian and German mass publics point to the erosion of political autonomy.

ECONOMIC REWARDS:
POVERTY AND POLITICAL INTEGRATION

The probability of political autonomy is affected not only by mass behavior and attitudes but by the structure of economic rewards as well. Voluntary sacrifices of political autonomy are most probable where economic rewards associated with strategies of political integration outweigh the rewards of continued political independence. Throughout the voluntaristic pattern the First Republic was beset by serious economic scarcities. Far-reaching attempts to achieve an extensive and effective coordination of Austrian and German policies provided a political strategy highly valued by the Austrian people and elites simply because such attempts constituted a promise of escaping the

---

11. See also Stanley Suval, *The Anschluss Question in the Weimar Era: A Study of Nationalism in Germany and Austria, 1918-1932* (Baltimore: Johns Hopkins University Press, 1974), pp. 190-202.

economic harshness of life in the First Republic and achieving full political unification with Germany at some future date.

With the crumbling of the Dual Monarchy the economic rewards of the empire vanished. After 1918 opportunities for economic gain and upward social mobility were far inferior to what the Austrians had known before. The First Republic amounted to little more than 10 percent of the Dual Monarchy in terms of geographical size and total population, and it faced serious territorial disputes, military conflicts, and threats of invasions from Yugoslavia, Hungary, Italy, and Bavaria. A critical shortage of food supplies, especially in Vienna, and the standstill of entire branches of the Austrian economy for lack of raw materials had disastrous consequences for the living conditions of the Austrian people no less than for their projection of the economic viability of the First Republic. Although the most immediate economic needs were met with the aid of emergency credits and supplies provided by the Allies, the structural readjustment of the Austrian economy to radical differences in the size of the domestic market and the unfavorable conditions for trade with the protectionist successor states to the Dual Monarchy beset the First Republic with continuous and enormous economic difficulties.[12]

Austria's endowment of natural resources was highly unbalanced and insufficient. Entire branches of the empire's industry, such as glass and textiles, were lost to other successor states. Austria had no coal deposits and relied entirely on foreign imports. Its agricultural production was totally inadequate to feed the population of the First Republic. Large deficits in its trade balance throughout the interwar period were the result. Budget deficits were chronic for the better part of the 1920s. A runaway inflation fueled a deceptive economic boom during the early 1920s but prevented the required structural changes in Austria's economy and, with them, an increase in the general standard of living. Unemployment was high and much of it was

---

12. The economic situation of the First Republic is discussed in Rothschild, *Austria's Economic Development*, and Gustav Otruba, *Österreichs Wirtschaft im 20. Jahrhundert* (Vienna: Österreichischer Bundesverlag, 1968).

structural, concentrated among blue-collar workers and those segments of the Austrian middle class that had benefited from the administration of the empire's far-flung affairs before 1914.

These structural problems largely negated the economic rewards that the First Republic could offer. It was, therefore, logical that the citizenry should seize on demands for unification with Germany, the Anschluss, as the most desirable policy. There is, however, considerable disagreement on how large a number of Austrians actually backed the Anschluss movement during the 1920s. The Socialist Otto Bauer, himself an avid proponent of the Anschluss policy and the first foreign minister of the Republic, estimated that perhaps less than one-half of the entire Austrian population supported his policy in 1919–1920; on the other hand, another estimate puts the corresponding figure at 95 percent for the year 1925.[13] It appears unlikely that mass sentiment would have shifted by so much in such a brief span of time. But these divergent estimates confirm one of the results of our analysis of changes in Austrian self-identification. Just as competing modes of self-perceptions as Austrian or German changed twice during the interwar years, so probably did the strength of the Anschluss movement.[14]

Judging by the behavior of the Austrians themselves, we can be reasonably certain that Anschluss sentiment was fairly widespread throughout the 1920s. Referenda held in the immediate postwar period revealed both in Styria and Salzburg an overwhelming desire to join Weimar Germany. The fiftieth anniversary of the German Empire was celebrated no less enthusiastically in Austria than in Germany. At the height of the Ruhr and the financial crises in Germany, the Austrians organized a Support-for-Germany movement which collected money for starving children in Germany and had 2,000 of them transported to Austria

---

13. Bauer, *Österreichische Revolution*, p. 150. Ernst Baumgärtner, "Die Österreichische Presse in ihrer Stellungnahme zur Anschlussfrage, 1918-1938" (unpub. diss., University of Vienna, 1950), p. 68.
14. See also Jan Krulis-Randa, *Das Deutsch-Österreichische Zoll-Unionsprojekt von 1931: Die Bemühungen um eine wirtschaftliche Annäherung zwischen Deutschland und Österreich* (Zurich: Europa Verlag, 1955), pp. 69-73. Suval, *The Anschluss Question*, pp. 42-54, 169-189.

in order to provide more adequate shelter and food.[15] During the seventy-fifth anniversary of the Frankfurt Assembly of 1848 the Austrian delegation was prominent in all the ceremonies. In 1925, 100,000 Viennese spontaneously greeted a delegation of 400 members of a nationalist organization from Germany; the emotional demonstration ended with the singing of the German national anthem. The eightieth birthday of the German president, von Hindenburg, was celebrated in Vienna by 75,000 who turned the occasion into a parade for Anschluss. The greatest Anschluss demonstration of all occurred during the Schubert Festival in 1928. Over a four-day period, political demands for Anschluss appeared to be as important as music. The festival was capped by a march of 200,000 Austrians which took them through the city of Vienna for an entire day. Judging by this evidence, then, the sentiment in favor of Anschluss was strong, particularly during the second half of the 1920s.[16]

Public sentiment was channeled through institutions dedicated to the task of furthering the cause of Anschluss. At the elite level there was the German Study Group, founded in 1920, and enlarged to the German-Austrian Study Group after an allied organization had been formed in Munich in 1925. Staffed and supported primarily by members of the university community (who were particularly impoverished and would have benefited greatly from an enlargement of the academic market), it worked quietly for the assimilation of bureaucratic practices in Austria and Germany.[17] The Delegation for Austro-German Economic Unification was founded in the fall of 1927. Somewhat broader

15. Karl R. Stadler, *The Birth of the Austrian Republic, 1918-1921* (Leyden: Sijthoff, 1966), pp. 83-163. Kurt Becsi, "Die auswärtige Pressepolitik Österreichs von Saint Germain bis Berchtesgarden" (unpub. diss., University of Vienna, 1948), III, 490.
16. Ball, *Post-War German-Austrian Relations*, pp. 51-73, 83-92. Franz Gartner, "Der Plan einer Deutsch-Österreichischen Zollunion und die Wiener Presse" (unpub. diss., University of Vienna, 1949), pp. 85, 132-133. Nikolaus von Preradovich, *Die Wilhelmstrasse und der Anschluss Österreichs, 1918-1933* (Bern: Lang, 1971), pp. 195-232.
17. Ball, *Post-War German-Austrian Relations*, pp. 40, 56. Ernst Hoor, *Österreich, 1918-1938: Staat ohne Nation, Republik ohne Republikaner* (Vienna: Österreichischer Bundesverlag, 1966), p. 71.

in membership, it worked without the support of an allied organization in the Weimar Republic, and in the end unsuccessfully, for the creation of an Austro-German customs union.[18] The most important mass organization was the Austro-German People's League. Established in 1925, it soon counted a membership of over a million and at its peak could rely on the support of 1.8 million members, almost one-third of the total Austrian population and more than three times as many as the Pan-German League of Germans before 1918.[19]

Two conclusions can be drawn from the timing of the establishment and the location of these institutional underpinnings of the Anschluss movement. First, Austrian interest at all times appears to have exceeded German commitment to the goal of Anschluss. The allied organization of the German-Austrian Study Group was founded only in 1925, five years after the Austrian organization had been created. The Delegation for Austro-German Economic Unification had no counterpart at all in the Weimar Republic. Lastly, the Austro-German People's League was founded and supported in Germany primarily by Austrians living abroad.[20] Also noteworthy is the relative weakness of those organized economic pressure groups in Austria that worked actively for the goal of Anschluss. The delegation was the only significant exception; founded only in the late 1920s, it was not particularly successful in its work. Cultural-nationalist organizations appear to have been considerably stronger and more popular as is attested by the long list of cultural associations that merged with or created German counterparts.[21] This finding should not come as a surprise. It

18. Karl Drexel, "Der Österreichisch-Deutsche Wirtschaftszusammenschluss," in Friedrich F. G. Kleinwächter and Heinz Paller (eds.), *Die Anschlussfrage in ihrer kulturellen, politischen, und wirtschaftlichen Bedeutung* (Vienna: Braumüller, 1930), pp. 575-579, 581.
19. Baumgärtner, "Die Österreichische Presse," p. 88. Preradovich, *Wilhelmstrasse und Anschluss*, pp. 155-194.
20. Hermann Neubacher, "Die Organisationen für den Österreichisch-Deutschen Zusammenschluss," in Kleinwächter and Paller *Die Anschlussfrage*, pp. 605-617.
21. Adolf Günther, "Die Anschlussfrage als soziales und soziologisches Problem," in Kleinwächter and Paller, *Die Anschlussfrage*, pp. 414-415.

merely demonstrates that the dominance of cultural over social and economic factors occurred during the interwar years not merely on the attitudinal and behavioral levels but on the institutional level as well.

The strength of the Anschluss movement was reflected in the very extensive and effective coordination of Austrian and German policy. Short of the unification of the political institutions of the two countries, the assimilation of Austrian to German political practices went far beyond anything witnessed in the previous patterns. But a change in the political objectives of the German Nazi government after 1933 led to a rapid decline in the effectiveness of policy coordination. On November 12, 1918, the Provisional Assembly of German-Austria adopted a resolution which stated that "German-Austria is a constituent part of the German Republic. Special laws shall regulate the participation of German-Austria in the law-making and administration of the German Republic, as well as the extension of the sphere of validity of the laws and institutions of the German Republic to German-Austria."[22] If given the chance in 1918–1919, the Austrian government would have opted for unification with Germany. Only the veto of the French government created "two states within one nation." Since it would have required renegotiation of the peace treaty of 1919, Chancellor Seipel refrained from challenging outright the French veto of the Anschluss, despite the strong domestic pressures for unification which existed throughout the 1920s. The Austrian government continued to stick to its policy of "no solution [in central Europe] without German participation" but did not insist on pressing the issue of unification in international negotiations. At no point during the fourth pattern did Austria and Germany form a political community in institutional terms. Even so, they succeeded in establishing a high degree of political integration in the coordination of their political objectives and the assimilation of their political practices.

This process became known as assimilation policy (*Angleichungspolitik*). Its major purpose was to prepare all practical

---

22. Quoted in Ball, *Post-War German-Austrian Relations*, pp. 8-9.

aspects in the legal, economic, and cultural life of the two countries for an eventual institutional unification. The effect of this policy was to provide noninstitutionalized methods of consultation and coordination of government policies. Even though there was no expansion in the joint capability for collective decision making of the Austrian and German governments, political integration measured in terms of the number of issues covered and the effectiveness in the coordination of government policies was definitely on the increase, especially during the second half of the 1920s. Table 13 summarizes the important measures of policy coordination which then occurred.

Two features of the policy of assimilation should be noted. First, Austrian policy was assimilated to, not with, German policy. With only one exception—Austrian influence on the reform of the German code of civil procedure—*Angleichung* described a process in which the Austrians accepted German practices as their model to imitate and with it all the costs of change. The role reversal from leader to led which the Austrian Empire had experienced during the nineteenth century was cemented by the incomparably weaker position of the First Republic. The asymmetry in the relationship between the two countries was so great and the lack in German responsiveness to Austrian needs and interests, at times, so glaring that in some instances the Austrian government sought to retard for a while rather than to accelerate this one-sided process of political integration.[23] The asymmetry in Austrian and German commitment that we discovered in the institutional underpinnings of the Anschluss movement can be found as well in the realm of government policy.

A second characteristic of the policy of assimilation is the absence of the commitment of substantial economic resources to the process of policy coordination. Table 13 illustrates that with only one exception—the harmonization of insurance systems in 1930—policy coordination did not involve substantial tangible resources. Instead, numerous and far-reaching changes in political behavior were agreed on which required costs not measurable

23. Krulis-Randa, *Das Deutsch-Österreichische Zoll-Unionsprojekt*, pp. 73-74.

TABLE 13. Political Coordination between Austria and Germany, 1922-1933

1922 — Mutual recognition of diplomas and educational certificates as legally valid in both countries.

1923 — Decisions of civil courts are accorded privileged treatment in the partner country.

— Attestation of documents mutually recognized.

1924 — Veterinary agreement.

1925 — Visa abolished.

1927 — Harmonization of laws dealing with guardianship and rights of succession.

— Austrian army adopts the uniforms and ranks of the German army.

1928 — Unification of Austrian and German railway systems.

— Standardization of traffic regulations.

— Expansion of education exchange programs at the university level.

— Exchange programs initiated among different parts of the German and Austrian bureaucracies.

1929 — Constitutional reform in Austria, which imitates some of the provisions of the German constitution regarding the strong position of the president.

1930 — Unified treatment of patents and industrial patterns.

— Standardization of air traffic regulations.

— Harmonization of insurance systems.

1932 — Reciprocal recognition of bankruptcy laws.

1933 — Still under negotiation but, in part, substantially completed:

    Assimilation of marriage legislation
    Assimilation of court procedures
    Assimilation of press laws
    Standardization of labor contract legislation
    Adoption of a reformed criminal code in both countries

Sources: Kleinwächter and Paller, *Die Anschlussfrage*, pp. 460-547. Ball, *Post-War German-Austrian Relations*, pp. 77-82. Ernst Baumgärtner, "Die Österreichische Presse," (unpub. diss., University of Vienna, 1950), pp. 49-77.

in direct economic terms. This conclusion corresponds with the previous finding of the prominence of cultural, not economic, institutions in the Anschluss movement. The predominance of community over society in the voluntaristic pattern was as evident along the governmental and nongovernmental dimensions as along the behavioral and attitudinal ones.

The relative weakness of the economic link between Austria and Germany throughout the fourth pattern is revealed also by prolonged negotiations over plans for the creation of a customs or economic union encompassing both countries. Although Austria and Germany initiated active negotiations on this issue at the end of World War I, Austrian indifference, reinforced by the perceived threat of French disapproval, prevented the conclusion of an agreement before 1930. But when the accord was finally signed, opposition abroad, particularly in France, was so strong and the bargaining position of Germany and Austria so weak that it was soon abandoned. But as important as international constraints was the reluctance of Austrian industry to be incorporated in one large Austro-German market. When polled in 1931, Austria's chambers of commerce voted against the customs union by a margin of four to one.[24] It is, then, no surprise that Austro-German trade negotiations were arduous and difficult throughout the 1920s, leading at times, as they did in 1928 for example, to a total breakdown and suspension.[25]

These joint decisions involved no issue in which substantial economic resources were committed. This is, at least in part, an explanation for the dramatic change in the political relations of Austria and Germany after 1933. Had important economic interest groups been directly affected by the downturn in Austro-German relations, that downturn might have been less abrupt or might have taken different forms. Although few of the different measures of policy coordination were unilaterally

---

24. Karl H. Werner, "Österreichs Industrie- und Aussenhandelspolitik 1848 bis 1948," in Hans Meyer (ed.), *Hundert Jahre Österreichischer Wirtschaftsentwicklung, 1848-1948* (Vienna: Springer, 1949), p. 463.
25. Drexel, "Der Österreichisch-Deutsche Wirtschaftszusammenschluss," pp. 581-586.

changed by either the Austrian or the German side in the years 1933—1938, these agreements proved no barrier to the escalation of conflict between Hitler and Dollfuss.

From 1933 on the political objectives of the German and Austrian governments were diametrically opposed. Hitler's main interest was not the Anschluss per se but effective political control over Austrian domestic politics guaranteed by an Austrian government in which the Nazis had a significant political influence. His tactics included propaganda, intimidation, and sabotage. His main worry for the future of his country of birth was the danger that "Germany might definitely lose six million people who were becoming something like the Swiss."[26] The reaction of the Austrian government was defensive. As soon as the direction a Nazi government in Germany might steer became clear in 1932–1933, the two large parties in Austria dropped the demand for unification from their party programs; to the sabotage and bombings of the Austrian Nazi party in Austria the government responded with harsh measures.

In the years 1933–1934 Austro-German relations were a classic case of an escalating conflict. The conflict spiral started with the passing of an Austrian ordinance forbidding the display of Nazi uniforms, flags, and emblems and ended with the assassination of the Austrian chancellor, Dollfuss, in an unsuccessful coup d'état undertaken by German and Austrian Nazis. Within another four years, Austria succumbed to German pressures.

If by political integration we understand the purposeful coordination of political behavior in the achievement of common tasks, the voluntaristic pattern reveals a substantial amount of political integration. The weakening of political autonomy in processes of integration does not require the institutionalization of government contacts or the unification of political structures. The voluntaristic pattern shows instead that, in a partial response to the negative economic rewards which characterized the First Republic, Austria's political autonomy eroded through an extensive and effective coordination of government policy.

---

26. Quoted in Jürgen Gehl, *Austria, Germany, and the Anschluss, 1931-1938* (London: Oxford University Press, 1963), p. 55.

POLITICAL REWARDS:
INTEGRATION AND AUTONOMY

Political autonomy is the result of nonpolitical and political variables. In the voluntaristic pattern, both the balance between community and society and the structure of economic rewards pointed to significant sacrifices in political autonomy in the form of an extensive and effective assimilation of Austrian to German political practices. But since it failed to distinguish between different political actors, the analysis of the fourth pattern has remained deceptively simple so far. Despite the widespread desire for unification with Germany, different classes and political elites stood to gain to different degrees from a strategy of political integration. In their defense of the Austrian Empire's centers of power since the middle of the nineteenth century, the German-Austrians had adopted partial integration as a useful political resource in their conflict with the Slavs. During the fourth pattern domestic political conflict centered on questions of class rather than ethnicity. And unlike the nineteenth century a strategy of integration was most ardently desired not by those in power but out of power. The Socialists in their role as permanent opposition and the German nationalists in their's as impotent partner to the ruling coalition advocated most strongly the unification of Austria with Germany. The Christian Socials, on the other hand, were much more content in the new political structure of the First Republic which proved so hospitable to their political needs. During the fourth pattern the structure of domestic politics, thus, shaped competing strategies of autonomy and integration. Political integration was a political crisis strategy for some groups in Austrian society but not for others.

The First Republic was marked by one condition above all, disunity.[27] It was evident in the lack of regional integration,

---

27. For this period, see Walter Goldinger, *Geschichte der Republik Österreich* (Vienna: Verlag für Geschichte und Politik, 1962); Felix Kreissler, *Von der Revolution zur Annexion: Österreich, 1918 bis 1938* (Vienna: Europa Verlag, 1970); Bauer, *Die Österreichische Revolution*; Alfred Diamant, *Austrian Catholics and the First Republic: Democracy, Capitalism, and the Social Order, 1918-1934* (Princeton: Princeton University Press, 1960).

social cohesion, and political cooperation. Otto Bauer rightly observed at the outset of the First Republic that the Austrians thought of themselves primarily as "natives of Styria, Carinthia, the Tyrol, and Salzburg."[28] Popular referenda revealed that the provinces had little inclination to support the new government in Vienna. Economic interests (in the case of the Vorarlberg) pointed toward a union with Switzerland. In the Tyrol the independence of a united Tyrol was deemed preferable to the amalgamation of only the northern part of the province with the Austrian Republic. In Salzburg and Styria the vote was overwhelmingly in favor of Anschluss with Germany. The differences between the capital and the provinces were so strong that not the wish of the vanquished but the will of the victors kept Austria united in these initial trying times.

The split between Vienna and the provinces had the character of a class conflict between workers and peasants. Concentrated in the provinces were the peasants with their strong support of the Christian Socials. The stronghold of the Austrian working class, on the other hand, was Vienna which was utterly dependent on the food supplies shipped in from the provinces. When these supplies were not forthcoming in the aftermath of World War I, it was a clear indication that the "black" provinces preferred to starve "red" Vienna into submission rather than support a Socialist government which seemed to threaten social and political revolution. The pauperization of Austrian society after 1918 encouraged not only secessionist movements in different regions of the First Republic but intensified class conflicts as well.

Regional fragmentation and social polarization were reflected in the cleavages between Austria's three political camps. The First Republic was a stalemated country without a political center. In terms of electoral support the distribution of political power between the camps remained relatively stable throughout

---

Charles A. Gulick, *Austria from Habsburg to Hitler* (Berkeley: University of California Press, 1948), 2 vols.

28. Otto Bauer quoted in Julius Braunthal, *Otto Bauer: Eine Auswahl aus seinem Lebenswerk* (Vienna: Volksbuchhandlung, 1961), p. 33.

the 1920s. Between 1918 and 1920 the formation of a coalition government of Socialists and Christian Socials was an indication of both the pressing needs of the immediate postwar period and the even distribution of power within Austria. When the coalition split on constitutional issues and problems of social legislation, a more permanent alignment was made between the Christian Socials and the Great German party, which later came to include fascist organizations. Although divided on many important issues, the coalition held together because the shared fear of socialism was a powerful glue. The rising importance of the fascist *Heimwehr* in the late 1920s—first a paramilitary organization of the Christian Socials, later an independent political force—was no break with the coalition's original raison d'être but merely accentuated its antidemocratic tendencies. The sharp differences between the governing anti-Socialist coalition and the Socialist opposition permeated every aspect of political life. Police and army were penetrated first by the Socialists, later by the Christian Socials.[29] Parties maintained large and well-armed paramilitary forces. Violence occurred first in 1927, and the domestic peace became increasingly more fragile until the government crushed the Socialist party in the brief civil war of 1934.

During the interwar years Austria consisted of a number of isolated political fragments. These fragments responded differently to the issue of unification with Germany. A uniform programmatic commitment of all parties to the goal of unification merely concealed that the Anschluss became a political weapon in the hands of different political actors seeking to shape the distribution of political power at home. Competing strategies of integration and autonomy depended on how the political institutions of the First Republic served the different needs of Austria's three political camps.

For the supporters of the nationalist camp and the Great German party, the sheer force of the ideology of German

---

29. Gulick, *Austria from Habsburg to Hitler*, I, 129-131, 751. Ludwig Jedlicka, *Ein Heer im Schatten der Parteien: Die militärpolitische Lage Österreichs, 1918-1938* (Graz: Böhlaus, 1955).

nationalism was a major factor in the advocacy of political integration with Germany. But there were other party needs that were simply not met by the First Republic; and these were of no small importance. Part of the problem was economic. A concealed wartime inflation was reinforced by serious economic shortages after 1918. Capital flight and large budget deficits fueled speculation against the Austrian currency and created runaway inflation in the early 1920s. For the large number of middle-class supporters of the nationalist camp in particular, the consequence of inflation was disastrous. The money-wealth of the old middle class was destroyed and the recipients of fixed salaries—typically members of the middle class—bore a disproportionate share of the inflation burden.[30]

The collapse of the Austrian Empire, furthermore, saddled the Austrian middle class with a serious structural unemployment problem. Recruited from the middle class before 1918, the officer corps of the imperial army became virtually jobless overnight. Retired army officers were counted among the most ardent and active supporters of the Anschluss in the Great German party. As traditional beneficiaries of the empire, civil servants and white-collar workers were also hit. A drastic reduction in the size of Austria's now bloated bureaucracy put as many as 100,000 of them out of work. Their strong support of the Great German party first and the Nazis later was a direct reflection of the overwhelming economic problems they faced in the First Republic.[31]

The needs of the nationalist camp were not only economic but political. Before 1918 the largest support of the nationalist *Lager* had come from areas excluded from the First Republic, from Bohemia, Moravia, and Silesia. In terms of organizational strength and electoral support the Great German party was

---

30. Bauer, *Die Österreichische Revolution*, pp. 205-213. Reinhard Kamitz, "Die Österreichische Geld- und Währungspolitik von 1848 bis 1948," in Mayer, *Hundert Jahre Österreichischer Wirtschaftsentwicklung*, pp. 172-179.
31. Johann Christoph Allmayer-Beck, "Die Träger der staatlichen Macht," in Otto Schulmeister (ed.), *Spectrum Austriae* (Vienna: Herder, 1957), pp. 278-282.

condemned to a permanent status of the smallest party in Austria. Apart from all other considerations it was, then, a perfectly rational strategy on the part of the Great German party to advocate the political integration of Austria into Germany, where its political chances as part of a larger nationalist party might be substantially improved.

The Great German party was part of the German political community in aspiration; its successor, the Austrian Nazi party, was an integral part of the German political system in fact.[32] Incorporated de facto into the German Nazi party as early as 1926, the Austrian Nazis coordinated all their political activities with the German party and became an instrument in Hitler's terrorist attacks culminating in the assassination of the Austrian chancellor, Dollfuss, in 1934. More determinedly and consistently than any other party, the Austrian Nazis worked for the political integration of Austria with Germany.[33]

Nor did the First Republic serve well the needs of Austria's Socialist party. When a deflationary policy stopped Austria's inflation from 1922—1923 on, the burden of the new economic policy was transferred from the middle to the working class. During the interwar years Austria had the highest unemployment rate in Europe. At the height of the economic boom of the years 1925—1929, about 10 to 15 percent of Austria's labor force was out of work. At the worst time of the depression the total number of unemployed amounted to more than one-third of Austria's labor force.[34]

Austria's Socialists perceived the Anschluss as a question of class. The case was spontaneously made in October 1918 when a speaker's demand for early unification with Germany prompted the German nationalists to sing the unofficial German national anthem, the "Wacht am Rhein," and the workers the "Marseil-

---

32. Hoor, *Österreich, 1918-1938*, pp. 56-60. Gordon Shepherd, *The Austrian Odyssey* (London: Macmillan, 1957), pp. 119-122.
33. On the role of one of Austria's leading Nazis, see Wolfgang Rosar, *Deutsche Gemeinschaft: Seyss-Inquart und der Anschluss* (Vienna: Europa Verlag, 1971).
34. Alois Brusatti, *Österreichische Wirtschaftspolitik vom Josephinismus zum Ständestaat* (Vienna: Jupiter, 1965), p. 112, fn. 5.

laise."[35] In Otto Bauer's own analysis, class considerations dominated. He wanted a union with the workers of Germany. Unification with Germany was to bring socialism.[36]

To the Austrian Socialist party political integration with Germany was a highly valued resource for escaping the political isolation into which the party had slid in the early 1920s. The Christian Social policies of financial stabilization of 1922 and 1932 met the strongest Socialist opposition not merely because they distributed unequally the costs of stabilization between different classes. Rather, those policies were opposed because the international agreements signed then reiterated that there would be no unification with Germany for the duration of some long-term international loans. To the Austrian Socialists that stipulation must have appeared as the expropriation of their most prominent growth stock in what to them was an exceedingly tight market for raising additional political capital inside Austria.[37]

The Christian Socials were the one political group in Austria whose needs were met by the First Republic. At the same time that all other parties preached political strategies of integration, the Christian Socials practiced autonomy. To some extent the strength of the party and the success of its policy can be explained by the economic circumstances of the First Republic. Since Austria had an overwhelming need to import food supplies after 1918, a strengthening of the agricultural sector was a structural prerequisite for the very existence of the First Republic. From this fact the Christian Socials derived substantial political benefits, since the large majority of their supporters were peasants in the Austrian provinces.[38]

---

35. Franziska Brückl, "Die Probleme des neuen Österreichs im Spiegel der Wiener Presse" (unpub. diss., University of Vienna, 1952), p. 258.
36. Bauer, *Die Österreichische Revolution*, pp. 147-149.
37. Karl Stadler, *Austria* (London: Benn, 1971), pp. 109-111.
38. Friedrich Thalmann, "Die Wirtschaft in Österreich," in Heinrich Benedikt (ed.), *Geschichte der Republik Österreich* (Munich: Oldenbourg, 1954), p. 540. Karl Bachinger, "Mittelstand und Bauernorganisationen als neue politische Kräfte in Österreich nach dem Ersten Weltkrieg," in Richard G. Plaschka and Karlheinz Mack (eds.), *Die Auflösung des Habsburgerreiches: Zusammenbruch und Neuorientierung im Donauraum* (Vienna:

For the very reason that the Socialists favored the Anschluss, the Christian Socials opposed it. As the political center of the monarchists, proponents of a Danubian Confederation, and most of Austria's conservatives, the Christian Socials had little to gain from a policy in which they would risk their firm entrenchment in the centers of power in Austria for an uncertain future in an enlarged Austro-German political community.[39] To be sure, the party was not strong enough to govern Austria without the political support of the Great German party, and that coalition required that the Christian Socials and their leader, Prelate Seipel, adhere to the rhetoric of the Anschluss movement. But throughout the 1920s the party's policy did not betray an undue haste in seeing the Anschluss emerge as a serious political alternative. Political autonomy, not political integration, was its most valued objective.[40]

This was quite clear from the very beginning of the First Republic. In the fall of 1918 the Christian Socials were the party least willing to relinquish the institutional structures of the empire. As long as the radical Left in Germany seemed like a serious revolutionary force, the party advocated a Great Austrian Confederation as the most desirable successor to the Dual Monarchy. Like all other parties, the Christian Socials found themselves voting for the Anschluss declaration in Parliament but they did so with much greater hesitation.

The party's preference for autonomy from Germany and the beneficial effects of that autonomy on the distribution of political power at home were dramatically illustrated by the Geneva Protocol of 1922. Austria's stabilization policy was financed by

---

Verlag für Geschichte und Politik, 1970), pp. 462-467. Frederick Hertz, *The Economic Problem of the Danubian States: A Study in Economic Nationalism* (London: Gollancz, 1947), pp. 118-123.

39. Goldinger, *Geschichte der Republik Österreich*, pp. 71, 171-174. Hoor, *Österreich, 1918-1938*, pp. 53-57, 68.

40. The 1926 party program avoided the concept of Anschluss altogether. Goldinger, *Geschichte der Republik Österreich*, p. 115. Even so most Christian Socials were agreed on Austria's being a part of the German cultural nation. See also Klemens von Klemperer, *Ignaz Seipel: Christian Statesman in a Time of Crisis* (Princeton: Princeton University Press, 1972). Suval, *The Anschluss Question*, pp. 203-225.

an international consortium headed by France and Britain. Austria's government was asked to renounce the Anschluss as a political goal for the twenty years' duration of the loan. But even more important than this restriction were the effects of the international financial community on the balance of power between the different *Lager* in Austrian politics.

The policy adopted to restore financial stability in Austria was relatively straightforward. Government expenses were cut primarily by reducing the number of civil servants by 100,000 and by cutting social services stemming from legislation passed in 1919—1920 when the Socialists still shared power. On the other hand, an increase in revenues was sought by lowering direct taxes and increasing indirect taxes, a shift toward a more regressive system of taxation which put the burden almost entirely on low-income earners. A strictly deflationary policy was then adopted which succeeded in restoring financial stability rather quickly but at the cost of a very high rate of unemployment.[41]

The autonomy from Germany that the Christian Socials' policy established in 1922 had momentous effects on the party's consolidation of power in Austrian politics. The Christian Socials handed a triple defeat to the Socialists, who favored Anschluss, the consolidation of the social legislation of the early 1920s, and a better life for the Austrian working class. Supervision of the implementation of the policy by the League of Nations, furthermore, led to a shift of power away from Parliament, the last bastion the Socialists held in national politics. By convincing the Great German party to vote for the ratification of the Geneva Protocol, the Christian Socials managed to stigmatize that party as having voted against Anschluss, which permanently damaged its credibility in national politics. The Christian Social strategy of autonomy paid off handsomely.

The Christian Social preference for autonomy was obvious also at later points in time. When the Anschluss movement gained

---

41. Kurt W. Rothschild, "Wurzeln und Triebkräfte der Entwicklung der Österreichischen Wirtschaftsstruktur," in Wilhelm Weber (ed.), *Österreichs Wirtschaftsstruktur: Gestern, heute, morgen* (Berlin: Duncker, 1961), I, 79-82.

ground in Austria from the mid-1920s onward, the policy of the Austrian government and foremost its Christian Social chancellor, Seipel, was consistently to downplay the possibility or desirability of economic or political unification with Germany.[42] In fact, Seipel's negotiations with Czechoslovakia over a preferential trade agreement as a possible first step for an eventual economic arrangement among the states of the Danubian Basin failed only because Germany threatened economic reprisals which the Austrian government thought to be too costly.[43] Only after Seipel's ouster from the government and after a weakening of the cohesion of the Christian Social party did Austria—now represented by the leader of the Great German party as its foreign minister—and Germany enter serious negotiations over the establishment of an Austro-German customs union.

Regional, social, and political fragmentation of the First Republic were the result of one overriding condition, disunity. But this disunity affected Austria's political parties differently. For dissimilar reasons, neither the Great German party nor the Socialists could hope to achieve their objectives in the evolving First Republic. Both took, therefore, recourse to political integration as a crisis strategy designed to improve their positions in Austria's domestic politics. The Christian Socials, on the other hand, found the First Republic surprisingly hospitable to their political needs. As a result, political autonomy rather than political integration was their most favored political strategy. The distribution of political power inside Austria, thus, shaped competing political strategies of integration and autonomy.

Political autonomy can be explained by nonpolitical and political variables. For the first time since 1815 most of these variables worked toward an erosion of Austria's political autonomy during the voluntaristic pattern. Behavioral and

42. Ball, *Post-War German-Austrian Relations*, pp. 64, 92. Krulis-Randa, *Das Deutsch-Österreichische Zoll-Unionsprojekt*, pp. 75-76, 86. Goldinger, *Geschichte der Republik Österreich*, pp. 115, 157.
43. Rothschild, *Austria's Economic Development*, p. 41.

attitudinal indicators of community and society pointed to integration. Large-scale poverty which characterized the First Republic further intensified the process of Austro-German integration at the mass level. Finally, the scarcity of the political resources and rewards that they could control or enjoy in Austria prompted two of Austria's three political camps—the Socialists and the German nationalists—to pursue strategies of political integration.

But the Christian Social preference for autonomy illustrates clearly that these cumulative interlocking processes of integration did not determine political behavior. They simply made the determined pursuit of a strategy of autonomy quite improbable. Austria's domestic politics created constraints and choices which shaped the political responses of different actors. In their preference for political autonomy the Christian Socials, in particular, added to the voluntaristic pattern the one feature most characteristic of relations among disjoined partners.

VII

STRUCTURAL PATTERN
(1938-1945)

THE STRUCTURAL pattern of Austro-German relations differed from its predecessor in two important ways. After the Anschluss of 1938, common tasks were pursued under the total commitment of all German and Austrian resources, and the political institutions of the two countries were unified.

An analysis of the structural pattern reveals traces of Austria's past. On the one hand, this pattern was a consummation of mutually reinforcing processes which generated copressures and political integration in the voluntaristic pattern; the Anschluss of 1938 was conquest by consent. On the other hand, this pattern was also a continuation of mutually opposing processes which had generated counterpressures and political autonomy throughout the nineteenth century; the Anschluss of 1938 was conquest by coercion. The Austrian response in the years 1938—1945 shows that elements of both consent and coercion were present. In a commitment, which remained partial to the aims of the German Nazi government, the Austrians responded to the accumulation of past experiences. The empirical evidence suggests that in response to these heterogeneous experiences the Austrians, if given a choice, would have opted for the preservation of partial autonomy in the structural pattern.

CONQUEST BY COERCION

Almost without exception Austrian historians have attempted since 1945 to prove that the Anschluss occurred against the wishes of the Austrian people. Evidence cited in support of this view consists of generalized accounts of resistance and sabotage. According to one writer, "Public opinion in Austria was against the occupation . . . which can be demonstrated by studying the attitudes and the resistance of the population as well as the statements of the important political actors."[1] Similar opinions were voiced by other students of the Austrian resistance movement.[2] Since these views conflict directly with the analysis in the last chapter, they merit special attention.

One argument points to the behavior of the German Nazis as evidence for Austria's status as a conquered country. The Austrian army, for example, was purged before its incorporation into the German army. By the middle of 1939, 55 percent of the generals, 40 percent of the colonels, and 14 percent of the lieutenant-colonels had been retired and, in a few instances, arrested.[3] Many faculty members of the Austrian universities

---

1. Emanuel Guber, "Österreichischer Staatsvertrag und öffentliche Meinung" (unpub. diss., University of Vienna, 1955), p. 185.
2. Friedrich Engel-Janosi, "Remarks on the Austrian Resistance, 1938-1945," *Journal of Central European Affairs*, XIII, 2 (July 1953), pp. 109-110. Gordon Shepherd, *The Austrian Odyssey* (London: Macmillan, 1957), p. 154. Maria Szecsi and Karl Stadler, *Die NS-Justiz in Österreich und ihre Opfer* (Vienna: Herold, 1962), p. 7. Leopold Voller, "Le Mouvement de Résistance Autrichien et les Alliés," in *European Resistance Movements, 1939-1945: Proceedings of the Second International Conference on the History of the Resistance Movements Held at Milan, 26-29 March 1961* (New York: Macmillan, 1964), p. 570. Erika Weinzierl, "Der Österreichische Widerstand," in Erika Weinzierl and Kurt Skalnik (eds.), *Österreich: Die Zweite Republik* (Graz: Styria, 1972), pp. 109-128. Christine Klusacek, Herbert Steiner, Kurt Stimmer (eds.), *Dokumentation zur Österreichischen Zeitgeschichte, 1938-1945* (Vienna: Verlag Jugend und Volk, 1971). See also the papers and discussions in *Transactions of the Conference Group for Social and Administrative History*, IV (Oshkosh, Wisconsin, 1974). Unfortunately, Radomir Luza's book *Austro-German Relations in the Anschluss Era, 1938-1945* (Princeton: Princeton University Press), was not yet available as this manuscript went to press.
3. Ludwig Jedlicka, "Heer und Demokratie," in Jacques Hannak (ed.), *Bestandsaufnahme Österreich, 1945-1963* (Vienna: Forum, 1963), p. 243.

were dismissed. An incomplete estimate of the number of offenses committed against the state between 1938 and 1945 puts the figure at about 17,000, many of which probably occurred during the very first weeks after the Anschluss.[4] Austria's Jewish population either fled or was exterminated. And Austria was abolished as an administrative unit in 1939 and divided instead into seven regions governed directly from Berlin.[5]

Economically, Austria was also treated like a conquered country. To be sure, there were immediate economic gains. Unemployment dropped sharply in 1938 from 22 to 13 percent, and Austria's gross national product grew in real terms by 10 percent in the same year.[6] New plants, geared to the needs of the German war economy, were built in western Austria, and its industrial capacity was greatly enlarged. But there were direct economic losses as well, and in the end they turned out to be much larger. The expropriation of Austrian Jews, the takeover of the Austrian banking sector and large parts of Austrian industry, the conversion of Austrian bonds at a net loss to the Austrian owner, the cancellation of the credits which Austria had accumulated in her trade with Germany during the preceding years, and finally the great losses in human life and property suffered during World War II—all of these facts have been cited as indirect evidence in support of the view that the Anschluss was nothing but conquest by coercion.[7]

This line of reasoning is unconvincing. Undoubtedly the German Nazis revealed an even greater lack of responsiveness

---

4. Stadler and Szecsi, *Die NS-Justiz*, p. 21. A slightly higher estimate is given in Karl Stadler, *Österreich, 1938-1945: Im Spiegel der NS-Akten* (Vienna: Herold, 1966), pp. 29-30.
5. Erika Weinzierl, *Zu wenig Gerechte: Österreich und die Judenverfolgung, 1938-1945* (Graz: Styria, 1969). Christa Altenstetter, *Der Föderalismus in Österreich: Unter besonderer Berücksichtigung der politischen Verhältnisse von 1945-1966* (Heidelberg: Quelle, 1969), p. 20.
6. Gustav Otruba, *Österreichs Wirtschaft im 20. Jahrhundert* (Vienna: Österreichischer Bundesverlag, 1968), p. 30.
7. See, for example, Felix Romanik, *Der Leidensweg der Österreichischen Wirtschaft, 1933-1945* (Vienna: Österreichischer Bundesverlag, 1957), pp. 19-21.

than might have been expected on the basis of the asymmetric dependence relationship that had evolved between Austria and Germany during the preceding two generations. Yet, not only was Austria treated much better than the other occupied states in central and eastern Europe, but German-Austrians enjoyed a privileged position compared with Austria's Czech, Polish, and Jewish citizens.[8] Seventeen thousand legal proceedings covered less than 0.3 percent of Austria's total population; there appears, then, to have been little resistance to speak of, at least in statistical terms. In any case, from the mere fact that the Nazis, at times, behaved like an occupying power it is a leap of faith to conclude that Austria was an occupied country. That question can be answered only by assessing the sentiments and behavior of the Austrian people themselves.

On this point the judgement of participants and informed observers differs considerably. One student of the Austrian resistance has estimated that four- to five-sevenths of the Austrian people were prepared to wage a campaign of active resistance, another two-sevenths favored a strategy of passive resistance, and but one-seventh were Nazis actually in favor of the Anschluss; the Austrian people were endowed with a "fanatical will to resist."[9] If this were true, six million Austrians carried the art of deception to its highest perfection in 1938. Other estimates are more reasonable (but still questionable) in putting the number of Nazi supporters on the eve of the referendum in April 1938 at about one-third of Austria's population.[10]

8. Szecsi and Stadler, *Die NS-Justiz*, p. 22.
9. Otto Molden, *Der Ruf des Gewissens: Der Österreichische Freiheitskampf, 1938-1945* (Vienna: Herold, 1958), pp. 52, 40-45.
10. Ernst Hoor, *Österreich, 1918-1938: Staat ohne Nation, Republik ohne Republikaner* (Vienna: Österreichischer Bundesverlag, 1966), pp. 59-60. It is doubtful whether Hoor is correct in assuming that the entire Socialist camp, defeated by the clerical-fascist regime in the civil war of 1934, would have voted for Schuschnigg in 1938. See also John Mair, "Austria," in *Survey of International Affairs, 1939-1946: Four-Power Control in Germany and Austria, 1945-1946* (London: Oxford University Press, 1956), pp. 292-293. Bruce F. Pauley, "The Fascist Resistance: Anti-Nazism in Austria before the Anschluss," *Transactions*, IV, 67.

In addition to these assessments of Austrian attitudes there are, of course, many acts of resistance, which seem to support the argument that the Anschluss was conquest by coercion. Seven thousand Austrians fought against the Germans in the French and the British armies. The Austrian resistance movement, to the extent that it was organized, was independent from the resistance in Germany. Furthermore, the Moscow Declaration of 1943 served to strengthen the opposition forces inside Austria since it made the future of the country dependent on its own contribution to the liberation. Secret reports of the Gestapo give a vivid picture of Austrian discontent, and in many of these reports the notion of an independent Austria recurs time and again as a rallying point for opposition to the Nazis. Even the Austrian Nazis appear to have been disappointed by some features of the Nazi policies. They had envisaged a somewhat more autonomous status for Austria and somewhat more privileged one for themselves in the new political order.[11] In the most detailed study of this period published to date, the Austrian resistance has been identified as a national one.[12] To prove that point conclusively, the relative amount of resistance to Nazi policies needs to be analyzed together with the relative amount of consent.

CONQUEST BY CONSENT

When Austrians talk or write today about the experience of the years 1938—1955, phrases such as "the lost war" or "ten years of occupation" are not uncommon;[13] the unconscious identification with the war effort of the German Nazis remains strong and the years experienced as occupation occurred

---

11. Johann Christoph Allmeyer-Beck, "Die Österreicher im Zweiten Weltkrieg," in *Unser Heer: 300 Jahre Österreichisches Soldatentum in Krieg und Frieden* (Vienna: Fürlinger, 1958), p. 344. Engel-Janosi, "Remarks on the Austrian Resistance," pp. 105, 107. Karl Stadler, *Austria* (London: Benn, 1971), pp. 154-171. Ulrich Eichstädt, *Von Dollfuss zu Hitler: Geschichte des Anschlusses Österreichs, 1933-1938* (Wiesbaden: Steiner, 1955), pp. 389-391.
12. Stadler, *Österreich, 1938-1945*.
13. Ernst Joseph Görlich, *Die Österreichische Nation und der Widerstand* (Vienna: Europa Verlag, 1967), pp. 36-37.

after rather than before and during, World War II. This use of language accords well with the spontaneous enthusiasm that greeted Hitler and the German troops as they entered Austria in March 1938. In fact, the enthusiasm was so great that Hitler changed his mind on what to do about Austria only after the occupation had taken place; instead of the loose personal union he had envisaged, he decided in favor of complete unification.[14]

In Vienna Hitler was greeted by a crowd estimated at about a quarter of a million, but in purely Catholic areas as well turnout was extremely heavy. In statements released separately to the public, the Catholic and the Protestant churches supported the Anschluss and encouraged the Austrian public to vote for unification with Germany at the impending plebiscite of April 1938. In the words of the National Council of the Lutheran Church: "We support the actions of the Führer without any reservations and thank God that in the most desperate hour he has brought salvation to the German people."[15] Public support for the Anschluss came also from Karl Renner, the Socialist president of both the First and the Second Republics. With mass and elite support of that magnitude it came as no surprise that the referendum organized by the Nazis in April 1938 brought a resounding vote in favor of unification.

The 99 percent vote for unification was a gross exaggeration of the actual distribution of preference of the Austrian people at that time. Many people did not participate in the celebration of unification; some fled the country; others were arrested. But contemporary observers and a number of historians estimate that probably a majority of the Austrians and perhaps as many as two-thirds of the population favored the Anschluss in the spring of 1938.[16] Undoubtedly the motivations underlying that preference varied greatly, and no one has succeeded better in summarizing in one word the entire range of Austrian emotion than

14. Hoor, *Österreich, 1918-1938*, p. 138.
15. Quoted in Eichstädt, *Von Dollfuss zu Hitler*, p. 435. The Catholic church used similar language.
16. *Ibid.*, p. 436. Shepherd, *Austrian Odyssey*, p. 134. Walter Goldinger, *Geschichte der Republik Österreich* (Vienna: Verlag für Geschichte und Politik, 1962), pp. 254-255.

Structural Pattern (1938-1945)

Berthold Brecht who called the Austrians *freudeschlotternd* (fearfully trembling with joy).[17] But one important political fact is indisputable whether we subscribe to minimum estimates of one-third or maximum estimates of two-thirds support for unification with Germany. If one-third of the Austrian population supported the Anschluss and Nazi rule, this was enough to make an informal system of supervision, control, and repression highly effective. In no other country the Germans "occupied" after 1938 could they hope for support from one-third of the population, and in no country but Austria was the problem of political control solved as easily.

Three times during the preceding two hundred years—in the eighteenth century, in 1809, and in 1866—German troops (Prussian and Bavarian) had crossed the Austrian border, and three times the Austrians had resisted. But by the end of the nineteenth century, Austria and Germany had become a peace community; and despite the political conflict between 1933 and 1938, war remained a solution for which neither the Austrians nor the Germans were actively prepared in 1938. As for the German side, there were no plans for an invasion of Austria when Hitler ordered the tanks to move, and the German army improvised the entire campaign.[18] The Austrians had a defense plan (the Jansa plan), but preparations were woefully inadequate. Troops were not concentrated for the defense of any one border; and equipment was so insufficient that active fighting, under the best of all circumstances, was not expected to last longer than two days.[19]

More important was the low morale of the Austrian troops. When mobilized, many Austrians entered army barracks displaying Nazi flags and raised their right arms defiantly in the

---

17. Berthold Brecht, "Der aufhaltsame Aufstieg des Arturo Ui" (scene 15): "Die Wahl is aus, Chef, Ciceros Grünzeughändler/ Und die Chicagos danken tiefbewegt/ Und freudeschlotternd dir für deinen Schutz." *Stücke gegen den Faschismus: Deutschsprachige Autoren* (Berlin: Henschel, 1970), p. 423.
18. Eichstädt, *Von Dollfuss zu Hitler*, p. 366.
19. Peter Gschaider, "Das Österreichische Bundesheer 1938 und seine Überführung in die Deutsche Wehrmacht" (unpub. diss., University of Vienna, 1967), p. 98.

German salute.[20] After the German invasion, Austrian troops stationed in the Innsbruck and Salzburg areas put themselves under German command immediately and participated in joint victory parades.[21] But most important of all was Chancellor Schuschnigg's unwillingness to resist. Undoubtedly many of the foregoing considerations must have weighed heavily on his mind. But in addition there was the compelling image of Austria and Germany as two brother nations, which prompted him to conclude his last radio speech with the words: "Because we do not want at any price and even in this somber hour that German blood be shed we ordered our army . . . to retreat without resistance."[22]

At no time was a government-in-exile formed between 1938 and 1945. Another piece of evidence which suggests that the unification of Austria with Germany in 1938 was not totally involuntary is the degree of support the Nazi party received in Austria during the 1930s. In the absence of electoral data for the years after 1932, we have to rely on the party membership figures presented in Table 14. This table reveals that the Nazi party experienced a continuous growth in Austria throughout the 1930s. The peak values in the average monthly entry figures (column three) were achieved when the party was not operating underground, in 1933 and in 1938. But the figures in Table 14 show also that growth in the support of the party accelerated from 1934 on. Judging by this evidence, an increasing number of Austrians backed the Nazis and through them a policy of unification.

Other fragmentary pieces of evidence suggest that the Austrians did not seriously resist the Germans. In World War II Austrians did well in terms of military honors, with 326 earning the *Ritterkreuz*, one of the highest military awards the German army offered. In response to Nazi pressures, 300,000 Austrians left the Catholic church between 1938 and 1945. The attempted

---

20. *Ibid.*, pp. 78-79.
21. Friedrich Fritz, "Der Deutsche Einmarsch in Österreich 1938," in *Militärhistorische Schriftenreihe*, VIII (Vienna: Österreichischer Bundesverlag, 1968), p. 20.
22. Quoted in Kurt Steiner, *Politics in Austria* (Boston: Little Brown, 1972), p. 18.

TABLE 14. Membership Figures of the Austrian Nazi Party, 1928-1938

	(1) Cumulative Absolute Membership Figures	(2) Cumulative Relative Membership Figures	(3) Entry per Month
1928	4,466	2	
January 20, 1933 (Hitler becomes German chancellor)	43,129	21	644
June 19, 1933 (Nazi party declared illegal in Austria)	67,980	33	5,323
August 4, 1934 (Nazi putsch in Austria)	88,690	43	1,534
July 11, 1936 (Austro-German agreement)	115,612	56	1,171
February 12, 1938 (Berchtesgarden agreement)	148,747	72	1,744
March 11, 1938 (Anschluss)	161,173	78	12,426
Fall 1938 (active and inactive membership)	203,627[a]	99	1,311

Source: Computed from Stadler, *Österreich, 1938-1945*, pp. 34-35.
[a]Slight inaccuracy because of rounding errors.

plot of July 1944 was crushed as easily in Vienna as in Berlin, and Austrian participation in the country's final liberation was haphazard at best.[23]

23. Allmeyer-Beck, "Die Österreicher im Zweiten Weltkrieg," p. 358. Erich Zöllner, *Geschichte Österreichs: Von den Anfängen bis zur Gegenwart*, 4th ed. (Vienna: Verlag für Geschichte und Politik, 1970), p. 524. Antony Evelyn Alcock, *The History of the South Tyrol Question* (London: Michael Joseph, 1970), pp. 103-104. Ludwig Jedlicka, *Der 20. Juli in Österreich* (Vienna: Herold, 1965). Molden, *Ruf des Gewissens*, pp. 220-259.

A similar picture emerges from other evidence. Although the data on court-martials with death penalties are incomplete, they provide a rough measure of the degree of Austrian resistance in the German army. A total of 523 death penalties were passed on Austrian citizens as compared with roughly 6,000 on Germans.[24] Since the ratio between these two figures is roughly equal to the ratio between the total Austrian and German populations in 1937, the intensity of Austrian opposition did not differ significantly from that of the Germans. We reach a similar conclusion if we take the total of civilian and military death sentences. The Austrian figure is again about 10 percent of the corresponding German figure of 26,000.[25] On the basis of this evidence one might be tempted to conclude that conquest by consent describes the Austrian experience between 1938 and 1945.

COERCION AND CONSENT: AUSTRIA'S PARTIAL COMMITMENT

These contrasting views of the structural pattern as conquest by coercion or conquest by consent reflect the dissimilar stream of Austrian experience before 1938. Political autonomy in the first three patterns was replaced by political integration in the fourth. If, therefore, our previous analyses were correct, attempts to label the structural pattern either coercion or consent are both in error. Instead, Austria's past experience of autonomy and integration seems to indicate a combination of coercion and consent.

If one compares the Austrian resistance with that of Germany on the one hand and with that of other occupied countries in Europe on the other hand, Austria holds an intermediary position. As was true of Germany, material grievances were the major source of complaint and unrest; but many police reports show that Austrian national consciousness played an important role as well.[26] On the other hand, if one compares Austria not to

---

24. Szecsi and Stadler, *Die NS-Justiz*, pp. 23-24. Kurt Stadler, *Austria* (New York: Praeger, 1971), p. 159.
25. *Ibid.*, pp. 24-28. It should be noted, though, that these data are incomplete.
26. Stadler, *Österreich, 1938-1945*. On Germany's resistance see Heinz Boberach (ed.), *Meldungen aus dem Reich: Auswahl aus den geheimen Lage-*

countries such as Yugoslavia or France (which experienced active resistance movements) but to a country such as Czechoslovakia (where things were reasonably quiet), there is a significant difference. In Czechoslovakia the Germans were greeted not by jubilant but by quiet and embittered crowds. Symbolic boycotts and silent mass demonstrations recurred frequently even though in Czechoslovakia, as in Austria, habitual compliance dominated. One of the top leaders of the Nazi party, Heydrich, was assassinated in Prague, not Vienna.[27] Compared with the Germans, the Austrians may have behaved like an occupied people at times; compared with the Czechs, they did not.

One rough, quantitative estimate of the degree of Austrian commitment to the objectives of Nazi policy can be made on the basis of the casualties different countries sustained in World War II. Table 15 illustrates that, compared with other successor states of the Dual Monarchy, Austria was strongly committed to help achieve German objectives. The relative share of fatal military casualties (indicating the degree of commitment) was two to three times as high as for the other four states, and the relative number of civilian deaths (indicating the degree of resistance and actual fighting) was among the lowest. Compared with other states in central and eastern Europe, Austria fought more in World War II and suffered less under German occupation.

How do these Austrian figures compare with those for Germany? The ratio of Austrian to German war dead, which was 15 percent in World War I, fell to 10 percent in World War II.[28] Even though the 10 percent figure approximates the ratio of the two population totals, there occurred, then, an appreciable reduction in Austria's commitment to help reestablish a German-Austrian hegemony over central and eastern Europe.

---

berichten des Sicherheitsdienstes der SS, 1939-1944 (Neuwied: Luchterhand, 1965). Hermann Graml et al., *The German Resistance to Hitler* (Berkeley: University of California Press, 1970).

27. Vojtech Mastny, *The Czechs under Nazi Rule* (New York: Columbia University Press, 1971), pp. 110-111, 179, 207. The Nazis fully appreciated the difference between the Czech and Austrian resistance. In contrast to the Austrians, the Czechs were not admitted to military service in the German army.

28. Sources are the same as for Table 16.

TABLE 15. Casualties Sustained by Five Countries in World War II (in percentages)

	Armed Forces Dead as Percent of Population		Civilian Dead as Percent of Population
Austria	0.03[a]	Yugoslavia	0.09
Yugoslavia	0.02	Hungary	0.03
Hungary	0.02	Roumania	0.01
Roumania	0.01	Czechoslovakia	0.01
Czechoslovakia	0.01	Austria	0.01

Source: Helmut Arntz, "Die Menschenverluste im Zweiten Weltkrieg," *Bilanz des Zweiten Weltkrieges: Erkenntnisse und Verpflichtungen für die Zukunft* (Oldenburg: Stalling, 1953), p. 445.
[a]This figure represents a minimum estimate.

That finding is confirmed further if we disaggregate the overall casualty figures as is done in Table 16. The two ratios presented in this table—dead/injured and injured/prisoner—might be regarded as rough indicators of commitment: the higher the value of the ratio, the higher the degree of commitment. For both sets, the Austrian figures are significantly below the German ones (column four). Thus, the overall casualty figures as well as their breakdown into more specific categories point to the same conclusion. The Austrians appear to have been less committed to the establishment of a German-Austrian hegemony over Europe than the Germans.

On the basis of these figures it appears, then, that the structural pattern was neither conquest by coercion nor conquest by consent. It was, rather, a combination of coercion and consent in response to Austria's past experiences of autonomy and integration. In the eight years in which it appeared to be most complete, Austro-German political integration remained partial.

For only 8 of its 800 years' history was Austria fully united with Germany—under Nazi rule. Through the Anschluss, Hitler tried to force into one mold a heterogeneous set of

TABLE 16. Austrian and German Casualties in World War II

(1) Degree of Commitment as Indicated by Ratio	(2) Austria	(3) Germany	(4) Austria as Percent of Germany
Military dead/ civilian and military injured	1.25	1.87	67
Civilian and military injured/ military taken prisoner	0.63	1.15	55

Sources: Austrian figures: Wolfgang Oberleitner, *Politisches Handbuch der Republik Österreich, 1945-1960* (Vienna: Guardaval, 1960), pp. 84-85.
German figures: Arntz, "Menschenverluste im Zweiten Weltkrieg," p. 443. Hans Sperling, "Deutsche Bevölkerungsbilanz des Zweiten Weltkrieges: Einführung und Zusammenfassung," *Wirtschaft und Statistik*, N.F. VIII, 10 (1956), p. 494.

processes which had left the two countries above the level of indifference and below the level of unification since 1815. The Nazi policy of extending German rule over all of Europe was much more ambitious than what either Metternich or any of his successors had ever attempted to achieve in the name of Austria. World War II offered the Austrians a second chance to achieve what they had not succeeded in securing during World War I: the cementing of a strong position in central Europe. Reliance on Germany's formidable capital resources and military potential gave the attempt some chance of success at the outset. The habit of thinking of Austria's identity in large spatial terms made it attractive. As my data reveal, the Austrians fought hard for the achievement of this tempting objective. But they did not fight as hard as the Germans.

Austria's limited participation in Germany's imperialist venture was doomed by the twin factors that had made Austria's previous attempts in this direction falter: overcommitment abroad and neglect at home. An examination of the structural pattern, thus, supports my previous analysis of the other four patterns of Austro-German relations. The mixture of coercion and consent was a reflection of past experiences. Among those experiences autonomy had figured prominently. Thus, elements of disjoined partnership were traceable also in the structural pattern.

VIII

PLURALISTIC PATTERN
(1945-1970)

A CENTRAL problem of the postwar period—and the problem which motivated this research in the first place—is the German Question. Can a smaller culturally assimilated Austrian state withstand the magnetism of a larger and more dynamic West German one? Is the political fragmentation of this part of central Europe here to stay? The pluralistic pattern answers these questions in the affirmative, and the mode of explanation employed throughout this book helps in understanding why. As was true of the interwar years, the structure of the international system after 1945 did not permit a far-reaching policy coordination between Austria and Germany. But this surface similarity conceals that the sixth pattern is marked by three different features diametrically opposed to the voluntaristic one of the interwar period. The balance between standardization and differentiation, between community and society, points not to integration but autonomy. The structure of economic rewards associated with autonomy is positive instead of negative. And the political strategies of all major actors in Austrian politics are served by an Austria politically autonomous from West Germany instead of integrated with it. Nonpolitical and political variables, thus, reinforce each other in pointing to autonomy, not integration—to a relationship, in short, of disjoined partnership.

COMMUNITY AND SOCIETY: COPRESSURES

Just as its preference for political integration during the voluntaristic pattern, so Austria's choice of autonomy during the pluralistic pattern is grounded in a distinct relationship between community and society. That relationship is revealed in mass behavior and attitudes, which provide the context in which political actors pursue their competing strategies. The data suggest that since 1945 the behavioral and attitudinal changes of the Austrian public moved in parallel directions and created copressures as the precondition of political autonomy characteristic of the pluralistic pattern.

Behavioral Disintegration The nationalization of the Austrian banking sector and much of the country's heavy industry after 1945 sharply reduced the level and scope of foreign capital. Yet the West German share in the total foreign capital invested in Austria rose from 7 percent in 1959, to 10 percent in 1962, to 28 percent in 1969.[1] Compared with the interwar years, the role of West German capital in Austria thus seems to have become more important. Sharp increases are observable also in the flow of Austro-West German trade as a second indicator of social transactions. The West German share in Austria's total imports increased from 22 percent in 1952, to 43 percent in 1961, to 41 percent in 1969; the corresponding figures for Austria's export trade were 20, 27, and 24 percent.[2] Only in the 1960s,

---

1. Eckard P. Imhof, "Ausländische Investitionen in Österreich im Rahmen eines internationalen Vergleichs unter besonderer Berücksichtigung der Direktinvestitionen" (unpub. diss., University of Vienna, 1960), pp. 49, 55. Wiener Arbeiterkammer, *Das Eigentum an den Österreichischen Kapitalgesellschaften* (Vienna: Vorwärts Verlag, 1962), pp. 6, 20. Oskar Grünwald and Ferdinand Lacina, *Auslandskapital in der Österreichischen Wirtschaft* (Vienna: Europa Verlag, 1971), p. 62. It should be noted that these figures overstate somewhat the actual involvement of West German capital in Austrian industry especially in the late 1960s, because a large part of West German capital was invested in limited liability companies not directly engaged in production but interested in sales promotion in Austria.
2. *Statistisches Handbuch für die Republik Österreich*, N.F., IV (1953), p. 118; XIII (1962), p. 98; XXI (1970), pp. 182-183. A general discussion of Austrian trade is given in Gerhard Frey, "Die Handelsverflechtung Ös-

then, has the expansion of Austro-West German trade stopped at a level that far exceeds corresponding figures for the interwar years.

The relative number of migrants is a third indicator of Austro-German transactions. Before 1945 the slogan of Austrians moving to Germany was *heim ins Reich* (return to the German Empire); after 1945 it became *reich ins Heim* (rich at home).[3] The great magnetism of the West German economy since 1945 caused a sizable and increasing flow of labor from Austria to West Germany. In the late 1960s the net loss of Austrians moving to the Federal Republic was estimated as high as 10,000 a year.[4] The relative number of West Germans among all foreigners residing in Austria rose at the same time from 15 percent in 1934 to 42 percent in 1961 before declining again to 27 percent in 1971.[5] These figures far exceed the level of Austro-German transactions attained during the interwar years.

The relative number of tourists traveling between the two countries is a fourth and final indicator of social transactions. The number of West German tourists in Austria has increased dramatically since 1945. It rose from 38 percent in 1952, to 65 percent in 1961 before leveling off at about 64 percent in 1971. The relative number of Austrian tourists in West Germany, on the other hand, has remained at a constant 5 percent throughout the postwar period.[6] The evidence presented so far points, then,

---

terreichs mit Deutschland" (unpub. diss., University of Graz, 1960); also see Egon Matzner, *Trade between East and West: The Case of Austria* (Stockholm: Almqvist and Wiksell, 1970), pp. 18-44.
3. Andreas Kirschhofer-Bozenhardt, "Die Wohlstandslegion: Materialsammlung für die Fernsehdokumentation 'Österreicher in der Bundesrepublik' " (MS, Allensbach, West Germany, 1970).
4. *Ibid.*, p. 27. The relative share of Austrians among all foreigners in West Germany has, however, decreased simply because there are now more than two million foreign workers in the Federal Republic.
5. Bundesamt für Statistik, "Die Ergebnisse der Österreichischen Volkszählung vom 22. März 1934," *Statistik des Bundesstaates Österreich*, II, 20. Österreichisches Statistisches Zentralamt, *Volkszählungsergebnisse, 1961*, XIII, 68. *Beiträge zur Österreichischen Statistik*, 309/1 (1971), p. 9; and 309/15 (1974), p. 13.
6. *Statistisches Handbuch*, N.F., IV (1953), pp. 149-150; XIII (1962), pp. 147-148; XIX (1968), p. 234. *Statistisches Jahrbuch für die Bundesrepublik Deutschland, 1955*, p. 350; *1964*, p. 307; *1969*, p. 268.

to general increases in Austro–West German transactions, which were much stronger in the 1950s than the 1960s.

Transactions lead to differentiation, communications to standardization. Table 17 shows that the relative amount of attention Austria has paid to events in the Bonn Republic has declined considerably. Since 1945 Austrian attention has shifted decisively to a world of independent and interdependent states. Compared with the interwar years, Austria's attention to extra-European affairs more than trebled. This reorientation came at the expense of the two traditional foci of attention, the successor states to the Dual Monarchy and Germany. Austrian attention to both areas was less than one-half of what it had been during the interwar period. West Germany no longer commanded the interest and respect it had enjoyed in Austrian eyes during the interwar years, and the absence of any perceived need for coordination of Austrian policies with those of the Federal Republic helped to accentuate the drop in attention.

Other measures also point to the decline or stagnation of Austro–West German communications between 1952 and 1969. But there existed a difference between considerable increases in Austro–West German communication flows during the 1950s and stagnation and decline during the 1960s. The West German share of the foreign students in Austria, for example, rose from 23 percent in 1951 to 34 percent in 1961; in 1969 that figure was substantially unchanged.[7] Changes in the sum of personal mail, telegrams, and telephone calls also point in the same direction. Between 1952 and 1961 the West German share of the total number of Austrian messages received increased from 27 to 39 percent; but by 1969 that figure had declined again to the 1952 level (29 percent). The corresponding figures for Austrian messages sent to West Germany in these three years were 44, 55, and 37 percent, respectively.[8]

---

7. *Statistisches Handbuch*, N.F., III (1952), pp. 258-259; XIII (1962), pp. 286-287; XX (1969), pp. 368, 372.
8. Universal Postal Union, *Statistique des Expéditions dans le Service Postal International, 1952* and *1961; idem, Statistique des Services Postaux, 1969*; letter from the German Ministry for Postal Affairs, February 1973; Bundesministerium für Verkehr, *Geschäftsbericht, 1952, 1961, 1969; United*

TABLE 17. Relative Distribution of Austrian Attention: Average Foreign News Coverage in Two Austrian Papers, 1933-1969 (in percentages)[a]

	1933-1938	1946-1955	1958-1969
Germany	25	14	10
Northern Europe[b]	9	11	7
Western Europe[c]	15	12	15
Eastern Europe[d]	5	4	7
Southern Europe[e]	12	8	12
Successor States[f]	21	16	8
Rest of world	13	34	41

Sources: *Wiener Zeitung; Presse.*
[a]The method of calculation is explained in Chapter III, fn. 28. Because of rounding off, percentages do not always add to 100.
[b]Scandinavia and Britain
[c]France, Benelux, and Switzerland
[d]Russia, Poland, and East Germany
[e]Spain, Portugal, Italy, and Greece
[f]Czechoslovakia, Hungary, Roumania, Yugoslavia, Bulgaria, and Albania

The large percentage increases in Austro–West German interdependence along the social and cultural dimensions in the 1950s and a flattening of all curves in the 1960s appear to have been the result of two sets of conditions, one related to Austria and West Germany in particular, the other to changes in the European state system in general. First, Austria's experience of unification with Germany between 1938 and 1945, brief though it was, greatly enlarged both transactions and communications. After the restoration of the channel capacities destroyed in World War II, transactions and communications flows were, therefore, bound to increase greatly in the 1950s. But changes in Europe were also important. The division between eastern and western

---

Nations Statistical Yearbook, 1954, 1963, 1970; International Telecommunications Union, *General Telegraph Statistics,* 1952, 1961; *General Telephone Statistics,* 1952, 1961; *Telecommunications Statistics,* 1969.

Europe, which closed Austria off from the other successor states to the Dual Monarchy as its traditional partners for communications and transactions, led to an initial transfer of excess capacities to Austro–West German relations in the 1950s. But the disparate experience of Austria and West Germany in the evolving blocs inside western Europe during the 1960s helped to arrest and, at least in part, to reverse the trend of the previous decade.

The probability of political autonomy is affected by the balance between community and standardization, on the one hand, and society and differentiation, on the other. Changes in different indicators of social transactions and cultural communications since 1945 suggest that the erosion of the gains of the 1950s since 1961 was stronger for cultural communications than for social transactions. The behavioral indicators of community and society thus point to a process of relative disintegration of the Austrian and West German mass publics since 1945.

Attitudinal Disintegration Autonomy is affected also by attitudinal measures of community and society. Social integration is measured by changes in evaluations, cultural integration by changes in identifications. Table 18 summarizes the results of the content analysis of government speeches and New Year's Eve editorials for the pluralistic pattern. It shows that a sharp increase occurred in Austria's positive evaluations of West Germany.

This finding is supported by public opinion polls available for the postwar period. When asked in 1947 to identify the foreign country they liked most, only 16 percent of the Viennese respondents mentioned Germany. Between 1959 and 1970, on the other hand, between 45 and 50 percent of national samples of Austrians mentioned the Federal Republic, more than twice the number preferring any other country.[9]

9. Headquarters, United States Forces in Austria, Information Service Branch, APO 777, U. S. Army, *Bericht Nr. 11* (Vienna: October 20, 1947), p. 2. Österreichisches Meinungs- und Marktforschungsinstitut, *Pressedienst*, Nr. 47 (Vienna: November 26, 1959), p. 1. Manfred Koch, *Das Deutschlandbild im Ausland* (Bad Godesberg: Inter Nationes, 1969), p. 25. Sozialwissenschaftliche Studiengesellschaft, "Statistische Auswertung des

TABLE 18. Evaluation of Germany in Government Speeches and Newspaper Editorials in Austria, 1946-1970[a]

	(1)	(2)	(3)			(4)	(5)	(6)		
	No. of Government Speeches	Government Evaltns.: Positive−Negative/Positive+Negative	Government Evaluations (in percent)			No. of Press Editorials	Press Evaltns.: Positive−Negative/Positive+Negative	Press Evaluations (in percent)		
			Pos.	Neu.	Neg.			Pos.	Neu.	Neg.
1946-55	11	−1.00	−	−	73	19	−0.52	5	16	16
1956-70	10	0.30	20	20	10	20	1.00	5	15	0

[a]The method of calculation is explained in Chapter V, fn. 11.

Mutual identification provides the attitudinal basis of community. Among the more than 1,500 references to a collective Austrian identity that can be counted in the major government speeches since 1945, one cannot find one German one. More slowly the Austrian people have also come to identify themselves as Austrian rather than German since 1945. These changes are summarized in Table 19. The data in this table document the assimilation of Austrian public opinion into an overarching consensus on the question of an Austrian identity. By 1970, the deep schisms that divided the Austrians in 1956 had become minor differences. An overwhelming majority identified themselves as a distinct group no longer tied to the German people. Furthermore, Table 19 shows also that the process advanced further and faster among those groups of Austrian society dominant in politics. As is shown in columns three and six, the greatest amount of attitude change occurred among what might be called the centers of Austrian society and politics, the young, the better educated, and the upper classes. By this evidence, then, the decline in mutual identification with West Germany became cemented into the very structure of Austrian society. Attitudinal disintegration between Austria and West Germany along this cultural dimensin coincided with the growth of the commitment of the Austrians to their own new nation.[10]

Behavior and Attitudes: Copressures The probability of autonomy is affected by the balance between community and society. The results of an analysis of the pluralistic pattern of Austro–West German relations point to two mutually consistent conclusions. After 1945 social transactions between Austria and West

---

Fragebogens Nr. 42" (MS, Vienna, 1965). Österreichisches Gallup-Institut, "Nationalitätsbewusstsein der Österreicher" (MS, Vienna, April-May 1970).

10. This process is analyzed at greater length in William T. Bluhm, *Building an Austrian Nation: The Political Integration of a Western State* (New Haven: Yale University Press, 1973), pp. 177-207, 220-241. See also Peter J. Katzenstein, "The Last Old Nation: Austrian National Consciousness since 1945," Paper prepared for presentation at the 1975 annual meeting of the American Political Science Association, San Francisco, September 2-5.

TABLE 19. The Growth of Austrian Self-Identification, 1956-1970 (in percentages)

	(1)	(2)	(3)	(4)	(5)	(6)	(7)	(8)
	Austria Is a Nation			Austria Is Not a Nation			Undecided	
	1956	1970[b]	Net Shift	1956	1970	Net Shift	1956	1970
Total	49	82	33	46	8	38	5	10
Age								
Under 30[a]	44	87	43	51	3	48	5	10
30-50	48	79	31	48	15	33	4	6
Over 50	65	83	18	26	6	20	9	11
Education								
High-School	40	86	46	58	10	48	2	4
10th Grade-Elem.	52	82	30	42	8	34	6	10
Occupation								
Professional	32	82	50	61	10	51	7	8
White collar	48	89	41	48	9	39	4	2
Farmers	56	74	18	37	4	33	7	22
Blue collar	62	79	17	32	12	20	6	9
Pensioners	n.a.	83		n.a.	5		n.a.	12

Sources: Dr. Walter Fessel (ed.), *Querschnitte der öffentlichen Meinung*, 15-16 (May 8, 1956), pp. 1-2. Gallup-Institut, "Nationalitätsbewusstsein," pp. 14-15.

[a]The age brackets for the 1956 figures are 18-39, 40-59, and over 60.

[b]In the 1970 poll, a distinction was made between "Austria is a nation" and "Austria is slowly becoming a nation"; both response categories were added for the purpose of this analysis. The figures are, therefore, slightly inflated estimates of the present consensus on an Austrian nation.

Germany became relatively more important than cultural communications. The same is true of attitudes. Positive evaluations of West Germany increased with a simultaneous decline in mutual identifications. Multiple interlocking copressures toward the relative disintegration of Austrian and West German mass publics point to the expansion of political autonomy.

ECONOMIC REWARDS:
PROSPERITY AND POLITICAL AUTONOMY

The probability of autonomy is affected by the structure of economic rewards and reward perceptions. The more rewards offered by national economic and political structures, the higher the probability of autonomy. Throughout the pluralistic pattern of Austro-West German relations, the Second Republic enjoyed a spectacular economic recovery from the stagnation obtained in the interwar period and the destruction that occurred in World War II. Economic pressures toward unification with West Germany were absent from all parts of Austrian society.

Inflation and unemployment had constantly bedeviled the economic viability of the First Republic. At the outset the problems of the Second Republic were no less serious than those of the First, but its capabilities to deal with them successfully were much greater.[11] German occupation had significantly enlarged Austria's industrial sector. The production capacities of its heavy and chemical industries and its extractive industry (mining and oil) were either newly created or greatly expanded between 1938 and 1945. Geared to the needs of the German war economy, Austria's new industrial base was too large for the domestic market and provided an indispensable ingredient for the export drive after the end of World War II. Austria's new endowment with German capital is reflected in the industrial statistics of the immediate postwar period. Despite large-scale destruction, industrial output reached 92 percent of the prewar level as early as 1948, compared with West Germany's 52

---

11. Recent analyses of the Second Republic include Bluhm, *Building an Austrian Nation*; Kurt Steiner, *Politics in Austria* (Boston: Little, Brown, 1972); Karl Gutkas, Alois Brusatti, and Erika Weinzierl, *Österreich, 1945-1970* (Vienna: Österreichischer Bundesverlag, 1970); Karl-Heinz Nassmacher, *Das Österreichische Regierungssystem: Grosse Koalition oder alternierende Regierung?* (Cologne: Westdeutscher Verlag, 1968). Alexander Vodopivec, *Der verspielte Ballhausplatz: Vom schwarzen zum roten Österreich* (Vienna: Molden, 1970); Karl Stadler, *Austria* (London: Bonn, 1971); Anton Pelinka and Manfried Welan, *Demokratie und Verfassung in Österreich* (Vienna: Europa Verlag, 1971). Rodney P. Stiefbold, "Segmented Pluralism and Consociational Democracy in Austria: Problems of Political Stability and Change," in Martin O. Heisler (ed.), *Politics in Europe: Structures and Processes in some Postindustrial Democracies* (New York: David McKay, 1974), pp. 117-177.

percent.[12] Since the Austrian government had nationalized much of industry and all banks, this increase in economic capacity greatly strengthened the government. Directly or indirectly it controls about three-quarters of Austrian industry today, a proportion higher than in any other western European state.[13]

Foreign aid, given at the barest minimum after World War I, flowed freely into Austria after World War II. Austria received about 1.4 billion dollars of the funds of the European Recovery Program after 1945, almost ten times as much per capita as West Germany and enough to offset a very substantial part of the monetary loss the country incurred because of World War II.[14]

The economy was, then, much better equipped to deal with problems arising from reparation payments and preferential trade agreements concluded with the Soviet Union, and with the problems of inflation and unemployment. The dramatic increase in the economic capacity of the Second Republic is reflected in the growth rates of the Austrian economy. Between 1924 and 1937, per capita gross national product, measured in real terms, stagnated; between 1948 and 1966 it increased by a factor of three.[15]

This strong economic performance of the Second Republic shaped reward perceptions. In 1959, 87 percent of the citizenry evaluated positively the preceding decade, and the answers given largely referred to the country's growing economic prosperity.[16] The increasing economic attachment of the Austrians to the Second Republic is reflected clearly in the figures presented in Table 20.

---

12. Kurt W. Rothschild, "Wurzeln und Triebkräfte der Entwicklung der Österreichischen Wirtschaftsstruktur," in Wilhelm Weber (ed.), *Österreichs Wirtschaftsstruktur gestern, heute, morgen* (Berlin: Duncker, 1961), I, 35.
13. Friedrich Thalmann, "Die Wirtschaft in Österreich," in Heinrich Benedikt (ed.), *Geschichte der Republik Österreich* (Munich: Oldenbourg, 1954), p. 520.
14. Gustav Otruba, *Österreichs Wirtschaft im 20. Jahrhundert* (Vienna: Bundesverlag, 1968), p. 39.
15. *Ibid.*, p. 83.
16. Österreichisches Meinungs- und Marktforschungsinstitut, *Pressedienst*, Nr. 51 (December 22, 1959), p. 1.

TABLE 20. The Growth of Austrian Economic Attachment to the Second Republic (in percentages)

	1956[a]	1959	1964	1970[b]
Before 1918	19	9	5	4
1918-1938	34	8	3	3
1939-1945	16	6	5	1
Since 1945	35	74	83	92
Undecided	8	3	4	—

Sources: Dr. Walter Fessel (ed.), *Querschnitte*, 13 (March 13, 1956), p. 15; Österreichisches Meinungs- und Marktforschungsinstitut, *Pressedienst*, Nr. 33 (August 20, 1959), p. 1; Sozialwissenschaftliche Studiengesellschaft, "Statistische Auswertung des Testfragebogens Nr. 36" (MS, Vienna, 1964), p. 11. Gallup-Institut, "Nationalitätsbewusstsein," p. 19.

[a]The percentages add to more than 100 percent since respondents in some instances indicated different time ranges.
[b]There was no undecided category in the 1970 poll.

Economic growth and prosperity also helped to bridge the regional, social, and political cleavages that had made the different fragments of the First Republic favor a sacrifice of autonomy. Demographic changes and migration reduced the concentration of the population in the eastern part of the country and accelerated the shift of the labor force from the primary and secondary to the tertiary sector of the economy.[17] Because of both developments, traditional regional and social cleavages in Austrian society diminished after 1945.

At the elite level it was not change but its absence that produced a similar result. Political cleavages were narrowed not by social change but by an ideological reorientation. In contrast to the Federal Republic, the continuity of Austria's political elite was striking. In 1956, 55 percent of the Socialists (SPÖ) in Parliament and 43 percent of the delegates of the successor of the

17. Hans Seidel, Felix Butschek, Anton Kausel, *Die regionale Dynamik der Österreichischen Wirtschaft* (Vienna: Österreichisches Institut für Wirtschaftsforschung, 1966).

Pluralistic Pattern (1945-1970) 189

Christian Socials, the Peoples Party (ÖVP), had been politically active before 1934. Only the political leaders of the Free Party (FPÖ), the inheritors of the nationalistic camp which was more tainted with the experience of Nazism, were significantly younger and less experienced in politics.[18] Elite circulation in the Second Republic was low, which contributed to the homogeneity and stability of Austria's political structures.

Elite stability was reinforced by ideological change. Virtually the entire political elite that returned to Austrian political life from concentration camps, prisons, exile, and private life had by 1945 discovered that they had more in common with their fellow Austrians of opposing political convictions than with the Germans. The condition of relative economic abundance prevailing in the Second Republic only reinforced that feeling. The continuing, if abating, vertical division of Austrian society into different political camps was countered by the horizontal bracket provided by a political elite with a more consensual orientation. Because of economic and ideological factors, the dynamics of the Austrian political system changed from centrifugal in the First Republic to centripetal in the Second.[19]

Scarcity marked the voluntaristic and abundance the pluralistic patterns. The striking difference between the two is illustrated by the sharp drop in the Austrians' desire to leave

18. Norbert Freytag, "Die Struktur des Österreichischen Nationalrates in der Gegenwart" (unpub. diss., University of Vienna, 1958), pp. 114-115, 117. See also the discussions in Hans Heinz Fabris, "Demokratische Auswahl: Führungsschichten im Parteienstaat am Beispiel der Zweiten Republik, 1945-1967" (unpub. diss., University of Salzburg, 1968). Peter Gerlich and Helmut Kramer, *Abgeordnete in der Parteiendemokratie* (Vienna: Verlag für Geschichte und Politik, 1969).
19. For an application of the concept of consociational democracy to the Austrian case see Steiner, *Politics in Austria*, pp. 409-426. See also Eric A. Nordlinger, *Conflict Regulation in Divided Societies*, Occasional Papers in International Affairs, Number 29, Harvard University, Center for International Affairs, January 1972. G. Bingham Powell, Jr., *Social Fragmentation and Political Hostility: An Austrian Case Study* (Stanford: Stanford University Press, 1970). Rodney P. Stiefbold, "Elite-Mass Opinion Structure and Communication Flow in a Consociational Democracy (Austria)" (paper presented to the meeting of the American Political Science Association, Washington, D.C., 1968).

home. During the sixth pattern of Austro-German relations, the average annual number of emigrants dropped to one-half of what it had been during the fourth, from 4,000 to 2,000. But change was even more dramatic with regard to the Austrians' preference to become German. The ratio between the number of Germans naturalized in Austria over the number of Austrians expatriated to Germany shifted from 0.69 for the years 1919–1936 to 624.00 for the years 1946–1968.[20] Judging by these figures, autonomy was favored by a change amounting to several orders of magnitude.

POLITICAL REWARDS:
AUTONOMY AND INTEGRATION

Political autonomy is the result of nonpolitical and political variables. In sharp contrast to the interwar years, in the pluralistic pattern of Austro—West German relations both the balance between community and society and the structure of economic rewards pointed to political autonomy as the expected outcome. Analysis reveals that the decay of the partial political community that had existed between Austria and Germany occurred rapidly. After 1945 all major actors in Austrian politics were for the first time in agreement with the principle and practice of autonomy.

As had been true of the interwar years, the international system directly affected Austro–West German relations. While international forces accentuated the similar experiences of Austria and Germany as maligned and defeated countries after 1919, they provided dissimilar streams of political experience after 1945. Unlike the Federal Republic, Austria enjoyed the status of a country occupied by rather than allied with Nazi Germany.[21] Unlike Berlin, Vienna remained an undivided

---

20. *Beiträge zur Statistik der Republik Österreich*, VIII (1923), pp. 139-140. *Statistisches Handbuch für die Republik Österreich*, XIII (1932). *Statistisches Jahrbuch für Österreich, 1938. Statistisches Handbuch für die Republik Österreich*, N. F., VI-XX (1955-1969).
21. For a general discussion, see William B. Bader, *Austria between East and West* (Stanford: Stanford University Press, 1966). Kurt Waldheim, *Der Österreichische Weg* (Vienna: Molden, 1971). William Lloyd Stearman,

capital in which free political activity was permitted. Unlike the Federal Republic, Austria had had the experience of Soviet troops stationed on Austrian territory. And unlike West Germany, Austria succeeded in 1955 in ridding herself of all occupation forces and reestablishing an independent, united, and neutral Austria. While the Federal Republic pursued a policy of western integration and a policy of strength in the hope of eventual reunification with East Germany, Austria jealously guarded its precious new neutrality. The difference in the political experiences and objectives of the Austrian and West German governments constituted an important brick in the edifice of Austria's political autonomy.

These dissimilar conditions and political experiences left their traces on the public mind. After 1945 the war experience that Austria had shared with Germany was no longer perceived as a common responsibility. More than two-thirds of the Austrian respondents denied in 1947 that Austria—in contrast with the Federal Republic—had to share in the guilt for World War II.[22] And because the problems in Austria were so pressing, the predicaments of Berlin did not meet with any special sympathy in Austria in the late 1940s.[23]

Furthermore, political conditions inside Austria strongly supported the country's new autonomy. The party whose commitment to an independent and neutral Austria appeared to be most in doubt after World War II, the FPÖ as inheritor of the nationalist camp in Austrian politics, gradually lost support, from 12 percent of the popular vote in 1949 to 6 percent in 1971.[24]

But the two major parties, the ÖVP and the SPÖ, underwent equally important changes without a corresponding erosion in

---

The Soviet Union and the Occupation of Austria: An Analysis of Soviet Policy in Austria, 1945-1955 (Bonn: Siegler, 1961).

22. Headquarters United States Forces in Austria, Information Service Branch, *Bericht Nr. 7* (May 17, 1947), p. 11.
23. Headquarters, *Bericht Nr. 54* (June 27, 1948), pp. 3-4. Meinrad Peterlik, "Republik und Tradition," in Erhard Busek and Meinrad Peterlik (eds.), *Die unvollendete Republik* (Vienna: Verlag für Geschichte und Politik, 1968), p. 114.
24. *Statistisches Handbuch*, N. F., XXII (1971), p. 446.

their electoral base. During the interwar years their behavior in Austrian politics and in particular their stand on the most vital political issue of the day, the Anschluss, was heavily influenced by changes in the political constellation in Germany. In many instances one could have predicted Austrian political affairs quite accurately by studying German politics. After 1945 that was no longer possible. The mutual sensitivity of the two political systems decreased sharply, and in their new encapsulation the Austrian parties strengthened Austria's autonomy. For most of the postwar period the Austrian and West German political systems responded to different political needs. In Austria the two large parties formed a coalition government until 1966, the very year the West Germans, for the first time since 1949, adopted that political formula. Domestic political calculations in both countries, thus, were out of phase, and there was never any ground for political coalitions across borders.

Austria's political autonomy was the result of both the low effectiveness and the low extent of Austro–West German political coordination. This is partly revealed by the low and declining proportion of diplomatic personnel that the two partner countries assigned to one another after 1945. In 1969 only 3 percent of Austria's diplomats were stationed in the Federal Republic, as compared with 9 percent in 1936; and the share of the West Germans in the total number of foreign diplomats accredited in Vienna declined from 6 percent in 1936 to 2 percent in 1969.[25]

Throughout the sixth pattern Austria's political autonomy is best understood by looking at the absence of any significant attempts to find objectives that might merit political coordination with West Germany. Political issues that had been prominent in the past, such as the policy of assimilation during the interwar years, remained fossils of Austria's past, devoid of political content.[26] The one important economic problem stemming from the nationalization of the "German Property" in

25. *Österreichischer Amtskalender für das Jahr 1936*, pp. 45-47, 126-128; *1969*, pp. 86-96, 116-120.
26. See, for example, Kurt L. Shell, *The Transformation of Austrian Socialism* (Albany: State University of New York Press; 1962), pp. 182-183, 230.

Austria after 1945 was resolved with relative ease in 1957. And occasional slips of the West Germans not yet accustomed to think of the Austrians as a people in their own right provided political issues that barely lasted a week.[27]

But if the past failed to provide Austria and Germany with common political objectives, so do the present and future. The modernization of antiquated Austrian practices, once achieved through imitation of Germany, now occurs in response to pressures from the international environment. Austria's old judicial arrangements, for example, are modified not by policies implemented in West Germany but by rulings of the European Court of Justice.[28] As for the future, no bilateral political objectives appear on the horizon that might offer Austria and West Germany once again an opportunity for effective policy coordination. The important political objectives have either been renationalized, that is, reduced to the jurisdictional authority of the Austrian government, or they have been internationalized beyond the bilateral level on which Austro-German policy coordination took place during the interwar years.

The recurrent bankruptcy of the attempts to secure or reestablish an Austro-German hegemony over central and eastern Europe left the Austrians with a businesslike efficiency in dealing with outstanding debit items after 1945. When the balance sheet with Germany was cleared, there were simply no political objectives that merited joint action. The depoliticization of Austro–West German relations is a strong guarantor of Austria's political autonomy.

But this conclusion needs modification. Although Austria desires more autonomy today than it did during the interwar period, long previous experience with partial sacrifices of autonomy could be expected to shape, in part, Austrian political practices today. As had been true of the first five patterns, in the sixth, competing strategies of integration and autonomy were

---

27. One example is described in *Keesing's Contemporary Archives*, IX, 2 (November 20-27, 1954), p. 13,896B.
28. Scott N. Wolfe, "The European Court of Justice" (MS, Cambridge, Mass., 1972).

used as instruments for shaping the distribution of political power in Austrian politics. That political process was acted out, however, in the context of Austria's relations not with West Germany but with a western Europe undergoing different forms of economic and political integration. Austria's problem of autonomy, in short, was seen not in terms of West Germany but of Europe.

Austrian actors and analysis alike have done the obvious in interpreting the political debate on Austria's role in European integration in terms of that country's uncertain national past. Possible arrangements with the European Economic Community (EEC) were often regarded as unification with Germany in disguise (*kachierter Anschluss*).[29] The continuation of established modes of thinking, of traditional hopes and fears, was a major source of the appeal of European integration especially for the (German) national camp in Austrian politics. But with the passing of time and a firmer implantation of an Austrian self-identification, that appeal gradually weakened. By the late 1960s, even the supporters of the FPÖ had become largely immune to the concealed appeal of German nationalism on this particular issue.[30]

In the face of widespread public indifference to the issue of Austria's relation to the European integration process, the intensity of conflict among Austria's political elites is striking. This was, in fact, the only issue in postwar Austria that led to an ideologically significant divergence between the ÖVP and the SPÖ, the two large parties in Austria.[31] Existing accounts of the

29. The important literature on this topic includes Friedrich Wlatnig, *Krise der Integration: Europa und Österreich* (Vienna: Europa Verlag, 1967); Wilhelm Weber and Dieter Bös, *Ökonomische Probleme eines Vertrages zwischen Österreich und EWG* (Vienna: Jupiter, 1966); Felix Butschek (ed.), *EWG und die Folgen: Die Auswirkungen eines Abkommens zwischen Österreich und der Europäischen Wirtschaftsgemeinschaft* (Vienna: Molden, 1966); Bundesministerium für Handel und Wierderaufbau, *Zehn Jahre Österreichische Integrationspolitik, 1956-1966* (Vienna: Staatsdruckerei, 1966); *Österreichische Integrationspolitik, 1956-1966* (Vienna: Staatsdruckerei, 1966); Otto Wanke (ed.), *Integrationsgeschehen im Überblick* (Vienna: Verlag des Österreichischen Gewerkschaftsbundes, n.d.).
30. Institut für Marktforschung Dr. Walter Fessel, "Europa Studie, 1967/1968," courtesy of Handelsministerium.
31. Rodney Stiefbold, "Elite-Mass Opinion Structure," p. 9.

consensus in Austrian politics since 1945 have failed so far to give a convincing explanation of why on this one issue, the issue of autonomy or integration, elite conflict was so prominent. My analysis of the first five patterns points to the interpenetration of domestic and foreign policy as the main reason. In contrast to the previous patterns, the partial sacrifice of autonomy no longer involved Germany but Europe as the potential partner. But as had been true before, different political actors adopted contrasting strategies on the issue of autonomy or integration because it served their different political needs at home.

Although this conflict was intense, it was based on one premise shared by all three parties in Austria, the unwillingness to sacrifice Austria's neutrality for full integration. But neutrality meant different things to different political actors. The FPÖ interpreted it strictly in legal, the ÖVP in military, the SPÖ in broader political terms. These different conceptions, and with them the different degrees of autonomy deemed desirable, were reflected in the contrasting political stances adopted on the issue of European integration by Austria's two largest parties.

Since the late 1950s the ÖVP has been a stronger advocate of a policy of partial integration than has the SPÖ. The primary justification given for this policy was economic. If Austria was to maintain economic prosperity, or so the argument ran, and with it a viable foundation for neutrality, it had no choice but to join a prosperous and dynamic western Europe.[32] But in the demonstrable absence of virtually any economic contribution of western European integration to Austrian economic prosperity, other considerations as well shaped the ÖVP's preference for partial integration; and those considerations were primarily geared to domestic politics.[33]

32. See, for example, the remarks of the ÖVP minister in charge of negotiating an agreement between Austria and the EEC. Fritz Bock, "Wirtschaftsintegration als innenpolitisches Problem," *Österreichische Monatshefte*, XXIII, 3 (March 1967), pp. 11-13. Fritz Bock, "Integrationspolitik zwischen heute und morgen," *Österreichische Monatshefte*, XXII, 7-8 (1966), pp. 5-7.
33. An overview of the economic consequences of different arrangements between Austria and the EEC is given in Hans Mayrzedt, "Zwei Hypothesen über die globalen ökonomischen Auswirkungen einer Nahverbindung mit der EWG," in Hans Mayrzedt and Hans Binswanger

Between 1945 and 1966 the ÖVP was the major partner in a coalition government with the SPÖ. In that coalition the SPÖ controlled Austria's nationalized industries, about two-thirds to three-quarters of the country's total industrial capacity. European integration, the business wing of the ÖVP argued, might weaken this position of the SPÖ by stimulating the inflow of foreign capital and strengthening the political authorities in Brussels at the expense of Vienna. And those authorities were to the liking of the ÖVP. In the 1950s integration in western Europe was spearheaded by cooperation among the sister parties of the ÖVP, the Christian Democrats, in West Germany, Italy, and France. Political alignment with these forces abroad could only help the ÖVP in its limited, but real, conflict with the SPÖ at home. Technocratic or economic arguments pointing to the necessity of things (*Sachzwang*) enforcing an integration beyond the level of the nation-state were welcome tools for aligning the ÖVP with political forces abroad which might help to weaken the entrenched position of power of the SPÖ in Austrian politics.[34]

For the very reason that the ÖVP backed a policy of partial integration with the EEC, the SPÖ opposed it. The requirements of this party in domestic politics were not an Austrian alignment with the "black" EEC but with the "red" European Free Trade Association (EFTA).[35] As a free trade association EFTA did not in any way endanger Austria's neutrality, which the Socialists

---

(eds.), *Die Neutralen in der Europäischen Integration: Kontroversen, Konfrontationen, Alternativen* (Vienna: Braumüller, 1970), pp. 263-276. See also Egon Matzner, "Österreich und die Integration Westeuropas," *Die Zukunft*, 1 (1967), pp. 7-10. The political aspects of Austrian integration policy are discussed in greater detail in Peter J. Katzenstein, "Trends and Oscillations in Austrian Integration Policy since 1955: Alternative Explanations" (unpublished paper, Cornell University, 1974).

34. Bock quoted in *Die Furche*, 46 (1963), p. 3; see also *Die Furche*, 11 (1967), p. 16; Chancellor Klaus quoted in *Kronen Zeitung*, June 30, 1969, p. 3.
35. The SPÖ was less clear about its policy preference than the ÖVP. Haleh Esfandiari, "Die Diskussion um die Gültigkeit des staatsrechtlichen Begriffes Neutralität in den ideologischen publizistischen Führungsmitteln: Die Neutralität Österreichs im Spiegel der Wiener Tagespresse (1955/1956 bis 1960)" (unpub. diss., University of Vienna, 1963), p. 147.

interpreted in broad political terms. Nor did it threaten to intervene in Austria's domestic economic policy greatly influenced by the Socialists.[36] The SPÖ's aversion to an ideological form of anti-Communism (as opposed to a political one) and the party's sensitivity to the political aspects of Austria's institutional involvement in the EEC also made the Socialists opt for greater stress on the importance of Austria's political autonomy.

On the issue of the choice between different degrees of autonomy, both parties behaved, then, in a fashion predictable from our earlier analyses. Deadlocked in a grand coalition which made the raising of additional political support inside Austria virtually impossible, in the early 1960s both parties favored strategies of partial political integration abroad which would have modified Austria's autonomy to different degrees and which would have had different political payoffs in Austrian domestic politics. The primacy of domestic concerns was of still greater importance once the political balance in Austria had tipped in favor of the ÖVP, which formed a government on its own after its election victory in 1966. In 1966–1967, the ÖVP opened a political offensive abroad in order to involve Austria with the EEC on the ÖVP's terms, thus hoping to settle in its favor, once and for all, the one political issue that had created a real stir in Austrian domestic politics since 1945. The SPÖ quickly caught on and strongly pressed its claim that nothing but a preferential trade agreement was acceptable if Austria's political interests were to be served.

In the end the constellation of political factors in international affairs—the Italian veto of the Austrian effort in Brussels over the issue of southern Tyrol, the opposition of the Soviet Union to a partial sacrifice of Austria's neutrality, the conflict between France and Britain over the relation between the EEC and EFTA, and the unwillingness of the EEC to undercut its institutional powers by granting qualified political codetermination to assoc-

---

36. Bruno Kreisky, *Die Herausforderung: Politik an der Schwelle des Atomzeitalters* (Vienna: Europa Verlag, 1965), p. 52. Bruno Pittermann quoted in Josef Hindels, "Sozialistische Ideologie und Europäismus," *Die Zukunft*, 3 (1960), p. 78.

iate members—all were decisive in accounting for the failure of the ÖVP policy. In the early 1970s, with the SPÖ in control of Austrian domestic politics, the dampening effects of these foreign factors are reinforced by domestic ones. Austria was now willing to settle for little else but a preferential trade agreement with the EEC.

The sixth pattern of Austro-German relations confirms, then, the analysis of the previous five, which had shown competing strategies of autonomy and integration to depend on the structure of domestic politics. But signifying a crucial change, the sixth pattern witnessed the choice between autonomy and integration as relevant no longer to Austro–West German but to Austro-European relations. Since the expected political payoffs were smaller than they had been during the interwar period, interparty conflict was less intense. But even though the ÖVP and SPÖ reversed their political stances of the fourth pattern, both continued to act according to the same political maxim, the requirements of their position in domestic politics.

Throughout the pluralistic pattern, Austria's political autonomy was never at stake in its relations with West Germany. Mutually reinforcing processes of disintegration created numerous pressures conducive to the persistence of political autonomy. Behavioral and attitudinal indicators of community and society, of standardization and differentiation, pointed to autonomy instead of integration. The experience of continuous prosperity greatly strengthened the economic attachment of the Austrians to the Second Republic. Finally, none of Austria's three parties saw its interests served by strategies of integration with Germany, even though in Austria's relations with western Europe each party continued to behave according to the requirements of its position in domestic politics. Despite multiple interdependencies, the disjoinedness of the Austro-German partnership has never been more prominent than since 1945.

IX

COUNTERPRESSURES AND POLITICAL AUTONOMY

THE PRECEDING analysis of six patterns of Austro-German relations has focused on the particularity of each and has disregarded continuities in long-term trends. But since 1815, these trends, reflecting as they do the process of modernization, have affected the nonpolitical and political variables which explain political autonomy and disjoined partnership. Even if one considers changes in the size of Austria and Germany, many of these trends point also to counterpressures and, thus, in the same direction as the six patterns of Austro-German relations, toward political autonomy, not integration.

COUNTERPRESSURE (I): FOREIGN AND DOMESTIC

An explanation of political autonomy can be given without regard for the analytical distinction between society and community. It treats social transactions and cultural communications as a homogeneous set of indicators of interdependence. Divergent trends in the balance between foreign and domestic activity (transactions and communications) and attention create a first type of counterpressure conducive to autonomy. Interdependence and attention could be thought of as processes occurring "vertically" within Austrian society of "horizontally" between Austria and the rest of the world. The stronger the vertical link within, rather than the horizontal link between, the greater the probability of autonomy. The data suggest that since 1815 the foreign-domestic ratio has increased for measures of interdependence and declined for measures of attention.

Table 21 reveals Austria's growing attention to domestic affairs. World War I and the change in the size of Austria had the effect of shifting Austria away from its overwhelming preoccupation with domestic affairs in the late nineteenth century. Although this shift slowed the overall decline in the twentieth century, it did not halt it.

Table 22 reports the foreign-domestic ratio of different measures of interdependence. The data point to three distinct phases. Throughout the nineteenth century the share of the foreign sector increased. During the interwar years, on the other hand, the dominant trend was downward as the depression caused people to economize on foreign rather than domestic transactions and communications. Since 1945, however, with growing prosperity, the foreign share again increased, at least until the 1960s. The process of modernization has, then, created

TABLE 21. Austrian Attention to Domestic and Foreign News, 1815-1970[a]

	(1) Domestic	(2) Foreign	(3) Foreign/ Domestic
1816-1849	20%	80%	4,00
1852-1867	55%	45%	0,82
1870-1912	76%	24%	0,32
1921-1938	60%	40%	0,67
1946-1969	65%	35%	0,54

Sources: *Wiener Zeitung; Österreichischer Beobachter, Neue Freie Presse, Presse.*
[a]The method of calculation is explained in Chapter III, fn. 28.

TABLE 22. Austria's Foreign Communications and Transactions as Percent of Domestic Total

	(1) Mail	(2) Telegrams	(3) Telephone Calls	(4) Migrants	(5) Students	(6) Tourists	(7) Trade
1831	22						
1846	18						
1855		43					
1867/69	23	75		1.01	15		
1885/93	31	72			37		
1910/12	40	87		2.04	15	50	10-15
1924/25	52	185	33		50	51	66
1934/36	34	187	42	4.28	15	42	31
1952	19	58	3[a]	4.65	11	56	32
1961	53	98	1	1.47	55	150	48
1969/71	66	98	1	2.37	23	266	53

Sources:
Column (1): Chapter III, fn. 51; Chapter IV, fn. 17; Chapter V, fn. 9; Union Postale Universelle, Le Bureau International, *Relevé des Tableaux Statistiques du Service Postal International (Expédition), 1893*; Chapter VI, fn. 9; Chapter VIII, fn. 8.
Column (2): *Statistische Mitteilungen*, XVIII, 1 (1871), p. 133; Chapter V, fn. 9; *Nachrichten über Industrie, Handel, und Verkehr aus dem statistischen Department im K.K. Handelsministerium, 1891*; Chapter VI, fn. 9; Chapter VIII, fn. 8.
Column (3): Chapter VI, fn. 9; Chapter VIII, fn. 8.
Column (4): Chapter V, fn. 6; Chapter VIII, fn. 5. Österreichisches Statistisches Zentralamt, *Volkszählungsergebnisse 1951*, XII, p. 126. *Beiträge zur Österreichischen Statistik*, 309/1 (1971), p. 9; and 309/15 (1974), p. 13.
Column (5): *Statistisches Jahrbuch, 1867*, pp. 268-271; *Österreichische Statistik*, XVI, 2 (1887), pp. 2-8; Chapter VI, fn. 7; Chapter VIII, fn. 7.
Column (6): *Statistisches Jahrbuch, 1912*, p. 43; *Statistisches Handbuch für die Republik Österreich, 1925*, p. 29; *1937*, p. 38; Chapter VIII, fn. 6.
Column (7): Alois Brusatti, *Österreichische Wirtschaftspolitik vom Josephinismus zum Ständestaat* (Vienna: Jupiter, 1965), p. 81. *Monatsberichte des Österreichischen Institutes für Wirtschaftsforschung*, 14. Sonderheft (Vienna: Selbstverlag, 1965), p. 41; *Monatsberichte*, 15. Sonderheft (Vienna: Selbstverlag, 1971), p. 9.
[a]The figure is low because all local calls are included in the calculation.

two divergent developments: a decline in the share of Austrian attention to foreign events, on the one hand, and an increase in the foreign part of the total of Austria's transactions and communications on the other. These divergent trends constitute the initial type of counterpressure conducive to the persistence of political autonomy.

COUNTERPRESSURE (II): INTERDEPENDENCE AND ATTENTION

If we relate changes in interdependence to changes in attention, conditions favorable to the erosion or expansion of political autonomy can be deduced. If economic, social, and cultural interdependencies grow faster than attention facilities required to deal with them politically, attention deficits create conditions favorable to the persistence of political autonomy. On the other hand, if attention facilities grow faster than the volume of transactions, attention surpluses create conditions favorable to a decline in political autonomy.[1] The analysis of the Austro-German case since 1815 reveals an increase in interdependence in the nineteenth century and fluctuations in the twentieth century. Parallel to these changes there occurred a long-term decline in Austrian attention to Germany since 1815. These two divergent developments define a second type of counterpressure conducive to political autonomy.

Indicators of the relative size of Austro-German interdependence were the shares of Austro-German transactions and communications measured as a percentage of Austria's total foreign transactions and communications. Table 23 summarizes the long-term trends in these indicators since 1815. Row three of Table 23 shows that the level of Austro-German interdependence has rarely fallen below 20 percent and rarely risen above 50 percent. A gradual growth in interdependence since 1815 is evident. This growth took place in two phases. The first phase occurred during the nineteenth century and was completed by 1900, when

---

1. This section and the next are based on a *ceteris paribus* assumption since, by itself, interdependence says nothing about the probability of integration or autonomy.

Austro-German interdependence leveled off at a high plateau. The second phase commenced with a change in the size of Austria in 1918. During the interwar years, changes in Austro-German interdependence were more moderate than the shift that occurred during World War II and in the 1950s. By the late 1960s Austro-German interdependence again approached the level of the early decades of the twentieth century.

These increases and fluctuations in Austro-German interdependence were accompanied by a consistent decline in Austrian attention to Germany. Figure 4 depicts this decline and relates it to the two centers of attention that came to substitute for Austria's traditional emphasis on Germany. During the nineteenth century, Austrian attention shifted gradually away from the industrialized states in northern and western Europe, including Germany, and toward the backward parts of the continent in the east and southeast. Austria's relations with Germany were not sufficiently salient for it to withstand this reorientation of attention within Europe.

An analogous process can be traced in the twentieth century. Because of the reduction in Austria's size, the decline in Austrian attention to German affairs started at a level that was considerably higher in 1921 than it had been in 1912. But it occurred nonetheless as part of a broader reorientation of Austrian attention which now took place, not from one part of Europe to another, but from Europe to the rest of the world. This decline in Austrian attention to German affairs may have been accentuated by the Austrian exposure to the German Nazi government in the 1930s and 1940s. But it is likely that the overall reorientation of attention away from Europe to a world of independent states would have occurred after 1945 whatever the Austrian experience during the preceding two decades. The decline might have been less sharp but, judging by the trend of the nineteenth century, it would still have occurred.

In the Austro-German case interdependence and attention have moved in opposite directions since 1815. Interdependence increased at the same time that attention declined. If increasing demands for the coordination or regulation of behavior are to be met successfully, increases in interdependence require corre-

TABLE 23. Transactions and Communications between Austria and Germany, 1815-1970 (coded by the author)

	I 1815-1848	II 1849-1870	III A 1871-1900	III B 1901-1912	IV A 1918-1932	IV B 1933-1938	VI A 1945-1955	VI B 1956-1970
(1) Transactions								
Trade	ML(0)	M(+)	MH(+)	MH(0)	ML(+)	ML(−)	MH(+)	MH(0)
Capital	ML(0)	ML(+)	MH(+)	MH(0)	ML(0)	ML(0)	L(+)	M(+)
Labor[a]			MH(+)	H(+)	ML(0)	L(−)	ML(+)	MH(+)
Migrants[a]			MH(+)	H(+)	ML(0)	L(0)	MH(+)	MH(+)
Tourists				H(0)	H(+)	ML(−)	H(+)	H(0)
Average	ML(0)	M(+)	MH(+)	MH(0)[b]	ML(0)	ML(−)	MH(+)	MH(0)
(2) Communications								
Mail	MH(+)	H(+)	M(−)	M(0)	M(−)	M(−)	MH(+)	M(−)
Telegram			MH(−)	MH(0)	M(+)	ML(−)	MH(+)	M(−)
Telephone					M(+)	ML(−)	H(+)	H(0)
Students					MH(+)	M(−)	M(+)	M(0)
Average	MH(+)	H(+)	M(−)	M(0)	M(+)	M(−)	MH(+)	M(0)
(3) Transactions and Communications								
Average	M(0/+)	MH(+)	MH(0)	MH(0)	M(+)	ML(−)	MH(+)	M(0)

Source: Table 22.
Key: L = 0-15%; ML = 16-25%; M = 26-35%; MH = 36-50%; H = 50-100% of foreign total. (+) = increasing trend; (−) = decreasing trend; (0) = unchanged trend.
[a] The difference between labor and migrants is here defined as the difference between short-term and long-term migration.
[b] The figures for labor and migrants have in this instance been weighted less heavily because many of the people moving are known to have been of Slavic ethnic stock.

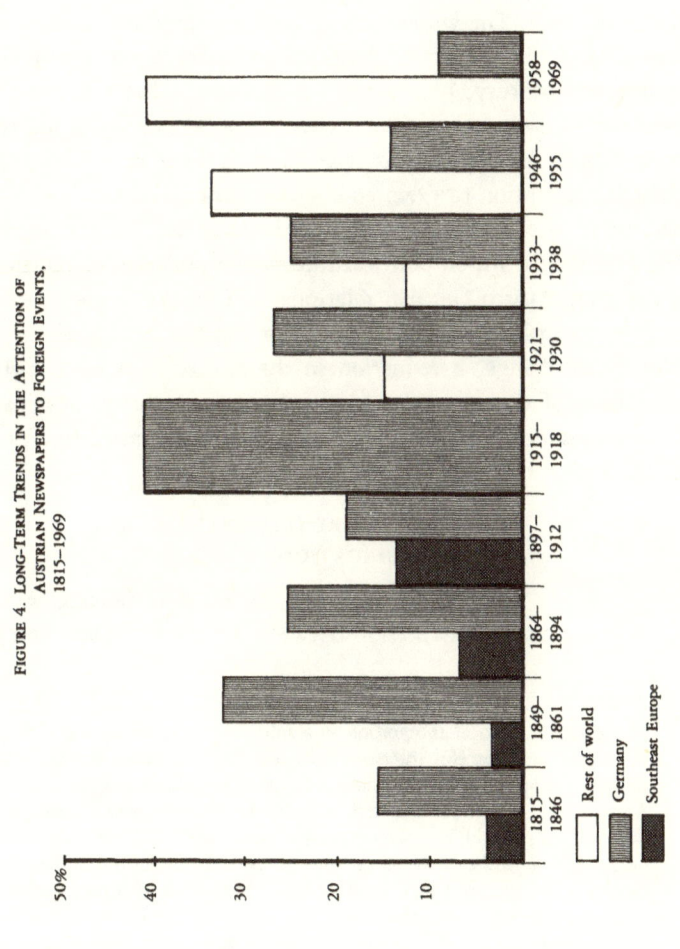

FIGURE 4. LONG-TERM TRENDS IN THE ATTENTION OF AUSTRIAN NEWSPAPERS TO FOREIGN EVENTS, 1815–1969

sponding gains in attention. Counterpressures between rising interdependence and declining attention created conditions favorable to the persistence of political autonomy.[2]

This conclusion is confirmed by the one case in which political autonomy was seriously eroded, the voluntaristic pattern of the interwar years. The widening gap between interdependence and attention occurred in two phases, the first three patterns in the nineteenth century, on the one hand, and the last three in the twentieth, on the other. The experience of World War I and the reduction in Austria's size after 1918 made for an upward shift in Austria's attention to German affairs and caused a simultaneous decline in the average level of interdependence. That is, in the one instance in which political integration outweighed political autonomy, Austro-German relations were marked by a relative attention surplus instead of deficit. But this was due largely to an exogenous change, a reduction in the size of Austria. For the remainder of the nineteenth and twentieth centuries, however, counterpressures between interdependence and attention prevailed and with them political autonomy.

COUNTERPRESSURE (III): TRANSACTIONS AND COMMUNICATIONS

The first two counterpressures were deduced without relying on the distinction between society and community,

---

2. If one views political integration as a subclass of a more general category of cooperative, peaceful interstate relations, this conclusion can be linked to recent empirical findings concerning conflict relations between states. According to a large-scale investigation of the incidence of war since 1815, the success ratio of the war-initiating party decreased over time. This declining probability may result from the same feature of the modernizing international system which inhibits the achievement of highly extensive and effective policy coordination. The widening gap between growing interdependences which increase the loads imposed on governments, on the one hand, and decreasing attention spans which reduce governmental capabilities to deal with these loads, on the other, may well have decreased the probability of success of strategies of extreme conflict as well as cooperation. See the figures quoted in Karl W. Deutsch and Dieter Senghaas, "Die Schritte zum Krieg: Systemebenen, Entscheidungsstadien, Forschungsergebnisse," *Aus Politik und Zeitgeschichte*, B47/70 (November 27, 1970), p. 19.

Counterpressures and Political Autonomy

which has provided one basis for this analysis of the Austro-German case. That distinction introduces the potential for tracing numerous additional counterpressures. In our analysis of the Austro-German case, the balance between society and community pointed to political integration unambiguously only once, during the voluntaristic pattern of the interwar period. Numerous counterpressures conducive to political autonomy were not only expected theoretically but ascertained empirically.

By affecting transactions and communications as behavioral measures of society and community, two long-term trends have created a third type of counterpressure conducive to political autonomy and disjoined partnership. The first is a reversal in the political important attached to communications and transactions. Prior to the establishment of regular communications channels between Austria and Germany, as seen in the aristocratic pattern, the control of communications was an important stake in politics for which Metternich fought tenaciously in his defense of the old order. Once these channels had been established, however, this aspect of Austro-German relations became quickly depoliticized. Social transactions, on the other hand, and in particular the flow of capital and trade, acquired increasing prominence only in the second half of the nineteenth century, after governments had come to appreciate more fully the political benefits of economic dominance as well as the economic benefits of economic dominance as well as the economic benefits of political dominance.

This reversal in the political priority of communications and transactions affected the Austro-German case twice. In the conflict pattern during the middle of the nineteenth century and in the voluntaristic pattern during the middle of the twentieth, successive Austrian governments were correct in deliberately trying to enlarge communications flows between Austria and Germany as helpful for gains in Austro-German political integration. In both instances they adopted what one might call a poor man's strategy of integration. Mass communications preferences were thought to be changeable not by the commitment of economic resources but by the stroke of a pen, not by the creation of positive incentives but by changes in rules and regulations. But the long-term reversal of the political importance of transactions and communications meant that the cheap way for strategies of political integration was no longer the effective way.

The growing complexity and diversity of society and economy in the process of modernization is the second development that has affected the probability of political autonomy. This change is illustrated in Table 24.

Since 1815 the relative homogeneity of indicators of Austro-German society and community has changed. Measures of community have become increasingly homogeneous at the same time that measures of society have grown increasingly heterogenous. A comparison of the voluntaristic with the pluralistic pattern of Austro-German relations, in particular, points to a striking gain in the heterogeneity of indicators of social transactions during recent decades.

The interaction of these trends—of the decreasing political prominence of communications and their increasing homogeneity as a measure of community and of the increasing political importance of transactions and their decreasing homogeneity as a measure of society—has created a third type of counterpressure. The very objectives that have come to matter most politically,

TABLE 24. Changes in the Heterogeneity of Austro-German Transactions and Communications since 1815

	Ratio of No. Indicators/ No. Categories[a]	
Pattern	Transactions (Society)	Communications (Community)
I-III	2.1	1.0
IV-VI	1.7	1.8
IV	2.5	2.0
VI	0.8	1.6

Source: Table 22.

[a]The ratio is based on the sum of the number of different categories per period given in Table 23.

society and economy, have become increasingly heterogeneous and, thus, increasingly difficult to direct politically. This analysis points to political autonomy as the expected outcome.

COUNTERPRESSURE (IV): EVALUATIONS AND IDENTIFICATIONS

A fourth type of counterpressure characterizes evaluations and identifications as attitudinal measures of society and community. The changes in these two measures since 1815 are depicted in Table 25. Long-term changes in Austrian self-identification as German could be likened to a wave that gradually swelled during the second half of the nineteenth century, crested during the interwar years, and broke quite rapidly after 1945. Austria's positive evaluations of Germany, on the other hand, showed a number of short-term fluctuations which often depended on the political relations of the two countries. Although many of these fluctuations are concealed by average figures taken over longer periods of time, they are readily apparent when these periods are disaggregated into shorter segments.[3]

Counterpressures between these different rates of change, between the faster rate for evaluations and the slower one for identifications, will generate repeated realignments in the balance between society and community, between differentiation and standardization. The resultant oscillations are conducive not to political integration but to autonomy.

COUNTERPRESSURE (V): NATIONAL AND INTERNATIONAL

An increasing divergence between two political processes, between the unchanged primacy of considerations of domestic politics on the one hand and the growing internationalization of Austro-German measures of bilateral policy coordination on the other, have created a fifth type of counterpressure. Autonomy is strengthened by the politics of integration and autonomy.

---

3. See above, Tables 7, 12, 18; Chapter VIII, fn. 9.

TABLE 25. Long-Term Trends in Evaluations and Self-Identifications in Austrian Newspapers (coded by the author)

Pattern	(1) Positive Evaluation	(2) Mutual Identification
I (1815-1848)	ML[a]	L[a]
II (1849-1870)	L[a]	ML[a]
III A (1871-1900)	M	MH
III B (1901-1912)	M	M
IV A (1918-1932)	ML	M
IV B (1933-1938)	M	ML
VI A (1945-1955)	L[b]	ML[b]
VI B (1956-1970)	MH[b]	L[b]

[a]Coded on the basis of the qualitative analysis with reference primarily to elite attitudes.
[b]Coded on the basis of public opinion polls.
Key Column (1): Net Amity Coefficient of Positive Evaluations: H = 1.0-0.60; MH = 0.59-0.50; M = 0.49-0.30; ML = 0.29-0.15; L = 0.14-(−)1.0.
Key Column (2): Mutual identification was classified on the basis of the ratio of direct and indirect German symbols over direct and indirect Austrian symbols: H = 1.0-0.60; MH = 0.59-0.40; M = 0.39-0.30; ML = 0.29-0.15; L = 0.14-0.00.

In all six patterns, the analysis points to one constant feature. In serving as a crisis strategy for political actors in Austria, the adoption of a political strategy of partial integration with Germany was always motivated primarily by considerations of domestic politics. Whenever an important political group could not obtain its objectives, it took recourse to a political strategy which sought to supplement its political resources in Austria with those from Germany. Integration policy was a standard feature of the emergency kit of all the major political coalitions in Austria after 1815. Each group that had gained political power at home relied on an integration policy abroad in defending its established position against others seeking a better representation of their own interests.

Analysis showed this to hold for ethnic and class conflicts alike. As one ethnic group among many, the German-Austrians came to rely increasingly on the political support of the German Reich in the defense of their elite position in the Austrian Empire against the political demands of the Slavs. By the turn of the century that political coalition had become an indispensable prop of the besieged German-Austrians. But the logic of political integration as a crisis strategy prevailed also in the conflict between different groups or classes of German-Austrians. The aristocratic pattern was nothing but a class coalition across political borders which sought to defend the ancien régime against Jacobin agitation. The coordination of policies served as an instrument to repress liberals and democrats as the most probable source of opposition to the ruling coalition of the court, the bureaucracy, and the aristocracy. In the conflict pattern the Austrian military attempted to secure and enlarge its domestic power base by incorporating the German states into a Great Austrian Empire. This political strategy was designed to serve the purpose of consolidating Austria-Hungary by keeping in check the instigators of the Revolution of 1848, the Slavs and the liberals.

The bourgeoisie was the next group to seize control of Austria's political machinery after 1866. Even though the middle class was tied firmly to the revamped empire, it advocated and pursued a policy of partial integration with Germany, especially in those provinces of the empire where German-Austrian supremacy was already seriously threatened by the demands of the Slavs, notably Bohemia, Moravia, and Silesia. The defense of their elite position became the central issue around which the three German-Austrian mass parties began to organize their political activities during the hierarchical pattern. Despite great policy differences, the three *Lager* of Austrian politics—the Christian Socials, the Socialists, and the Pan-German nationalists—were all agreed on the objective of keeping Austria a German state, preferably run by German-Austrians.

The adoption of integration as a political crisis strategy was evident also in the voluntaristic pattern during the interwar years. Here it was the political opposition, the Socialists and the Nationalists, that pressed hardest for political integration with Germany, in part because their position in Austrian politics was so unpromising. The Christian Socials, on the other hand, after they had seized effective control of the First Republic from the early 1920s on, preached integration but practiced autonomy to the extent possible under the circumstances of the time.

With lesser but still notable intensity, the same political process recurred most recently during the pluralistic pattern after 1945. Although the potential partner for political integration was no longer Germany but the EEC, actors in domestic politics again advocated competing strategies of integration or autonomy designed to further their objectives in Austria. The Peoples Party (ÖVP) favored partial integration with the EEC, at least in part, because of the political character of the integration process which had gotten under way in western Europe during the mid-1950s. It hoped to use European integration as an instrument to weaken the grip of the Socialists (SPÖ) over Austria's economy. Only the constellation of forces in international politics prevented the ÖVP from achieving for Austria the status of an associate member of the EEC.

The analysis of the six patterns points, then, to this conclusion. Despite the great intensity with which the objective of partial integration was pursued by any of the groups seeking to stabilize its political position in Austrian politics, it was quite moderate taken for the country as a whole. By definition, integration as a crisis strategy of select groups and coalitions in Austrian politics inhibited the emergence of broadly based alliances. Only during the interwar years was such a coalition approximated and even then, as the analysis showed, there existed significant differences. But in the remaining patterns, the advocacy or adoption of political integration abroad was highly divisive at home, since political integration was both a weapon and a stake in Austria's domestic politics.

The repetition of the same political process in all six patterns of Austro-German relations constitutes only one part of the fifth political counterpressure. The other is the decline in the bilateral ties between Austria and Germany since 1815 which can be linked to long-term changes in the international system. The magnitude of that decline is illustrated in Figure 5.

Even if one considers the effects of Germany's unification in 1871, this decline in bilateral ties between Austria and Germany is the result of a process of internationalization. That process is composed of two mutually reinforcing components, the internationalization of the European state system through the inclusion of a large number of new state actors, on the one hand, and a corresponding internationalization of bilateral political coordination, on the other. A comparison of the first with the last pattern makes readily apparent both of these components. The aristocratic pattern was marked by the concurrence of political interdependence and economic, social, and cultural isolation; the pluralistic pattern by political isolation and economic, social, and cultural interdependence of Austria and Germany.

Mirrored in the change from political interdependence to political isolation is the great expansion in the number of actors in international politics and the gradual encroachment of the expanding international system on the political relations between Austria and Germany. The increasing availability of new partners made the coordination of policies between the old less likely with the passing of time.[4]

Reflected in the change from economic, social, and cultural isolation to interdependence is the internationalization of bilateral political coordination between Austria and Germany. In the analysis of the Austro-German case we encountered this process twice, during the second pattern in the middle of the nineteenth century and during the sixth in the middle of the twentieth.

The replacement of the Austro-German Postal and Telegraph Unions by the Universal Postal and the International Telegraph Unions is a typical example of the internationalization of bilateral policy coordination. If the fruits of the development of a modern communications technology were to be exploited fully, technologically obsolete bilateral agreements had to be discard-

---

4. This analysis neglects important considerations of policy sensitivity such as strategic interdependence which do not require the presence of transactions of any sort.

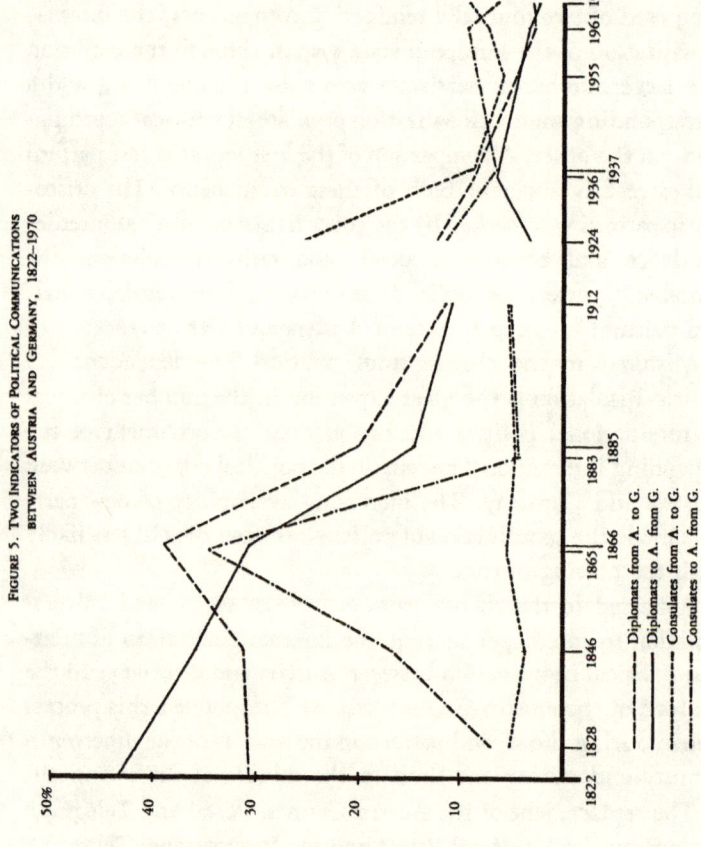

FIGURE 5. Two Indicators of Political Communications between Austria and Germany, 1822–1970

ed. Policy coordination between Austria and Germany was incorporated into and diluted in a more encompassing international framework. A similar process has probably also occurred since 1945. Although the relations between Austria and Germany were practically depoliticized, the two partner countries shared common political concerns now expressed, discussed, and, at times, acted upon by one or several of the many European or worldwide organizations existing today.[5]

The internationalization of Austro-German bilateral ties and its inhibiting effect on policy coordination between Austria and Germany could have been compensated for by political changes inside Austria. But as our analysis showed, it was not change but its absence that was the distinctive feature of all six patterns. The primacy of domestic politics and partial political integration as a crisis strategy was the driving force from the first to the last pattern. The decline of bilateral political ties abroad and the constancy of the Austrian political process at home, thus, resulted in a fifth counterpressure which has enhanced the probability of autonomy and relations of disjoined partnership.

COUNTERPRESSURE (VI): OLD AND NEW

The sequence of six patterns of Austro-German relations points to a last pair of trends. Established elites and old social conditions, and political counterelites and new social conditions define a sixth type of counterpressure conducive to political autonomy. There was a definite order to the transitions from one pattern to the next. These transitions were the result of processes of decay and growth. Unlike Darwinian theory, birth and death of new and old patterns occurred simultaneously; and unlike dialectic theory, political outcomes were combinatorial instead of deterministic. The application of old policies to new conditions created a syndrome permissive of partial integration in the short term and supportive of autonomy in the long term.

---

5. For an analysis that attempts to explain political autonomy not from a national but an international perspective, see John G. Ruggie, "Collective Goods and Future International Collaboration," *American Political Science Review*, LXVI, 3 (September 1972), pp. 874-893.

The overcommitment of political resources abroad was motivated in each of the patterns by the objective of reinforcing a policy of neglect at home. Taken together, overcommitment and neglect proved a recipe for the failure of all strategies of integration. Political autonomy prevailed by default of strategies of integration.

In the aristocratic pattern decay and growth were shown respectively in the gradual erosion of the difference between the cosmopolitanism of an international elite at the pinnacle of society and the segmentation of parochial publics at the base. In the face of increasing social loads and declining political capabilities, Metternich's crisis strategy of partial integration failed in the end because the overcommitment of scarce political resources abroad reinforced the neglect of social concerns at home. The Revolution of 1848 was the result of this policy.

The convergence of cosmopolitanism and parochialism and the divergence of capabilities and loads continued in the second pattern. The new government attempted to consolidate its own position not by sharing political power at home with the German-Austrian middle class and the Slavs as the major agents of the Revolution of 1848, but by pursuing an integration strategy abroad. Effective domestic control was to be maintained against existing sources of opposition by incorporating the German states into a Great Austrian Empire. Overcommitment abroad and neglect at home led to the defeat and dismissal of the military-bureaucratic regime by 1866.

In the face of the growing social mobilization of the Slavs and a corresponding increase in their national and political aspirations, middle-class and mass parties of the German-Austrians increasingly favored a partial political integration with Germany during the hierarchical pattern. The German-Austrian attempt to compensate for the absence of basic reforms in the structure of the Austrian Empire through a strategy of integration abroad eventually led to an intolerable overcommitment of Austrian resources, World War I, and the collapse of the monarchy.

Just as changing political actors and unchanged reward perceptions had been distinctive of the first three patterns, unchanged actors and changing reward perception were distinctive of the last three. But the concurrence in the growth of new and the decay of old elements in Austro-German relations continued, and with it integration as a political resource in domestic politics. A novel element of the voluntaristic pattern was the attempt to construct a modern welfare state in some parts of the First Republic, an undertaking never seriously entertained in the larger empire. Unchanged, however, was the reliance of the Austrian Socialists on a strategy of political integration. Instead of adjusting the party's strategy to the changed conditions in the First Republic, the Socialists looked upon the Anschluss as the remedy that would cure the party's ills in Austria.

Throughout the 1930s and the structural pattern, a sizable fraction of the Austrian population—national and national-socialist—adhered to old preferences in regarding unification with Germany as the only solution that would improve its position. But new was Austria's direct reliance on Germany's enormous economic and military resources in the attempt to reassert German and Austrian hegemony over central and eastern Europe. Hopelessly overcommitted, that attempt failed within a few years.

But these German resources, supplemented by generous foreign aid and the growing commitment of Austrians to their country's institutions, gave the Second Republic after 1945 a much greater chance to succeed where the First Republic had failed. Even so, Austria's political elites continued to view strategies of partial political integration abroad as an instrument with which Austria's domestic politics could be shaped. These strategies no longer applied in relation to Germany but to Europe undergoing rapid economic, ideological, and political change. But the adoption of a traditional political strategy in the context of a new situation in Austrian domestic politics revealed that change after 1945 had been less than total.

Counterpressures between processes of decay and growth occurred in each of the six patterns of Austro-German relations since 1815. Repeated applications of traditional strategies of partial political integration abroad to new conditions at home led to overcommitment or neglect, or both. The failures of policies of partial integration helped secure political autonomy.

Since 1815 the distinctive feature of the relations between Austria and Germany has been the presence, pervasiveness, and persistence of counterpressures and political autonomy. A focus on the long-term trends of some of the variables from which this explanation of disjoined partnership was fashioned helps in understanding why. Six counterpressures, in particular, were identified between the following elements: foreign and domestic, interdependence and attention, transactions and communications, evaluations and identifications, national and international, and old and new.

These six counterpressures point to structural features of the process of modernization since 1815 which have maintained the probability of political autonomy. "Partial political integration" adopted as a crisis strategy thus acquires a double meaning. In emphasizing crisis features it describes the attempt of political elites to improve their political positions in domestic politics. In stressing incompleteness it refers to a political strategy that conforms to important structural conditions confining modern politics. None of the theoretically specified variables, by itself, determined the outcome of any of the six patterns; correspondingly none of these structural conditions makes political integration impossible and political autonomy inevitable. But several or all of the variables in combination created a cumulative and interlocking pattern making political autonomy a probable outcome; and several or all of these structural conditions become cumulative in their impact on conditions favorable to a continuation of political autonomy. Although the process is probabilistic, it reveals a distinct structure. And for the Austro-German case that structure points to political autonomy and disjoined partnership.

X

CONCLUSION

ONE ASSERTION, shared alike by many actors in and analysts of contemporary politics, views the political integration of culturally cohesive areas to be both historically preordained and normatively prescribed, determined and desired. The point of departure of this book is the gap between aspiration and achievement, prediction and verification. With the growing interdependence among culturally cohesive states, why does political integration not follow political autonomy? Why do partners remain disjoined?

The reasons for the persistence of political autonomy were explored through the analysis of one particular case. The relationship between Austria and Germany affects the future shape of central Europe and is typical of the political relations among other culturally cohesive states. If political autonomy, not integration, is possible even when the partners belong to one overarching cultural community, as is true of Austria and Germany, some fears concerning the future of central Europe may be weakened; and the burden of proof on the prospects of culturally homogeneous areas in general is shifted to those embracing the logic of integration.

Theoretical considerations pointed not to an inevitable trend toward political integration but its absence. Political autonomy and relations among disjoined partners, it was reasoned, are the result of a probabilistic process. This process is composed of several components that are often marked not by copressures but counterpressures. These counterpressures can be found within and between two clusters of variables. The growth of the division of labor in society as measured by transactions and evaluations leads to increases in differentiation; gains in the sharing of meaning in community as measured by communications and identifications lead to increases in standardization. Asymmetries in the growth of interdependence in community and society define one set of nonpolitical variables affecting political autonomy. Economic and political rewards and reward perceptions, on the other hand, shape competing actor strategies of autonomy or integration. Multiple mutually reinforcing counterpressures within and between these two clusters of variables make for the persistence of political autonomy as they condition relations of disjoined partnership.

Empirical analysis of six distinct patterns of Austro-German relations since 1815 identified counterpressures and political autonomy as a more frequent result than copressures and political integration. The balance between community and society, between standardization and differentiation, pointed to autonomy more often than integration. Economic rewards and reward perceptions were tied to Austria more firmly than to Germany. Finally, the primacy of domestic politics made Austria's political elites choose partial integration abroad as a crisis strategy designed not to surrender but to secure their position at home. The prevalence of counterpressures among twelve long-term trends showed the process of modernization as a further powerful factor that favors political autonomy. As a result, in five of the six patterns analyzed, political autonomy prevailed. The theoretical argument put forth at the outset thus appears to be confirmed by a number of case studies which are important for the future shape of central Europe and illustrative of culturally cohesive regions in general.

The Austro-German case is not an exception in contemporary European politics. High degrees of cultural homogeneity, social and economic interdependence, and political diversity coincide in several instances. In northern Europe the Scandinavian countries are united by many cultural and economic bonds which seem to predestine them to full political integration. Yet, the political autonomy of the traditional nation-state has prevailed. In southern Europe, Spain and Portugal share a geographic cohesiveness and cultural and political affinities pointing toward extensive and effective political coordination. Yet political autonomy has prevailed here too. In western Europe, multiple cultural, social, and economic links among the Low Countries seem to predict political integration as the expected outcome. Here too, though, political autonomy has prevailed over political integration. The political fragmentation of the German culture area in central Europe, which has accelerated greatly since 1945, thus conforms to developments that characterize contemporary European politics in general.

The coincidence of cultural unity and political diversity is as persistent across time as it is pervasive across space. Historically, the political unifications of the German and Italian culture areas in the nineteenth century gave way to a recurrence of the political fragmentation of culturally cohesive areas in northern, western, and central Europe in the twentieth century. The fragmentation of Sweden-Norway in 1905 and of England-Ireland in 1921 were precursors of the current experience of central Europe. The incidence of political integration has thus diminished over time. A broadening of the perspective to include the Anglo-Saxon cultural area outside Europe points to the same conclusion. In the eighteenth century the emergence of a distinct American national consciousness contributed greatly to the political fragmentation of Britain and the colonies. Between 1890 and the middle of the twentieth century, that fragmentation appears to have accelerated along numerous dimensions.[1] Similar trends are discernible in other parts of the Anglo-Saxon world.[2] Political coordination between the Anglo-Saxon core of the Commonwealth—Great Britain, Canada, South Africa, Australia, and

1. Richard L. Merritt, *Symbols of American Community, 1735-1775* (New Haven: Yale University Press, 1966). Bruce M. Russett, *Community and Contention: Britain and America in the Twentieth Century* (Cambridge, Mass.: M.I.T. Press, 1963).
2. A few of these cases are discussed in Karl W. Deutsch et al., *Political Community and the North Atlantic Area: International Organization in the Light of Historical Experience* (Princeton: Princeton University Press, 1957).

New Zealand—has weakened noticeably over the last century. And relations between the United States and Canada have become a growing source of friction in recent years.[3] These developments suggest increasing political autonomy within the Anglo-Saxon cultural community.

The persistence of political autonomy in the Austro-German case thus is part of a broader pattern spanning continents and centuries. Culturally homogeneous areas appear to have a high resistance to sustained and effective drives toward political unification. This conclusion raises a problem that points beyond this book with its focus on political affairs in central Europe as an example of other culturally cohesive regions. There is no reason to believe in the similarity of processes of unification and fragmentation in culturally homogeneous and heterogeneous areas. But the assumption is plausible that the barriers against integration are at least as high and the probability of political autonomy is at least as great in regions that are culturally diverse rather than united. This assumption is supported by a cursory look at the incidence of political unification and fragmentation of Europe's culturally heterogeneous states. The data suggest that here, too, the logic of autonomy is at least as prominent as the logic of integration. Between 1815 and 1918 the successful unification of France-Savoy in 1860 contrasts with the fragmentation of Austria-Hungary, the Ottoman Empire, Russia-Poland, and Russia-Finland at the end of World War I. Since 1919 there has been no instance of either unification or fragmentation in Europe. In most of these cases, to be sure, political fragmentation was imposed by the international system rather than the free choice of political elites. Yet when that system changed, elites and masses normally continued to opt for independence instead of reunification. Like the experience of Austria and Germany and many culturally homogeneous areas, the overall picture of Europe's culturally heterogeneous regions points to autonomy instead of integration.

3. Andrew Axline et al. (eds.), *Continental Community? Independence and Integration in North America* (Toronto: McClelland & Stewart, 1974). Annette Baker Fox, Alfred O. Hero, Jr., and Joseph S. Nye, Jr. (eds.), "Canada and the United States: Transnational and Transgovernmental Relations," *International Organization*, XXVIII, 4 (autumn 1974).

Conclusion

This historical perspective is important for a proper understanding of the European unification movement since 1945. In the past the core problem of western Europe has always been the reconciliation of diversity with peace, hegemony with justice. In a world of growing interdependence it is widely assumed that mutually reinforcing copressures among numerous factors within and between states create conditions conducive to political unification. Since, in the past, villages have integrated into regions and regions into nation-states, what, it is being asked, will come beyond the nation-state?

At the close of World War II the "founding fathers" of western Europe, men like Adenauer, de Gasperi, and Schumann, thought they could push the old states quickly into a new Europe. Their efforts, as we know, remained unsuccessful. But the example they set provided a compelling image for the political leaders of western Europe in the 1960s and early 1970s, men like Brandt, Heath, and Pompidou, to continue along the same path with undiminished hopes for the future.

In his maiden speech before Parliament in 1969, Chancellor Brandt expressed his strong commitment to working toward a unified Europe: "Europe's peoples are waiting and demand that the statesmen match the logic of history with the will to succeed."[4] An ardent backer of European unity throughout his political career, Prime Minister Heath made his strong support of a united Europe the first substantive point of the opening of the British Parliament in 1970.[5] And in his first year in office, President Pompidou argued, "Europe does have a chance to be united and thus to find again on all levels, including the political level, the means for its development and its influence enabling it to make its voice heard in all areas of international politics."[6]

Political analysts have taken a very similar view. In his widely acclaimed book, *The American Challenge*, J. J. Servan-Schreiber

---

4. Willy Brandt, "Regierungserklärung, 28. Oktober 1969," in Bundesministerium für innerdeutsche Beziehungen (ed.), *Texte zur Deutschlandpolitik* (Bonn: Vorwärts, 1970) IV, 37.
5. *The Times*, July 3, 1970, p. 7.
6. Ambassade de France, Service de Presse et d'Information, *French Foreign Policy: Official Statements, Speeches, and Communiqués, July-December 1969* (Paris: La Documentation Française, n.d.), p. 97.

saw the general conditions for a unified Europe as given and urged "strong-willed men who care about politics" to do the rest.[7] Functionalist theorists of international politics, in their own way, agreed. In his writings during the interwar years, David Mitrany predicted and valued the depoliticization of an increasing number of issues as a path toward political integration. After World War II, Ernst Haas reversed this view. The politicization of controversial issues, he thought, would lend to the integration process its own dynamic. Despite these differences, Mitrany and Haas both expected political integration to occur almost automatically.[8]

During the last decade, however, the belief in an inevitable trend toward European integration has weakend. An increasing number of research findings and the experience of the European unification movement itself have diminished early hopes and have corrected some misconceptions. In his summary of a substantial body of theoretical and empirical literature on regional integration schemes in different parts of the world, Joseph Nye spoke pessimistically of the prospects of political integration: "Our major hypothesized expectation is inertia."[9] Reflecting on the western European experience in particular, Leon Lindberg and Stuart Scheingold concurred: "The findings of our case-study analyses show a Community which is clearly tending toward an overall equilibrium or plateau."[10] What is striking about western Europe today is not political integration but its absence. Since until the mid-1960s most academic research in this field had started with the wrong question—what propels the process of European integration?—it arrived at wrong answers. The more

---

7. Jean-Jacques Servan-Schreiber, *The American Challenge* (New York: Atheneum, 1968), p. 201.
8. David Mitrany, *A Working Peace System* (Chicago: Quadrangle, 1966). Ernst B. Haas, *The Uniting of Europe: Political, Social, and Economic Forces, 1950-1957* (Stanford: Stanford University Press, 1958). Ernst B. Haas, *Beyond the Nation-State: Functionalism and International Organization* (Stanford: Stanford University Press, 1964).
9. J. S. Nye, *Peace in Parts: Integration and Conflict in Regional Organization* (Boston: Little, Brown, 1971), p. 63.
10. Leon N. Lindberg and Stuart A. Scheingold, *Europe's Would-Be Polity: Patterns of Change in the European Community* (Prentice-Hall: Englewood Cliffs, N. J., 1970), p. 279.

recent studies of Nye and Lindberg and Scheingold suggest that the counterpressures identified as causes of political autonomy in this analysis of the Austro-German case might well be present in western Europe as well. But to the extent that European political integration occurs during the next three or four decades, this analysis suggests that the source of partial political integration should be sought not in inter- but intra-state politics, in the sequence of crisis strategies that political elites adopt to secure their political positions at home.

Finally, this book tenders a partial answer to the German problem, the problem that has troubled Europe for more than a century. That answer is partial for two reasons. It deals only with the Austrian part of the Austro-German partnership, and it is not based on a detailed analysis of the current international system. That system is a powerful force which strengthens the present fragmentation of central Europe. But throughout this book the primary focus of the analysis has been on domestic factors, on the incidence of copressures and counterpressures which shaped competing strategies of political integration and autonomy. Since the change of the contemporary international system is rapid, that analytical perspective permits a cautious projection of past developments and present conditions into the future. The first conclusion is the reversibility and variability of the components that shape processes of unification and fragmentation. There exists, then, no definite and final solution to the German Question. But, on the basis of an analysis of the Austro-German case, the fragmentation of central Europe looks more permanent today than at any previous time since 1815. Of all the now-autonomous states that once formed the German Reich, Austria more than any other should feel today the magnetism of the residual core of Germany, the Federal Republic. East and West Germany are separted because of the powerful impact of different political ideologies and the reinforcing effect of mutual self-encapsulation. The outcome has been the emergence of two Germanies, not one. In the Austro-German case a process more subtle but no less effective led to the same result. Above the level of indifference and below the threshold of integration, the Austro-German experience of the past points to the central Europe of the future, to the political autonomy of disjoined partners.

APPENDIX

POLITICAL UNIFICATION, POLITICAL FRAGMENTATION, AND CULTURAL COHESION IN EUROPE SINCE 1815

The detailed analysis of the persistence of political autonomy in Austro-German relations since 1815 might become one part of a broader comparative inquiry into the relations between culturally cohesive states. This book has stressed how in the Austro-German case different kinds of counterpressures enhanced the probability of the status quo at the expense of the probability of structural change. This interpretation makes it imperative that future inquiries devote special attention to the analysis of instances of political unification or fragmentation of culturally cohesive states. In Europe these states have experienced four decisive shifts in political boundaries since 1815. The unification of Germany and Italy in the middle of the nineteenth century was followed by the fragmentation of Sweden-Norway and England-Ireland at the beginning of the twentieth. This appendix applies one part of the explanation developed in Chapter II to these four cases. Only changing balances in cultural communications and social transactions, that is changing balances in standardization and differentiation, will be examined. Since they raise fewer theoretical questions, a discussion of economic and political rewards is lacking. This analysis, furthermore, is cursory. It is offered only tentatively as nothing more than an illustration of how work along the lines suggested in this book might be carried out in the future. But since the data presented in this appendix, by and large, support the ideas spelled out in Chapter II, they are further indirect evidence in support of the preceding analysis of Austro-German relations.

Cultural unity is an ideal which can only be approximated to different degrees of cultural cohesion. The cohesion that sets a group of people apart from others is defined by at least one of the following three characteristics: a high capacity for mutual cooperation, mutual predictability of behavior, and the development of mutual trust and identification. All of these factors contribute to and are a reflection of what appears as the key element of cultural cohesion, "the complementarity of the relative efficiency of communications among individuals—something that is in some ways similar to mutual rapport, but on a larger scale."[1]

France has often been viewed as the archetype of a culturally unified European state, but even France falls short of complete cultural unity. Religious divisions between Catholics and Protestants and between clericals and anticlericals cut deeply into French community as late as the nineteenth century. And today, in a predominantly Catholic country, pockets of Calvinists in the south and Lutherans in Alsace continue to flourish. Ethnically, the French are "a race of half-breeds," a mixture of Latin, Celtic, and Germanic tribes.[2] Finally, the persistence of France's linguistic diversity—of the languages spoken by the Germans in Alsace, Bretons, Corsicans, and Basques—is a poignant reminder that France is a culturally cohesive but not a culturally united state.

The three factors that contribute to the moderate divisions marking the French cultural community—religion, ethnicity,

1. Karl W. Deutsch, *Nationalism and Social Communication*, 2nd ed. (Cambridge, Mass.: M.I.T. Press, 1966), p. 188.
2. Charles Seignobos quoted in André Siegfried, "Approaches to an Understanding of Modern France," in Edward M. Earle (ed.), *Modern France: Problems of the Third and Fourth Republic* (Princeton: Princeton University Press, 1951), p. 4.

and language—are the three best indicators of complementary communication capacities as the most distinctive feature of a cultural community. The four cases here discussed—Germany, Italy, England-Ireland, and Sweden-Norway—score high at least on one of these three indices of cultural cohesiveness, but none score high on all three of them. Even though the divisive impact of their internal religious wars has greatly weakened since the seventeenth century, Germany and England-Ireland still lack the religious unity that characterizes Italy and Sweden-Norway. In ethnic terms Germany and Italy approximate much more closely the ideal of unity than do either England-Ireland or Sweden-Norway. But an index of ethnic fractionalization for Sweden-Norway—measuring the probability that two randomly chosen individuals from one country will belong to the same ethnic group—still lies more than six times below the worldwide average; and if comparable figures existed for England-Ireland, they would be of a roughly similar magnitude.[3]

The problems remaining are how to combine analytically the effects religion and ethnicity have on the complementarity of communication capacities and how to add the effect of other possible measures, such as language. Existing concepts and data do not permit the construction of a precise composite index. The fragmentary evidence on these two indicators suggests, however, that the degree of cultural cohesiveness of Germany, Italy, England-Ireland, and Sweden-Norway is substantial and, perhaps, greater than that typical of other areas of Europe or of most other parts of the world. But our present knowledge does not permit us to express that cohesiveness in unambiguous language or in precise quantifiable form.

This practical difficulty points to the use of language as a key indicator by which to judge the degree of cultural cohesiveness of

---

3. The index is discussed and the relevant data are presented in Charles L. Taylor and Michael C. Hudson, *World Handbook of Social and Economic Indicators*, 2nd ed. (New Haven: Yale University Press, 1972), pp. 214-217, 271-274. Equally weighted figures for the United Kingdom and Ireland are still less than half of the world average, and they exceed, of course, the degree of ethnic fractionalization of England-Ireland by a substantial margin.

this group of European states. Linguistic assimilation or differentiation is an intuitively plausible and empirically ascertainable measure of changes in the complementarity of communication capacities. As is illustrated by the Swiss case, linguistic assimilation is not a necessary condition for cultural cohesiveness. Conversely, linguistic homogeneity does not necessarily guarantee cultural cohesion. There is some scattered evidence, for example, that the political division between East and West Germany since 1945 may eventually lead to the emergence of two distinct cultures based on two different socioeconomic and political systems that share a common German language.[4] By and large, though, language is the single most adequate indicator of the complementarity of communications available to the student of unification and fragmentation processes. The correlation coefficient between linguistic and ethnic fractionalization is high, varying between 0.82 and 0.92 for different data collections.[5] For these reasons, the four cases under consideration here have been classified as culturally cohesive on the basis of their linguistic homogeneity.

In terms of that homogeneity Germany, Italy, England-Ireland, and Sweden-Norway rank very high in Europe. This is most evident for Germany and Italy. But since the virtual elimination of Gaelic as Ireland's indigenous language in the nineteenth century, the linguistic unity of England-Ireland has come to approach that of Germany and Italy. The growth of an indigeneous Norwegian language (*landsmaal*) in the nineteenth century has led to a smaller measure of linguistic homogeneity in the case of Sweden-Norway. But Norway's indigenous language spread slowly in the nineteenth century. Only about one-fifth of the Norwegian school districts had adopted *landsmaal* as the language of instruction by 1909 and since then the pace may well have been delayed further.[6] The available evidence, furthermore, suggests that what language barrier exists between Sweden and

4. Gebhard L. Schweigler, *National Consciousness in Divided Germany* (Beverly Hills, Calif.: Sage Publications, 1975), pp. 44-47.
5. Taylor and Hudson, *World Handbook*, p. 215.
6. Einar Haugen, *Language Conflict and Language Planning: The Case of Modern Norwegian* (Cambridge, Mass.: Harvard University Press, 1966), p. 39.

Norway is by no means insurmountable. In 1946, for example, only 15 percent of a national sample of Swedes indicated that they did not understand any Norwegian.[7] Thus, even in the area of least linguistic cohesion, complementary communication capacities, as indicated by linguistic homogeneity, were developed to a relatively high degree. In summary, the degree of cultural cohesion that marks this group of European culture areas is greater than that typical of other areas in Europe and most other parts of the world.[8]

Chapter II offered one particular formulation of the communications approach which principally has been developed by Karl Deutsch. Unlike other writings in the same research tradition, Chapter II did not focus on the gradual change in the level of interdependence but on the asymmetric reordering of two kinds of interdependence over time. The first kind describes mental factors, the sharing of meaning in community as indicated by the transfer of messages. The second kind of interdependence is based on material forces, the division of labor in society as indicated by the exchange of goods and services. In culturally cohesive areas the sharing of meaning in community leads to the convergence of regions and increasing homogeneity of people; the division of labor in society promotes divergence and heterogeneity. Changes in the balance between convergence and divergence, between standardization and differentiation, is one relevant set of factors that helps explain political unification and fragmentation.

Since it relies only on this set of factors the analysis of political unification and fragmentation offered in this appendix is partial. The choices of political elites and the constraints of the international system have an independent, direct effect on unification and fragmentation. But this part of a more encompassing explan-

---

Raymond Lindgren, *Norway-Sweden: Union, Disunion, and Scandinavian Integration* (Princeton: Princeton University Press, 1959), pp. 25, 275.
7. Lindgren, *Norway-Sweden*, p. 275.
8. Walker Connor, "Nation-Building or Nation-Destroying?" *World Politics*, XXIV, 3 (April 1972), pp. 319-355. See also the essays devoted to the topic in "Political Integration in Multinational States," *Journal of International Affairs*, XXVII, 1 (1973).

ation deserves to be tested in a preliminary fashion. How well does the balance between standardization in community and differentiation in society explain the four instances of unification and fragmentation that culturally homogeneous areas in Europe have experienced since 1815?

As will be argued at greater length in the next two sections, the unification of Germany and Italy and the fragmentation of Sweden-Norway and England-Ireland reveal distinct patterns of growth of the sharing of meaning in community and of the division of labor in society. In both instances this explanation would "postdict" an imbalance between interdependence in community and society. In Germany and Italy, standardization and increases in communication flows should exceed differentiation and gains in transaction flows. In the case of Sweden-Norway and England-Ireland, that relation should be reversed. There, differentiation should grow faster than standardization.

THE UNIFICATION OF GERMANY AND ITALY

In both the German and the Italian cases, the establishment of a cultural community predated the formation of a tightly knit society. As a result, communication capacities were sufficiently well developed to outweigh the differentiating impact of the increasing division of labor in society and economy during the Industrial Revolution. The major difference between the two cases was the degree of diffusion of community throughout the population. In Germany diffusion occurred early and was extensive; in Italy it took place late and was restricted. This difference was matched by a corresponding one between German and Italian society. German society modernized earlier and faster than Italian society. The result of these differences was in both cases similar, a balance between standardization and differentiation which favored the unification of both countries in the nineteenth century.

Both German and Italian histories reveal a wavelike pattern in attempted political unifications before the beginning of the nineteenth century. Although the early Holy Roman Empire and the Roman Empire provided historical models for imitation, most of these attempts were undertaken in modern times, after the emergence of German and Italian language communities around

1300. Both Germany and Italy experienced periods of general decline before a renewal of their vitality in the eighteenth century—Germany in response to the experience of the Thirty Years' War, Italy as a result of the shift of world commerce away from the Mediterranean toward the Atlantic. Finally, both countries were deeply affected by the ideological and political impact of the French Revolution and the Napoleonic occupation. These forces weakened established political and social structures in Germany and Italy without providing political unity to the increasingly cohesive German and Italian communities.

Although attempts at German and Italian unification go back many centuries, the nineteenth century experience of the two countries can be explained by reaching back no further than the seventeenth century. The growth of the German community occurred early. Revival of interest in the German language, manifested in the increasing popularity of literary groups and language reform associations, dates back to the second half of the seventeenth century. Germany's Augustan age of literature followed in the eighteenth century, culminating in the cosmopolitanism of the works of Goethe and Schiller. These changes in the realm of culture were accompanied and reinforced by changes in the structure of Germany's book trade. German literature was increasingly written in German. The proportion of books published in German to those in Latin changed from 1/2 in 1587, to 2/1 in 1714, to 10/1 in 1780.[9] The growth of a German periodical and newspaper press in the eighteenth century was a similar process of acceleration. The number of periodicals of all kinds increased from 58 to 410 between 1700 and 1770, an average rate of growth of 87 percent per decade. Toward the end of the eighteenth century, that growth rate increased futher. Between 1770 and 1790 the number of periodicals jumped from 410 to 1,225 for an average growth rate of 99 percent per decade.[10] These high rates of increase in a society not yet touched

---

9. Francis L. Loewenheim, "The German Unity Movement and the Rise of Political Community in the North Atlantic Area" (unpublished manuscript), Chapter III, p. 39.
10. Karl W. Deutsch et al., "Background for Community" (unpublished manuscript), Chapter IX, p. 11.

by the Industrial Revolution were influenced by a rise in the rate of literacy, the growth of public education in primary schools, and a trend toward scientific and German (rather than Latin or French) literary studies in secondary schools. To be sure, toward the end of the eighteenth century, particularism and parochialism still dominated the outlook of the German people. But the wave of nationalism that swept the German states between 1807 and 1815 in response to the French occupation reflected the considerable strength of the German community at the outset of the nineteenth century.

The growth of the German community accelerated further during the first half of the nineteenth century, spurred by the educational and cultural reforms adopted especially in Prussia in the years 1807–1815. Universal literacy was soon achieved. In 1820, 72 percent of the Prussian population was literate; the figure increased to 96 percent by 1850 and 98 percent in 1870.[11] Primary school education was virtually universal by 1830. In Prussia, school enrollment figures for the 5–24 year age group increased from 32 percent in 1822 to 41 percent in 1834 and stayed at that level throughout the rest of the nineteenth century.[12] Between 1834 and 1874 the total Prussian mail flow increased on the average by 283 percent per decade, compared to the 128 percent increase per decade for Germany as a whole between 1872 and 1910.[13] The number of titles published in

11. Wolfgang Zapf, "Indikatoren des sozialen Wandels 1760-1960: Vergleichende Übersichten" (unpublished paper, Cambridge, Mass., 1967), Table 27. The figure refers to Prussia only but can reasonably be assumed to hold approximately for the other German states as well.

12. Wolfgang Zapf and Peter Flora, "Zeitreihen als Indikatoren der Modernisierung: Einige Probleme der Datensammlung und Datenanalyse," *Politische Vierteljahresschrift*, XII (June 1971), p. 68.

13. Peter J. Katzenstein, "Political Integration and Partition in Nineteenth-Century Germany" (unpublished paper, Cambridge, Mass., 1969), Appendix. Friedrich Wilhelm von Reden, *Deutschland und das übrige Europa: Handbuch der Boden-, Bevölkerungs-, Erwerbs-, und Verkehrsstatistik: des Staatshaushalts und der Streitmacht. In vergleichender Darstellung* (Wiesbaden: Kreidel and Niedner, 1854), pp. 915-948. Königliches Statistisches Bureau (ed.), *Jahrbuch für die amtliche Statistik des preussischen Staats*, IV (1876), p. 365. Werner Sombart, *Die Deutsche Volkswirtschaft im 19. Jahrhundert und im Anfang des 20. Jahrhunderts: Eine Einführung in die Nationalökonomie* (Stuttgart: Kohlhammer, 1954), p. 495.

Germany between 1811 and 1850 almost trebled from roughly 3,200 to 9,100, as did the number of newspapers published in Prussia which increased from 845 in 1824 to 2,127 in 1869.[14] Similarly striking was the growth in the number of organized scientific congresses and conferences which brought together members of Germany's academic elite teaching in different German states.[15]

In contrast to Germany, the growth of community in Italy occurred later and did not diffuse as widely throughout the Italian population. At the outset of the nineteenth century the Germans reacted more strongly to the Napoleonic occupation than did the Italians. But the difference is also illustrated by the two countries' dissimilar experiences with linguistic assimilation. In short, it is the difference between Dante and Luther. Like Germany, Italy had achieved a large measure of linguistic unity by the thirteenth century. Dante was writing for a potentially nationwide Italian audience. But while Luther's prose was preached from the pulpit to the illiterate masses, Dante's poetry was praised in the parlors of the literate few. This difference was crucial. Prior to Italy's unification the emergence of an Italian language and the growth of an Italian community was largely confined to the elite. As late as 1951, one national sample survey showed that 35 percent of the respondents still used their dialect as their sole means of communications and that 13 percent were actually unable to use Italian.[16]

In the eighteenth century the growth of community was, therefore, less powerful in Italy than in Germany, but among members of the Italian elite that growth is clearly traceable. The eighteenth century witnessed a conversion from traditional Italian patriotism toward the type of Italian nationalism that was to mark the *Risorgimento* of the nineteenth century. Men like Antonio Genovesi, Vittorio Alfieri, and Pietro Verri expressed in

---

14. Sombart, *Deutsche Volkswirtschaft*, pp. 409, 412.
15. R. Hinton Thomas, *Liberalism, Nationalism, and the German Intellectuals (1822-1847): An Analysis of the Academic and Scientific Conferences of the Period* (Cambridge: Heffer, 1951), *p. 139*.
16. Raphael Zariski, *Italy: The Politics of Uneven Development* (Hinsdale: Dryden Press, 1972), p. 10.

their writings the growing sentiments favoring Italian unity. In the first half of the nineteenth century the growth of the Italian community continued to be restricted almost exclusively to the Italian elite, while the mass of the population lived on in its traditional and parochial ways. This gap between elite and mass explains the weakness of the Italian national consciousness and the unexpectedly gradual growth of the *Risorgimento* in a peninsula of considerable geographical and religious cohesion.[17]

Metternich's aperçu of Italy as a "merely geographical expression" was very applicable to the mass of the Italian population.[18] The spread of primary education and literacy among the population at large, which was largely completed in Germany by 1830, had hardly begun in Italy at the time of unification. Reforms, which in Prussia had been initiated in the first decade of the nineteenth century, were enacted on a much smaller scale in Piedmont, the political nucleus of modern Italy, only half a century later. Illiteracy had largely disappeared in Germany by 1850; the illiteracy figure for the Italian population stood at 75 percent in 1860.[19] Enrollment figures in Prussian primary schools had reached their peak as early as 1830; in Italy this was not to occur until the twentieth century.[20] Italy's average yearly book production between 1861 and 1870 was not higher than the Prussian production of 3,200 in 1811.[21] And while the number of Italian periodicals increased from 185 in 1836 to 450 in 1864, these figures were still hardly more than 20 percent of the respective Prussian totals for the years 1824 and 1869.[22] The

---

17. H. Stuart Hughes, *The United States and Italy*, rev. ed. (Cambridge, Mass.: Harvard University Press, 1965), p. 29. Dennis Mack Smith, *Italy: A Modern History* (Ann Arbor: University of Michigan Press, 1959), p. 5. Dennis Mack Smith (ed.), *The Making of Italy, 1796-1870* (New York: Walker, 1968), pp. 2, 6-7.
18. Quoted in Edgar Holt, *The Making of Italy, 1815-1870* (New York: Atheneum, 1971), p. 22.
19. Maurice F. Neufeld, *Italy: School for Awakening Countries* (Ithaca: Cayuga Press, 1960), p. 15.
20. Istituto Centrale di Statistica, *Sommario di Statistiche Storiche dell'Italia, 1861-1965* (Rome: Istituto Poligrafico, 1968), p. 40.
21. *Ibid.*, p. 46.
22. Neufeld, *Italy*, p. 130.

presence of the Catholic church, to be sure, provided a network of cultural and educational institutions which might have been used to accelerate the Italian unification process; but the church never became an advocate of political unity.

Since the growth pattern of the German and Italian communities was out of phase, how can this analysis explain political unification as the eventual outcome in both cases? The answer lies in a corresponding difference in the development of German and Italian society. During the eighteenth and nineteenth centuries, German society modernized more rapidly than Italian society. Slow social change exposed the moderate communication capacities of the Italian community to a weak differentiation effect. Rapid social change taxed more heavily the much greater communications capacity of the German community. But in both instances the balance between standardization and differentiation was favorable to political unification.

In the eighteenth century, German society looked dynamic in comparison with Italy's relative stagnation; but it was relatively slow to evolve in comparison with the growth of the German community. Although Germany was endowed with a superb grid of waterways and thoroughfares, in the eighteenth century technical and political factors prevented the net's full exploitation. Poor road conditions, dissimilar coinage systems, low labor mobility, and the absence of a large capital market provided barriers to the growth of social transactions. These barriers were reinforced by the large number of independent states and principalities, 1,789 in all, which exercised fully their rights to levy customs duties; the restrictive effect on the expansion of internal trade was enormous.[23] That expansion did not occur until the second quarter of the nineteenth century, that is, until after the growth of the German community had been substantially completed. The development of Germany's railways occurred rapidly—increasing from 400 miles in 1840 to more than 12,000

---

23. Wolfgang Zorn, "Binnenwirtschaftliche Verflechtungen um 1800," in Friedrich Lütge (ed.), *Die wirtschaftliche Situation in Deutschland und Österreich um die Wende vom 18. zum 19. Jahrhundert* (Stuttgart: Gustav Fischer Verlag, 1964), pp. 99-109.

miles in 1870. The economic unification of large parts of Germany through the German customs union (*Zollverein*) of 1834 was the second major factor contributing to the increase of social transactions.[24] Germany's delayed industrialization from a position of "relative economic backwardness" occurred rapidly only after the construction of railways on which goods could be shipped freely throughout Germany, that is, from about 1850 on.[25] The relative stagnation of German society during the first half of the nineteenth century and its change in the second half are reflected in the proportion of Germany's rural population which diminished only slightly from 74 percent in 1810 to 72 percent in 1850, but fell thereafter at an accelerating rate to 64 percent in 1870 and 40 percent in 1910.[26]

The division of labor in Italian society was less advanced than in Germany. The rapid expansion of Italy's population from 11.3 million in 1700 to 18.1 million in 1800 strengthened the agrarian character which marked Italian society until the end of the nineteenth century.[27] As all economic historians agree, Italian industrialization occurred late, and its impact on society was weak. Sustained economic growth did not set in until the end of the nineteenth century, a generation after the political unification of Italy had been achieved.[28] In 1806 less than 3 per-

---

24. William O. Henderson, *The Zollverein* (London: Cass, 1959). Arnold H. Price, *The Evolution of the Zollverein: A Study of the Ideas and Institutions Leading to German Economic Unification between 1815 and 1833* (Ann Arbor: University of Michigan Press, 1949).
25. The phrase was coined by Alexander Gerschenkron in his *Economic Backwardness in Historical Perspective: A Book of Essays* (Cambridge, Mass.: Harvard University Press, 1962), pp. 1-30. See also Helmut Böhme, *Deutschlands Weg zur Grossmacht: Studien zum Verhältnis von Wirtschaft und Staat während der Reichsgründungszeit, 1845-1881* (Cologne: Kiepenheuer & Witsch, 1966); and Theodore S. Hamerow, *The Social Foundations of German Unification, 1858-1871* (Princeton: Princeton University Press, 1969).
26. Zapf, "Indikatoren," Table 10. "Rural" is here defined as 2,000 inhabitants or less per community. Data for 1810 and 1850 refer to Prussia only. In 1870 the Prussian average was 4 percent above that for all of Germany.
27. Quoted in Deutsch et al., "Background for Community," Chapter VI, pp. 21-22.
28. See, for example, Shepard B. Clough, *The Economic History of Modern Italy* (New York: Columbia University Press, 1964), pp. 3, 20.

cent of the population held nonagricultural positions, and in 1860 manufacturing was still overwhelmingly artisan in character. Domestic transaction channels were poorly developed. Roads were in terrible condition; despite the construction of canals in some parts of the country in the eighteenth century, internal waterways were unimportant for Italy as a whole, and there were few ports for coastal shipping.[29] In contrast to Germany, the introduction of the railway was slow. In 1860, there existed only 1,200 miles of track (as compared to Germany's 7,200) and 90 percent of these were located in two provinces, Piedmont and Lombardy.[30] And in contrast to Germany, Italy did not experience economic unification before political unification; there was no Italian equivalent to the German *Zollverein*.

If applied to Italy's most advanced regions—to the prototypical cases of the growth of community and society inside Italy—the accelerated development of community as compared with society stands out even more clearly than for Italy as a whole. Piedmont was Italy's Prussia founded on rock, not sand; it exhibited a similar blend of authoritarianism, bureaucratization, militarism, and politically powerless liberalism. In this nucleus of Italy's political unification, society and economy stagnated in isolation from the rest of Italy and the world until the late 1840s.[31] In contrast, the Piedmontese education system, although poor at the primary level, improved greatly as one went to secondary and university levels. As a result the Piedmontese professional class, the strongest supporters of national and liberal sentiments and the strongest social link to other regions in Italy, was bigger than that of any other state in Italy. In 1861, 4.1 percent of Piedmont's population were professional men as compared with 3.1 percent in Lombardy, Italy's most advanced province, and 0.8 percent in the Papal States, Italy's most backward region.[32]

---

29. Neufeld, *Italy*, pp. 22-23.
30. Clough, *Economic History*, p. 66.
31. Bolton King, *A History of Italian Unity: A Political History of Italy from 1814 to 1871* (London: Nisbet, 1899), I, 41-51.
32. Deutsch et al., "Background for Community," Chapter XXV, pp. 13-14.

Lombardy presents the same picture of a more rapid development in cultural than social and economic affairs. Part of the reason for the province's economic stagnation must be sought in the tariff policy pursued by the Austrian occupation forces, which sought to shield Lombardy from the rest of Italy and tried to attach the province closely to the Habsburg Empire. But the main reason was the predominantly agricultural character of Lombardy's economy. This economic retardation embued Lombardy's weak industrial and commercial middle class with a spirit of conservatism and caution inimical to the growth of trade, commerce, and social transactions generally. To be sure, transport conditions in Lombardy improved considerably, and the pace in the founding of manufacturing industries and commerce quickened somewhat. But in the first half of the nineteenth century Lombardy remained a traditional society which modernized only gradually.[33] The same cannot be said of cultural communications which underwent much more dramatic expansion. Lombardy's education system was by far the best in Italy, comparable in many ways to that of France and perhaps even Germany.[34] Consequently, literacy was much more widespread than in the rest of Italy, and the size of Lombardy's professional class was second only to that of Piedmont. The growing sense of community, to be sure, in Lombardy as in the rest of Italy, remained almost exclusively restricted to the middle class. But in Lombardy that growth occurred very rapidly.[35] One indication is the expansion of journalism in the province, which by the late 1830s had become the primary propaganda weapon of the Risorgimento, evading skillfully the restrictions of the Austrian censorship system and pointing strenuously to the need for economic and institutional changes in Italy. To the extent that published opinion reflected public opinion, at least the public opinion of the middle class, the growth of cultural communica-

33. Ken Roberts Greenfield, *Economics and Liberalism in the Risorgimento: A Study of Nationalism in Lombardy, 1814-1848*, rev. ed. (Baltimore: Johns Hopkins University Press, 1965), pp. 9, 26, 35, 51-53, 66-67, 80-81, 100, 107, 124.
34. King, *Italian Unity*, I, 55. Greenfield, *Risorgimento*, pp. 212-214.
35. Greenfield, *Risorgimento*, p. 31.

tions in Lombardy was much more rapid, sustained, and pervasive than corresponding changes in Lombard society.[36] Thus, the relation between the sharing of meaning in community and the division of labor in society—between standardization and differentiation in Lombardy, Piedmont, and Italy at large—follows the same pattern, leading toward a growth rate that was relatively higher for cultural communications than for social transactions.

The German and Italian cases confirm a partial explanation of political unification in terms of the asymmetric growth of the sharing of meaning in community and the division of labor in society. Both cases reveal the predominance of community and its standardizing effect over society and its differentiating impact and a growth rate that was higher for cultural communications than for social transactions. The major difference between the German and the Italian experiences was the degree of diffusion of community among the mass of the population. In Germany the flow of cultural communications encompassed virtually the entire population; in Italy it was restricted to the elites. In both cases, then, the historical process proved variable, but that process revealed a distinct structure which supports this partial explanation of political unification.

THE FRAGMENTATION OF SWEDEN-NORWAY AND ENGLAND-IRELAND

Both the Norwegian and the Irish cases share the conditions most conducive to political fragmentation. Within Norway and Ireland the sharing of meaning and standardization grew faster than the division of labor and differentiation. But between Ireland and England, and Norway and Sweden that relation was reversed; the flow of social transactions grew faster than the flow of cultural communications, and with it differentiation increased faster than standardization.

As had been true of the comparison of Germany and Italy, the Irish-English and the Norwegian-Swedish cases show a marked difference in the relative strength of these relationships. In

36. *Ibid.*, pp. 147-287.

Norway, cultural communications were diffused widely throughout a basically agrarian society with a low level of social transactions. In Ireland's more industrialized, if stagnant, society, on the other hand, social transactions were more fully developed than in Norway, weakening the standardizing effect of cultural communications. An analysis of these domestic flows suggests, then, that demands for political independence should have been notably stronger in Norway than in Ireland. But this postulated effect was offset by a corresponding asymmetry in the relations between Norway and Sweden, and Ireland and England. Social transactions and differentiation were much stronger between Ireland and England than between Norway and Sweden. If, in comparison with cultural communications, the flow of social transactions had increased faster in Norway, political fragmentation would have occurred later; and if it had increased at a slower rate in Ireland, fragmentation would have occurred earlier. Conversely, if, compared with cultural communications, the flow of social transactions had been stronger between Norway and Sweden, fragmentation would have occurred earlier, and if it had been weaker between Ireland and England, fragmentation would have occurred later. These differences cancelled each other out. Differences in the relations between the internal and external transactions and communications flows help explain, therefore, the similar timing of the breakup of the two unions.

Ireland and Norway were both unwilling brides to marriages of convenience with their more powerful neighbors. Faced with a potentially revolutionary threat at home and abroad, England opted for union with Ireland as the most effective medicine against the Jacobin bacillus. It took a year's debate in the Irish Parliament and the puchase of the vote of a large number of parliamentarians to the tune of more than one million pounds to bring about Irish ratification of that union. Like Ireland, Norway was the victim of the instabilities created by the French Revolution and the Napoleonic Wars. Previously united with Denmark, one of Napoleon's defeated allies, Norway was given to Sweden in 1814. The Norwegians, who wanted no part of that arrangement, made a civilized revolution, wrote their own constitution, and bowed quickly to Sweden's military intervention. The Irish-English union was a tight one, with one king, one Parliament, and one system of taxation. The union of Norway and Sweden, in contrast, was much looser and depended only on the person of the Swedish king, the army he commanded, and the foreign policy he conducted. But whether tight or loose, in both cases unification at the outset of the nineteenth century was followed by fragmentation at the beginning of the twentieth.

In Ireland, community and standardization grew faster than society and differentiation. The linguistic assimilation of the Irish to English in the nineteenth century did not support the growth of an English-Irish community. But in comparison with nineteenth-century Norway, it probably slowed down the emergence of a distinct Irish political community. The relative retardation in the growth of an Irish community and its acceleration after 1860–1870 are reflected in the few quantitative data available. The proportion of the population between five and twenty-four years of age in school rose from less than 2 percent in 1830, to almost 8 percent in 1850, to 21 percent in 1880, and to 29 percent in 1910, with the greatest shift per decade occurring between 1860 and 1880.[37] Similarly, the proportion of the Irish labor force employed in the tertiary sector increased from 15 percent in 1840, to 26 percent in 1870, to 28 percent in 1910, with the greatest shift per decade occurring between 1850 and 1880.[38]

The growth of the Irish community accelerated significantly only during the second half of the nineteenth century. What happened at the same time to the flow of social transactions in Ireland? Here the picture is one of relative stagnation not uncharacteristic of other rural areas in Europe during the Industrial Revolution, but accentuated by Ireland's proximity to and

---

37. Zapf and Flora, "Zeitreihen," p. 68.
38. Simon Kuznets, "Quantitative Aspects of the Economic Growth of Nations: II. Industrial Distribution of National Product and Labor Force," *Economic Development and Cultural Change*, V, 4, Supplement (July 1957), p. 85. Between 1880 and 1910, the overall percentage for the tertiary sector declined slightly, while the relative share of those employed in transport and communications increased.

dependence on England as an industrial leader. Eighteenth-century Ireland had enjoyed a fair measure of economic prosperity and participation in the incipient industrialization process which had then been taking place in England. That development gradually halted during the first half of the nineteenth century as the crisis of domestic industry, coupled with a continued rise in population, gave Ireland once again a more agrarian social structure and a more decentralized economy.[39] After the famine of 1846, death and emigration contributed to the drastic decline of Ireland's population in the second half of the nineteenth century. The short-term impact of the famine was highly disruptive of social transactions and the potential long-term economic benefits of a declining population were soon more than offset by the industrial crisis of the 1870s and 1880s.[40] Compared with Norway, Ireland's channels for social transactions were in relatively good condition in the nineteenth century—a passable road and canal system first, reasonably quick and extensive railway construction later. But the halting progress in the division of labor in Irish society and economy during the nineteenth century was evident in the country's slow industrialization.[41]

In Ireland, community grew faster than society. Between Ireland and England that relation was reversed as social transactions grew faster than cultural communications. This is shown indirectly by the striking difference in the type of historical evidence available. Irish history is primarily the history of the growth of an Irish community; the history of English-Irish relations, on the other hand, deals mostly with the flow of social transactions. Here all indicators uniformly point to the great magnitude of Irish-English transactions, compared with the flow

39. L. M. Cullen, *An Economic History of Ireland since 1660* (London: Batsford, 1972), pp. 121, 127.
40. *Ibid.*, pp. 135, 141, 146-153.
41. *Ibid.*, 121-123, 125, 143-144. John F. Burke, *Outline of the Industrial History of Ireland* (Dublin: Browne and Nolan, 1946), pp. 272-273, 352-353. Joseph Lee, "Capital in the Irish Economy," in L. M. Cullen (ed.), *The Formation of the Irish Economy* (Cork: Mercier Press, 1969), pp. 56-57. Joseph Lee, "The Railways in the Irish Economy," in Cullen (ed.), *The Formation*, pp. 77-78. F. S. L. Lyons, *Ireland since the Famine* (New York: Charles Scribner's Sons, 1971), p. 46.

of cultural communications. During the eighteenth century, Ireland's trade dependence on England had increased greatly from 50 percent in 1700, to 81 percent in 1800.[42] Throughout the nineteenth century this trade link did not weaken. Free trade with England was established in 1825, with disastrous effects for Ireland's industrialization. In 1906, 80 percent of Ireland's export and 66 percent of its import trade was with England.[43] Capital flow between the two countries was also fully developed, due to Ireland's net contribution to the coffers of the British treasury, the transfer of rent by absentee landlords, and the repatriation of profits by British banks. And the evidence available suggests that the outflow of capital accelerated during the second half of the nineteenth century.[44] Lastly, a substantial amount of labor migration took place, especially during the first half of the nineteenth century; between 1780 and 1845, 750,000 Irishmen emigrated, most of them to England.[45]

The cultural relationship between Ireland and England, on the other hand, was more tenuous and weakened in the course of the nineteenth century. Before the political unification of the two countries, Ireland and England had formed a community at the top; their elites were united on questions of religion, indifferent to questions of nationality, and divided only on questions of their pocketbooks. Although empirical evidence is largely lacking for the nineteenth century, the English-Irish elite community appears to have eroded rapidly. The first of Ireland's four waves of political nationalism, led by Daniel O'Connell in the 1820s and 1830s, was distinguished by its inclusion of the clergy and the

---

42. L. M. Cullen, *Anglo-Irish Trade, 1660-1800* (New York: Kelley, 1968), p. 45.
43. Burke, *Industrial History of Ireland*, pp. 198-247, 264-270. Alice Effie Murray, *A History of the Commercial and Financial Relations between England and Ireland from the Period of the Restoration* (London: King, 1907), pp. 342-370. Cullen, *Economic History of Ireland*, pp. 103, 157-158. Lyons, *Ireland Since the Famine*, p. 57.
44. Cullen, *Economic History of Ireland*, pp. 105, 127-129, 169. Murray, *Commercial and Financial Relations*, p. 371. Lee, "Capital in the Irish Economy," pp. 53, 59-60. Lee, "Railways in the Irish Economy," p. 80.
45. Cullen, *Economic History of Ireland*, p. 119. Eric Strauss, *Irish Nationalism and British Democracy* (New York: Columbia University Press, 1951), pp. 118-131. Lyons, *Ireland since the Famine*, pp. 26, 112.

peasants, the two groups most opposed to the affirmation of the position of church and landlord in the Act of Union. Growing Irish hostility to England became permanently imprinted in the public mind by the mixture of incompetence and arrogance with which the English government handled the disastrous famine of 1846. Government policy in the 1840s was typical of the indifference and ignorance of English attitudes throughout the nineteenth century. That ignorance did not stem from an absence of facts—the English government collected copious information on the Irish question throughout the nineteenth century—but from a lack of understanding.[46] A community of meaning and shared preference may have been developed among the Irish and English elites at the outset of the nineteenth century. At the end of the century, however, only traces of a community bridging the Irish Sea could be found.

As had been true of Ireland, in Norway standardization grew faster than differentiation. But in contrast to the Irish case, the emergence of an indigenous language accelerated the growth of a Norwegian community, while Norway's more traditional society generated a smaller flow of social transactions. Between 1815 and the 1830s, the flow of internal Norwegian communications virtually stagnated; not until the 1830s did Norwegian literary life stir.[47] The traditional Norwegian peasant figured prominently as a theme in that literary revival. And in contrast to the mass of the Irish population, these Norwegian peasants were a well-educated lot.[48] In the eighteenth century, mass education had been largely

---

46. Nicholas Mansergh, *The Irish Question, 1840-1921; A Commentary on Anglo-Irish Relations and on Social and Political Forces in Ireland in the Age of Reform and Revolution*, rev. ed. (Toronto: Toronto University Press, 1965), pp. 50, 114, 295.

47. For a detailed and more contemporary view of Norway's community, see Harry Eckstein, *Division and Cohesion in Democracy: A Study of Norway* (Princeton: Princeton University Press, 1966), pp. 78-132. Theodore Jorgenson, *Norway's Relation to Scandinavian Unionism, 1815-1871* (Northfield: St. Olaf College Press, 1935), pp. 67-118, 433-456; Andreas Elviken, *Die Entwicklung des Norwegischen Nationalismus* (Berlin: Ebering, 1930); and Karen Larsen, *A History of Norway* (Princeton: Princeton University Press, 1948), pp. 416-417, 423, 431, 436-453.

48. Larsen, *History of Norway*, pp. 450-451; Lindgren, *Norway-Sweden*, p. 24.

the task of the church, which had done a reasonably effective job of creating semiliterate believers. Government reforms in the country's educational system in the 1820s could thus build on a good foundation. To be sure, Norwegian peasants hardly read anything but the Bible during the first half of the nineteenth century; but when in the middle of the century postage rates declined and newspaper circulation increased, the existence of a literate population made possible the large increases in the flow of communications.[49]

The last third of the nineteenth century witnessed a notable strengthening of the Norwegian community, as national sentiments were now universally shared in sharp contrast to the elite movements for Scandinavian unionism and romantic nationalism which had characterized the second third of the century.[50] A resounding defeat of a reform proposal of the union submitted to the Norwegian Parliament in 1871 set the stage for an increasing politicization of the Norwegian community in its demand for full sovereignty. The rising working class on the Left was fully imbued with a self-assertive nationalism, as indicated by a vigorous working-class press.[51] The growing cohesiveness of the Norwegian community during the last third of the nineteenth century was, finally, revealed by the rise of an indigenous Norwegian language.[52] Originally conceived by adherents of a romantic nationalism, such as Ivar Aasen, as an instrument to liberate Norway from intellectual domination by Denmark through a Danish-Norwegian elite language (*riksmaal*), the unification of Norway's diverse regional dialects into a new language of its own (*landsmaal*) soon served to increase friction between Sweden and Norway. *Landsmaal* spread slowly—in 1909 only

---

49. Lindgren, *Norway-Sweden*, p. 35; Larsen, *History of Norway*, p. 428; Brynjolf J. Hovde, *The Scandinavian Countries, 1720-1865: The Rise of the Middle Classes* (Ithaca: Cornell University Press, 1948), I, 269.
50. Oscar J. Falnes, *National Romanticism in Norway* (New York: Columbia University Press, 1933), pp. 42-44; Lindgren, *Norway-Sweden*, pp. 36-37, 49.
51. Lindgren, *Norway-Sweden*, pp. 36, 54-55; Larsen, *History of Norway*, pp. 454, 465-466, 486.
52. Haugen, *Language Conflict*; Lindgren, *Norway-Sweden*, pp. 25, 29, 275; Hovde, *Scandinavian Countries*, II, 466-469.

20 percent of Norway's school districts had chosen it as the medium of instruction—but it was more than a mere symbol of the distinctiveness of the Norwegian community.[53]

Compared with the growth of community, the evolution of Norwegian society and the flow of social transactions appear to have occurred at a markedly slower rate.[54] Norway was poor, a backwater of nineteenth-century Europe. After 1815 an internal transportation system began to develop very slowly; the modernization of the road system did not occur until after 1845. There were no canals, and the creation of a railway network did not start in earnest until the 1870s.[55] Norway's old guild system was abolished only in 1866, and domestic markets became more important only after the middle of the century.[56] Industrialization and the commercialization of agriculture occurred very slowly, as did the disintegration of the agrarian social order. Compared with the growing strength of its community, Norway's society was thus marked by relative stagnation.

In the relationship between Norway and Sweden, on the other hand, the relative strengths of communications and transactions flows were reversed. As had been true of the Irish-English case, social transactions were more fully developed than cultural communications; but in contrast to it, these social and cultural links were more tenuous. The absence of social interdependencies between Norway and Sweden after the union's formation was caused in part by geographical inaccessibility, in part by incompatible social structures.[57] Although the flow of social transactions between Norway and Sweden remained at a generally low level throughout the nineteenth century, increases were noticeable, especially toward the end of the century. Oslo and

---

53. Haugen, *Language Conflict*, p. 39; Lindgren, *Norway-Sweden*, pp. 29-30; Falnes, *National Romanticism*, pp. 365-372.
54. Larsen, *History of Norway*, pp. 398-403; Hovde, *Scandinavian Countries*, I, 261-270.
55. Larsen, *History of Norway*, pp. 427-428, 460; Lindgren, *Norway-Sweden*, p. 43; Hovde, *Scandinavian Countries*, I, 265.
56. Hovde, *Scandinavian Countries*, I, 240, 270; Lindgren, *Norway-Sweden*, pp. 31-32; Deutsch et al., "Background for Community," p. 528.
57. Lindgren, *Norway-Sweden*, pp. 18, 25, 29, 37, 39; Larsen, *History of Norway*, p. 396.

Appendix 249

Stockholm, for example, were connected by rail in 1867, an early date considering the relatively slow introduction of the railway in Norway itself. And as late as 1897–1903, the two partner countries cooperated in the construction of a railroad that was to carry iron ore from northern Sweden to Narvik.[58] Separate Norwegian and Swedish currency systems persisted for a long time because of Norwegian sensitivity, but in 1875 Norway decided to join the Scandinavian Monetary Union.[59] Sweden extended to Norway's growing merchant marine carrying privileges for Swedish foreign trade, and during the latter part of the nineteenth century a large and increasing portion of the Norwegian fleet was constructed in Swedish shipyards.[60] Some joint economic institutions emerged as late as the first decade of the twentieth century, indicating that the rising trend of social transactions persisted until the union's very end.[61]

The increases in social transactions between Sweden and Norway led to a differentiation that was not matched by corresponding gains in cultural communications. Norway's traditional cultural ties with Denmark declined gradually after 1815. But that decline was not matched by an increasing growth, depth, or amity in the cultural communications between Norway and Sweden.[62] No significant common cultural institutions emerged. The Norwegian and Swedish churches, for example, were both Lutheran but did not cooperate in any way.[63] Sharp differences between Norway's egalitarian and Sweden's hierarchical social structure, between democratic and aristocratic political practice, contributed to the weakness of the cultural links between the two middle classes. For a short time the pan-Scandinavian movement competed with the growth of a distinct Norwegian community, at least among the upper classes.[64] But

58. Lindgren, *Norway-Sweden*, pp. 37, 42.
59. *Ibid.*, pp. 28, 40; Larsen, *History of Norway*, p. 460.
60. Larsen, *History of Norway*, p. 429; Lindgren, *Norway-Sweden*, p. 40; Hovde, *Scandinavian Countries*, I, 264.
61. Lindgren, *Norway-Sweden*, p. 29.
62. Larsen, *History of Norway*, p. 396; Lindgren, *Norway-Sweden*, p. 34; Deutsch et al., "Background for Community," pp. 552-553.
63. Lindgren, *Norway-Sweden*, pp. 30-31.
64. *Ibid.*, pp. 33-35, 54-58; Deutsch et al., "Background for Community," pp. 530-532, 547.

more important was the mixture of hostility and indifference of large segments of the Norwegian population toward that movement.[65] Students, for example, should have been among its most enthusiastic proponents. But a majority of the Norwegian students decided to boycott a number of meetings called in Copenhagen, Lund, and Uppsala in the early 1840s.[66] The Norwegian estrangement from the union continued during the next decades. In 1898 Norway won its battle with Sweden over the right to display its own national flag. The growth of the Norwegian community had voided the union's importance even at the symbolic level.[67] By 1905 the real issue was no longer whether but how to dissolve the union. The Norwegian vote in favor of separation was practically unanimous: 367,149 yeas and only 184 nays.[68]

In both the Irish-English and the Norwegian-Swedish cases, political fragmentation resulted from a similar balance between community and its standardizing effect, on the one hand, and society and its differentiating effect, on the other. The relative dominance of cultural communications over social transactions pointed to the emergence of distinct Irish and Norwegian communities in the nineteenth century, marked by a relative abundance of internal communications capacities. The relative dominance of social transactions over cultural communications in the relations between Ireland and England, and Norway and Sweden pointed to an increasing relative scarcity in external communications capacities. Differences in the levels of internal and external transactions and communications flows were distributed asymmetrically. The relative strength of community was greater in Norway than Ireland, but the flow of social transactions was greater between Ireland-England than Norway-Sweden. These differential effects on political unification and fragmentation cancelled each other out and thus contributed to the roughly similar timing in the political fragmentation of the two unions. As had

65. Falnes, *National Romanticism*, p. 37; Larsen, *History of Norway*, p. 425.
66. Jorgenson, *Scandinavian Unionism*, pp. 115-117; Ingvar Andersson, *A History of Sweden* (London: Weidenveld and Nicolson, 1956), p. 340.
67. Lindgren, *Norway-Sweden*, pp. 47, 71.
68. *Ibid.*, p. 67.

Appendix

been true of the German and Italian cases, the historical process was variable but, confirming this partial explanation of political fragmentation, it had a distinctive structure.

SOME FURTHER TESTS

In the process of modernization, Europe's culturally cohesive areas have defied what is commonly thought of as a natural tendency of smaller political units to amalgamate into larger ones. Two instances of unification in the middle of the nineteenth century were followed by another two instances of fragmentation at the outset of the twentieth century. Although it proved variable, the historical process that led to these different political outcomes had a distinct structure. That structure was illuminated through an explanation drawn from the communications literature which focused on the balance between standardization and differentiation as one relevant set of factors that helps explain political unification and fragmentation. By way of summary, Table 26 specifies in a schematic fashion the conditions under which standardization and differentiation could be expected to occur in different political settings.

A systematic test of these hypotheses is made difficult by the limited amount of relevant and reliable historical data. For illustrative purposes a first attempt is made here only for the English-Irish and the Swedish-Norwegian cases. Table 27 summarizes long-term trends in two indicators of community and society.

The size of the economically active segment of the population is a rough measure of the growth of the division of labor in society. In Ireland as well as Norway, that growth accelerated from 1870 to 1910 and from 1920 to 1960, as is indicated by the deceleration of the negative Irish and the acceleration of the positive Norwegian growth rate. The total number of people enrolled in a country's school system, by way of contrast, provides one measure of the sharing of meaning in community. In Ireland and Norway that growth rate declined between 1870 and 1960. In the late nineteenth century, before the fragmentation of the English-Irish and the Swedish-Norwegian unions, communications grew faster than transactions. After these fragmentations had occurred, the relation between communications

TABLE 26. Political Unification and Fragmentation as Outcomes of the Balance between Communications and Transactions

	Politically United Culturally Cohesive Areas		Politically Divided Culturally Cohesive Areas	
	Standardization Effect	Differentiation Effect	Standardization Effect	Differentiation Effect
Within larger ◻ segment	?	?	*C↑ > T↑ Prussia Piedmont/Lombardy	T↑ > C↑
Between ◻ segments	C↑ > T↑	*T↑ > C↑ England-Ireland Sweden-Norway	*C↑ > T↑ Germany Italy	T↑ > C↑
Within smaller ◻ segment	T↑ > C↑	*C↑ > T↑ Ireland Norway	?	?

Key: C = Communications
T = Transactions
↑ = Increase
*Hypotheses preceded by an asterisk have been tested in the preceding sections of this appendix.

TABLE 27. Average Percentage Rates of Growth of Communications and Transactions per Decade in Ireland and Norway (1870-1910, 1920-1960)

Concept	Variable	Indicator	Ireland		Norway	
			1870-1910	1920-1960	1870-1910	1920-1960
Division of labor in society	Social transactions	Economically active population	-20.4	-2.3	5.5	6.8
Sharing of meaning in community	Cultural communications	Total school enrollment	8.0	3.9	11.5	8.8

Sources:
Row (1): Colin Clark, *The Conditions of Economic Progress* (London: Macmillan, 1957), p. 154; *Statistical Abstract of Ireland, 1963* (Dublin, 1963), p. 43; *Historisk Statistikk, 1968* (Oslo, 1969), pp. 36-37.
Row (2): Donald H. Akenson, *The Irish Education Experiment: The National System of Education in the Nineteenth Century* (London: Routledge and Kegan, 1970), pp. 276, 346; Arthur S. Banks, *Cross-Polity Time-Series Data* (Cambridge, Mass.: M.I.T. Press, 1971); *Historisk Statistikk*, p. 603.

and transactions flows was reversed. These countermoving trends as well as the relative magnitude of the two indicators in the two periods support this analysis.

Does a similar conclusion hold for the changes in the flow of communications and transactions between England-Ireland and Sweden-Norway? The data in Table 28 express the changing values of the Relative Acceptance Indicator (R. A.). Like a percentage figure, R. A. measures the relative intensity of communications and transactions flows. But in contrast to it, that intensity is compared not with the total foreign flows of each partner (for example, the percentage of Norwegian exports that are shipped to Sweden) but to the total flow among all countries of the world. R. A. measures the probability of a relation rather than its size.[69] Table 28 illustrates that the interdependence between England-Ireland and Sweden-Norway was high. But while the intensity of transactions increased, it declined in the flow of communications. Growing gaps in communications capacities and differentiation were the result.

The available data do not permit me to extend this analysis back into the nineteenth century. I cannot, therefore, be certain that these trends occurred also before the fragmentation of the two unions. But if this analysis is correct, trends in the intensity of transactions and communications flows in culturally cohesive areas that experienced political fragmentation should be different from trends in areas that did not. The data presented in Table 29 confirm that expectation. Since Table 29 summarizes information on only two indicators that cover different time periods, considerable caution is required in interpreting these data. Two conclusions can, however, be drawn unambiguously. Column A of Table 29 shows that eight of the ten trends in social transactions have moved downward in the twentieth century; they have moved, that is, in a direction opposite to what was observed for the Irish-English and the Norwegian-Swedish cases. Further-

---

69. The methodological literature has recently been summarized and discussed in Cal Clark and Susan Welch, "Western European Trade as a Measure of Integration: Untangling the Interpretations," *Journal of Conflict Resolution*, XVI, 1 (September 1972), pp. 363-382.

TABLE 28. Changes in the Relative Acceptance Indicator as a Measure of the Intensity of Transactions and Communications Flows between England-Ireland and Sweden-Norway, 1913-1968

	Social Transaction (Trade)				Cultural Communication (Mail)			
	UK to Ireland	Ireland to UK	Sweden to Norway	Norway to Sweden	UK to Ireland	Ireland to UK	Sweden to Norway	Norway to Sweden
1913	5.30	4.44	3.85	6.31				
1928	4.05	3.68	7.92	4.06	5.97	9.20	12.43	11.22
1937/8	5.34	6.69	5.38	3.58	6.60	8.49	13.80	11.91
1954/5	5.86	8.20	7.50	3.81	4.39	7.03	13.54	12.71
1961/3	7.21	9.10	8.78	5.57	4.41	7.16	10.80	8.43
1968[a]			8.52	6.60			9.72[b]	6.53
Trend	Up	Up	Up	Up or constant	Down	Down	Down	Down

Source: Trade data were provided by Richard W. Chadwick (University of Hawaii) and Karl W. Deutsch (Harvard University). Cal Clark (New Mexico State University) gave me access to his mail data.
[a] Preliminary data.
[b] 1958.

TABLE 29. Changes in the Relative Acceptance Indicator as a Measure of the Intensity of Culturally Cohesive Areas, 1913-1968

	(A) Social Transactions (Trade)		(B) Cultural Communications (Mail)	
	Trend	Period	Trend	Period
(1) US to UK	Down	1913-1963	Down[a]	1913-1958
(2) UK to US	Down	1913-1963	Down	1913-1961
(3) US to Canada	Down	1913-1963		
(4) Canada to US	Down	1913-1963		
(5) Spain to Portugal	Down	1913-1963	Up	1890-1961
(6) Portugal to Spain	Down	1913-1963	Down	1913-1961
(7) Germany to Switzerland	Up	1938-1963	Up	1913-1961
(8) Switzerland to Germany	Down	1938-1963	Up	1913-1955
(9) Australia to New Zealand	Up	1913-1963	Up	1920-1928
(10) New Zealand to Australia	Down	1913-1963	Down	1928-1958

Source: Trade data were provided by Richard W. Chadwick (University of Hawaii) and Karl W. Deutsch (Harvard University). Cal Clark (New Mexico State University) gave me access to his mail data.

[a] Russett, *Community and Contention*, p. 118.

more, the upward trend in the German-Swiss case (row 7) is due only to a later turning point; by the mid-sixties that R. A. also had declined below its 1938 level. In only one of the ten cases, then, in the case of Australia and New Zealand (row 9), did social transactions increase during the twentieth century. Column B, on the other hand, shows a mixed distribution of trends, with four increases and four declines; this is a clear contrast to the consistent declines in the communications between Norway-Sweden and Ireland-England shown in Table 28. The declining trends in social transactions and the mixed distribution of increases and decreases in cultural communications make for balances between social transactions and cultural communications which differ from the growing deficit in the communication capacities characterizing the Irish-English and Norwegian-Swedish cases. The signs of political fragmentation are, then, noticeable before as well as after the fact.

This appendix has tentatively extended one part of the previous analysis of the persistence of Austria's political autonomy to the political unification and fragmentation of other culturally cohesive areas in Europe since the beginning of the nineteenth century. The analysis has shown that the view of political unification as the normal outcome of the modernization process slights historical experience. Since it relied only on nonpolitical variables, this explanation of political unification and fragmentation is partial. As was abundantly illustrated by the Austro-German case, political choices and constraints have an independent, direct effect on political unification and fragmentation. But this discussion is in agreement with the theoretical analysis of Chapter II. Detailed political analysis, similar to the one offered for the Austro-German case, should enhance further the precision of analysis. In extending, revising, and refining it, broader comparative investigations into the relations between culturally cohesive states thus might rely on the line of reasoning proposed in this study.

INDEX

Adenauer, Konrad, 2, 223
Adler, Viktor, 122
Alfieri, Vittorio, 235
Andrássy, Julius, 126
Angleichungspolitik (1920s), 148–151
Anschluss, 12, 168–169; estimates of Austrian support for, 145–146; institutional structures of, 146–148
Army: after 1849, 68–69; mobilization strength, 88–89; ethnic composition of, 112; purged by Nazis, 164; low morale in 1930s, 169–170
Attention, of Austrian newspapers: to events in Germany 1816-1849, 53–55; 1831-1870, 77–78; 1873-1912, 100–101; 1900-1938, 134–136; 1933-1969, 180–181; 1815-1969, 203, 205; to events abroad, 200. *See also* Content analysis
Attitudes in Austria. *See* Attention, Content analysis, Evaluation, Identification, Public opinion
Augsburger Zeitung, 56
Austria: definition of territorial size, 5, 12–13; national anthem, 13; national consciousness, 172–173. *See also* individual topics
Austro-German People's League, relative size of, 147
Autonomy, political: definition of, 14; and changes in community and society, 25–26; and rewards, 26–32. *See also* Policy coordination

Bach, Alexander, 67

Banks: and government debt, 60–61, 73, 86–88; and industry, 115; nationalization of, 178, 187. *See also* Foreign investment
Bauer, Otto, 154
Bavaria, and the Napoleonic Wars, 39
Beust, Ferdinand von, 85, 126
Biedermeier culture in Austria, 11–12, 58
Bismarck, Otto von, 84, 85
Black, Cyril E., 19
Bosnia-Herzegovina, Austrian occupation and administration of, 128–129
Brandt, Willy, 2–3, 223
Brecht, Berthold, 169
Brezinski, Zbigniew, 3
Bruck, Karl von, 67, 80, 81
Brunn Congress (1899), 122
Bülow, Bernhard, 126
Bureaucracy: internal stalemate of, 59–60; expansion of its power, 69; German character of, 111; diminished size of, 156. *See also* Dynasty
Business organizations: fear of German imports, 47, 76; and Hungarian markets, 75–76; and German customs union, 76; growing power of, 82; and Austro-German economic union, 151. *See also* Commercial policy of Austria

Cabinet, ethnic composition of, 113
Carlsbad Conference, 41
Christian Social Party, 121, 158–161. *See also* ÖVP
Church: and Austria before 1815, 38, 51; in Austrian politics after 1848, 67–68;

259

attitude toward Nazis, 168; support by Austrians, 170
Clemençeau, Georges, 12
Coach Service, between Austria and Germany, 43–44
Coalition government, after 1945, 196
Commercial policy of Austria: in the 19th century, 46–47, 62–63, 78, 81–82; in the 20th century, 151. *See also* German Customs Union; Trade flow; Germany, economic unification
Communications: theory of integration, 16–19; between Austria and Germany, 202–206, *See also* Attention, Mail flow, Students, Telegrams, Telephone calls; in Germany, 233–235, *See also* individual topics under Germany and Prussia; in Italy, 235–237, *See also* individual topics under Italy and Lombardy; in Ireland, 243, 251, *See also* individual topics under Ireland; between Ireland and England, 245–246, *See also* individual topics under Ireland and England; in Norway, 246–248, 251, *See also* individual topics under Norway; between Norway and Sweden, 249–250, 254–257, *See also* individual topics under Norway and Sweden
Community: measurement of, 24–25, 36; theoretical description of, 19–22; and rewards, 28. *See also* Attention, Communications, Identification
Compromise (1866), 119
Concordat (1855), 68
Constitutional Assembly (1918), 148
Consulates: in Austria and Germany, 212–215; in Austria and Italy, 42
Content analysis, 53, 103, 106, 138–141. *See also* Attention, Evaluation, Identification
Counter-Reformation, effect on Austria's elite, 48
Cultural cohesion: and political autonomy, 4, 6, 20, 220–222; defined, 227–229
Cultural nationalism, 9, 10–12, 14, 16
Czechoslovakia, resistance against Nazi occupation, 173
Czernin, Ottokar, 129

De Gasperi, Alcide, 223
Delegation for Austro-German Economic Unification, 146
Deutsch, Karl, 16–17, 106, 231
Deutsche Gemeinbürgschaft, 122–123

Diplomatic agreements concluded between Austria and Germany: 1816-1847, 40; 1848-1865, 77; 1869-1912, 123–124; 1815-1970, 212–215
Diplomatic mail, transportation of, 57, 62
Diplomatic personnel exchanged between Austria and Germany: 1822-1846, 41; 1846-1866, 77; 1866-1912, 123; 1936-1969, 192; 1822-1969, 212–215
Divisions in Austria: interwar years, 153–155; since 1945, 188
Dollfuss, Engelbert, 135
Dual Alliance, 126; sacrifice of defensive character of, 129
Dual Monarchy. *See* Austria
Dynasty: and Napoleonic Wars, 38–39; coalition with bureaucracy, 67–68; German character of, 111; conflict with middle class, 118–119

Economic policy, 1860-1865, 88. *See also* Transactions between Austria and Germany; Rewards, economic
Education: reform of the 1850s, 69; discrimination in favor of Austro-Germans, 72. *See also* Students, Universities
Elite: migration between Austria and Germany, 48–50, 63, 100; continuity in Austria after 1945, 188–189; and integration policy, 215–218
Emigration from Austria: 19th century, 99; 20 century, 190
Erhard, Ludwig, 2
Erler, Fritz, 2
European Court of Justice, effect on Austria's judicial system, 193
European Economic Community, effect on Austrian domestic politics, 194–198
European Recovery Program, aid to Austria, 187
European unification movement, 223–225
Evaluation, of Germany in Austria: in the 1860s, 91–95; 1853-1918, 103–105; 1918-1938, 138–139; 1946-1970, 182–183; 1815-1970, 209–210. *See also* Content analysis, Public opinion

Federation of Germans, 123
Ferdinand I, Emperor of Austria, 60
Foreign investment of German capital in Austria: late 19th century, 98–99;

Index

interwar years, 133–134; 1959-1969, 178–180. *See also* Banks
FPÖ: loss of electoral strength since 1945, 191; and European integration, 194. *See also* Great German Party
France, 7; cultural cohesion of, 228
Francis I, Emperor of Austria, 59
Frankfurt Parliament (1848/49), Austrian delegation, 70–71
Franz Ferdinand (Archduke), assassination of, 128–129
Franz Joseph I, Emperor of Austria, 69

Galicia, uprising of 1846, 62
Geneva Protocol (1922), 141, 159–160
Genovesi, Antonio, 235
German-Austrian Study Group, 146
German Confederation: institutional strength, 39–40; suppression of opposition in Austria, 40; compared with Holy Roman Empire, 40; activity of, 77; after 1848, 83–84
German Customs Union, 27, 46–48, 80–82, 238. *See also* Commercial policy of Austria, Trade flow
German Federation, 83
German language: publications, 72, increasing use of, 233
German nationalism in Austria. *See* Attitudes in Austria, Communications
German National Union, 127
German Postal Union (1850), 79
German Property, nationalization of, 192–193
German School Club, 123
German Study Group, 146
German Telegraph Union, 79
Germany: Eastern policy, 2; definition of territorial size, 5, 12; national anthem, 13; railways, 44, 237–238; economic unification, 27, 46–48, 238, *See also* German Customs Union; support of German-Austrians, 125–126; casualties sustained in World War II, 173–174; cultural cohesion of, 229–231; history of political unification attempts, 232–233; books and periodicals published, 233, 235; elementary education, 234; literacy, 234; mail flow, 234; transport system, 237; urbanization, 238. *See also* individual German states
Government, intelligence service, 57, 61–62. *See also* Press censorship

Government revenues, 74–75, 115–116. *See also* Rewards, economic
Great German Party: and Anschluss, 155–157; economic base of, 157. *See also* FPÖ
Grillparzer, Franz, 58, 70
Gross, Nachum, 86

Haas, Ernst, 224
Habsburg. *See* Austria and individual topics
Heath, Edward, 223
Hesse, duchy of, 83
Heydrich, Reinhard, 173
Hitler, Adolf, 152, 168
Holy Roman Empire, decline of, 38–39
Hungary, trade dependence on Austria, 47–48, 75

Identification of Austria with Germany: in the 1860s, 91–95; 1853-1918, 105–110, 116–117; 1918-1938, 138–141; 1945-1970, 184; 1815-1970, 209–210. *See also* Content analysis, Public opinion.
Industrialization. *See* Rewards, economic; Transactions between Austria and Germany
Integration theory, 16–19, 224–225
International Telegraph Union, 80
Ireland: union with England, 242–243; primary education, 243; occupational structure, 243; transportation system, 244; famine of 1846, 244; nationalism, 245–246
Ireland and England: cultural cohesion of, 229–231; capital flow, 245; elite community, 245; labor migration, 245; trade relations, 245
Italy: Austrian occupation of, 43, 46, 74; cultural cohesion of, 229–231; history of political unification attempts, 232–233; books and periodicals published in, 236; literacy, 236; primary education, 236; population growth in the eighteenth century, 238; retarded industrialization, 238–239; professional class in the 19th century, 239; railways, 239; transportation system, 239

Jansa Plan, for Austrian defense in the 1930s, 169
Josefinismus, 58

Kiesinger, Georg, 2
Kissinger, Henry, 3
Kolowrat, Franz Anton, 60
Kotzebue, August von, 41
Kulturnation. See Cultural nationalism

Land reform (1848-1850), 69
Language policy, 122–123, 125
Liberal party, decline of, 120
Lindberg, Leon, 224
Linz Program (1882), 120–121
Lombardy: economic capacity of, 43; journalism, 240–241; professional class, 239

Mail flow between Austria and Germany: 18th century, 56; 1831-1846, 63; 1846-1867, 79; 1867-1912, 101–102; 1924-1936, 137; 1951-1969, 180; 1815-1970, 202–204
Marx, Karl, 22
Metternich: policy of restoration, 37–38, 59; censorship system, 52–57; opinion of Italy, 236
Middle Class: disenchantment with Metternich regime, 63; tacit support of neoabsolutist regime after 1849, 70; economic stakes in a unified Empire, 73–76, 118–119; ascendency in the bureaucracy, 112
Migration between Austria and Germany: 1869-1910, 100; 1925-1933, 134; 1934-1971, 179
Mitrany, David, 224
Modernization: definition of, 19–20; and nationalism, 35
Monetary Convention, Austria and Germany in 1857, 78

Napoleon, Bonaparte, 52
National debt, 60–61, 73, 86—88
Nationalist parties in Austria, 121, 123
Nationality conflict, 119–123, 125. *See also* Rewards, economic
Nazi party: support in Austria, 157, 170. *See also* Occupation
Neue Freie Presse, 117, 136
Neutrality: of Austria, 195
Newspapers in Austria, foreign influences, 55–56
Nieder-Österreichischer Gewerbeverein, 63
Norway: union with Sweden, 242–243; primary education, 246–247; nationalism, 247; emergence of *landsmaal*, 247–248; transportation system, 248; student movement, 250
Norway and Sweden: cultural cohesion of, 229–231; churches, 249; currency harmonization, 249; joint export strategies, 249; railway connections, 249
Nye, Joseph S., 224

Occupation: by Nazis, 169; by Allies, 190–191
Österreichischer Beobachter, 53, 55
ÖVP, 194–198. *See also* Christian Social Party

Pan-Scandinavian movement, 249–250
Parliament, ethnic composition of, 113
Parsons, Talcott, 21
Parties and integration policy: in the First Republic, 154–161; in the Second Republic, 194–198
Policy coordination between Austria and Germany: overview, 14–15, 32–34; 1815-1848, 37–41; 1848-1870, 76–85; 1870-1918, 123–127; 1919-1930, 148–152; 1945-1970, 191–193
Political nationalism, 9, 12–14, 16
Pompidou, Georges, 223
Press censorship: 19th century, 52–57; 20th century, 135–136, 141
Prosecution under Nazis, 165
Prussia: role in German economic unification, 27; and Napoleonic Wars, 39; armed forces as percent of total population in 1854, 89; military expenditure, 89; educational reforms, 234; literacy, 234; mail flow, 234
Public opinion as measured by polls after 1945, 182, 184, 186, 191. *See also* Evaluation, Identification

Radetzky, Johann J., Field marshal, 70
Railways: between Austria and Germany, 44–45, 89–90; sale of Austria's railways, 87
Rauscher, Joseph O., 67
Reform policies: in the eighteenth century, 42; in the 1850s, 69
Religion. *See* Church
Renner, Karl, 13, 168
Resistance: against Prussia, 91–95; against Nazis, 166–167, 172–175
Revolution of 1848, 67–71
Rewards: economic, 23–24, 26–28; 1815-1848, 43–50; 1848-1866, 72–

Index

75; 1870-1918, 110–118; 1919-1938, 143–145; 1938-1945, 165; 1945-1970, 185–188; political, of integration, 26–32. *See also* Policy coordination

Risorgimento, 235–236

Rothschild, Salomon, 60

Saxony, petition for Austrian tariff concessions, 46
Scandinavian Monetary Union, 249
Scheingold, Stuart, 224
Schlegel, Friedrich, 59
Schopenhauer, Arthur, 54
Schumacher, Kurt, 2
Schumann, Robert, 223
Schuschnigg, Kurt von, 135, 170
Schwarzenberg, Felix, 67
Seipel, Ignaz, 148, 159, 161
Serbia, conflict with Austria, 128–129
Servan-Schreiber, Jean-Jacques, 223–224
Socialist party: and support of the Empire, 122; and support of unification, 157–158. *See also* SPÖ
Society: measurement of, 24–25, 36; and rewards, 28, 31; theoretical exposition, 19–20, 22–24; *See also* Evaluations Transactions,
Soviet Union, 6–7, 15
SPÖ, 194–198. *See also* Socialist party
Staatsnation. *See* Political nationalism
Strauss, Franz Josef, 2
Students from Germany in Austria: 1912-1936, 136–137; 1951-1969, 180; 1918-1970, 202–204
Sudetenland, occupational distribution of Germans and Czechs, 114–115

Telegrams between Austria and Germany: 1867-1912, 102; 1924-1936, 137; 1951-1969, 180; 1871-1970, 202–204
Telephone calls between Austria and Germany: 1924-1936, 137; 1951-1969, 180; 1948-1970, 202–204
Tönnies, Ferdinand, 21
Tourism in Austria, 179, 202–204
Trade flow, between Austria and Germany: 1831-1848, 47–48; 1852-1864, 82; 1864-1912, 98; 1924-1936, 134; 1952-1969, 178-179; in printed materials, 102, 136
Transactions: between Austria and Germany, 202–206; *See also* Commercial policy, Elite migration, Emigration, Foreign investment, German customs union, Labor migration, Tourism, Trade flow; in Germany, 237–238; *See also* individual topics under Germany and Prussia; in Italy, 238–241; *See also* individual topics under Italy and Lombardy; in Ireland, 243–244, 251; *See also* individual topics under Ireland; between Ireland and England, 244–245; *See also* individual topics under Ireland and England; in Norway, 248; *See also* individual topics under Norway; between Norway and Sweden, 248–249, 254–257; *See also* individual topics under Norway and Sweden
Transportation system in Austria, 43–44. *See also* Railways
Treaties. *See* Diplomatic agreements
Turgot, Anne R., 20–21
Tyrol, incorporation into the Austrian market, 46

Unemployment during interwar years, 157
United States, 15
Universal Postal Union, 80
Universities: under Metternich, 57–58, 63–64; Austro-German domination of, 72; under German Nazis, 164–165

Venetia, economic capacity of, 43
Verri, Pietro, 235
Vorarlberg, incorporation into the Austrian market, 46

Wage differences in 19th century Austria, 72
War: history of, 38; with Denmark, 84; with Italy, 84; casualties in 1866, 85, 89; attitudes in 1866, 92–93; of 1870/71 in Austrian perspective, 93–94; effect on First Republic, 144; casualties in 1939-1945, 174
West Germany, Eastern policy, 2
Wiener Zeitung, 52–53, 55, 136
Württemberg, request for liberalization of agricultural trade, 46

Yugoslav, irredenta, 128

Zollverein. *See* German customs union

www.ingramcontent.com/pod-product-compliance
Lightning Source LLC
Chambersburg PA
CBHW021658230426
43668CB00008B/657